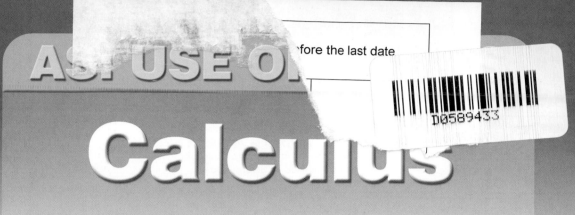

AS USE OF
Calculus

JUNE HAIGHTON • ANNE HAWORTH • GEOFF WAKE

Time t, seconds	Distance x, metres
0.0	0.00
0.1	0.04
0.2	0.23
0.3	0.69
0.4	1.45
0.5	2.57
0.6	4.00
0.7	5.60
0.8	7.62
0.9	10.12

Distance against time for accelerating car

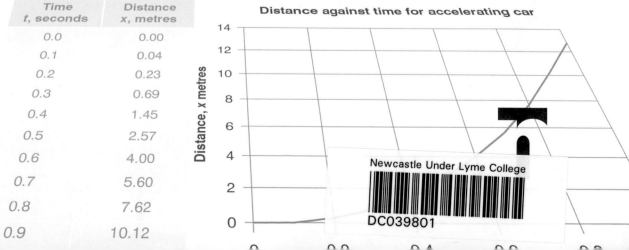

Published in 2004 by:
Nelson Thornes Ltd
Delta Place
27 Bath Road
CHELTENHAM
GL53 7TH
United Kingdom

10 11 12 13 / 10 9 8 7 6 5 4

A catalogue record for this book is available from the British Library

ISBN 978 0 7487 6978 0

Illustration by Mack Draisey
Page make-up by Tech Set Ltd

Printed in China by 1010 Printing International Ltd

Acknowledgements

The authors and publishers wish to thank Lawrence Wo for his help and assistance in checking and compiling the manuscript.
The publishers wish to thank the following for permission to reproduce copyright material:

Photodisc 54 (NT): v; Corel 605 (NT): v; American Institute of Physics/Science Photo Library, 1; Digital Vision XA (NT): 1,46; Cedar Point Amusement Park: 2; Corel 640 (NT): 4; Corel 640 (NT): 9,64; Corel 630 (NT): 13; Digital Vision 15 (NT): 13; Joe Cornish/Digital Vision LL (NT): 14; Imagin Lon (NT): 15; Digital Vision (NT): 18; John Howard/Science Photo Library: 18; NASA: 18; Photodisc 31: 19; Digital Vision XA (NT), 29; Peter Adams/Digital Vision BP (NT): 33; Digital Vision XA (NT): 39; Natures Images: 43, 44; Corel 519 (NT): 45; Photodisc 73 (NT): 62; Photodisc 54 (NT): 62; Digital Vision 6 (NT): 64; Photodisc 44 (NT): 68; Stockbyte 36 (NT): 71; Corel 458 (NT): 73; Corel 62 (NT): Corel 62 (NT): 47; Corel 709 (NT): 81; Peter Adams/Digital Vision BP (NT): 84; Photodisc 28 (NT): 78; Brain Yarvis/Science Photo Library: 89; Photodisc 72 (NT): 90; Dr R Morley/Science Photo Library: 92; Photodisc 31 (NT): 94; Corel 795 (NT): 94; Andrew McClenaghan/Science Photo Library: 98; Photodisc 41 (NT): 99; Corel 795 (NT): 99; George Bernard/Science Photo Library: 101; Corel 562 (NT) 101; Corel 485 (NT): 120; Corel 783 (NT): 131; Photodisc 68 (NT): 150; Photodisc 31 (NT): 150; Digital Vision 7 (NT). All other photographs Nelson Thornes Archive.

The publishers have made every effort to contact copyright holders but apologise if any have been overlooked.

Contents

Using this book

This book contains the material you need to study for the free-standing mathematics qualification *Modelling with calculus*. You may be studying this as a qualification in its own right or you may be studying it as part of the AS Use of Mathematics.

This unit will involve you in building on your knowledge of algebra, functions and graphs to consider the important branch of mathematics known as calculus. As well as learning new algebraic techniques associated with the topics of differentiation and integration you will learn to apply these in a variety of practical situations and eventually use these techniques to make sense of situations you investigate yourself.

You will investigate mathematical models of situations using the ideas that are contained in the free-standing mathematics qualification *Working with algebraic & graphical techniques* together with the additional material in this book.

Your consideration of mathematical models will involve you in:

- identifying an area or problem to investigate
- selecting appropriate data to use
- carrying out mathematical analysis
- drawing conclusions and summarising findings.

You will constantly be referring back and forth between your mathematics and the real world – this diagram attempts to summarise the mathematical modelling process. Central to your mathematical analysis will be the aspects of calculus covered in this book.

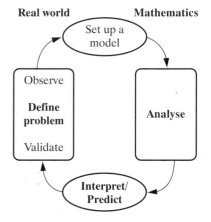

You will need to consider all aspects of the mathematical modelling process when completing work for your coursework portfolio. For example, you will need to consider whether the assumptions on which the model you are working with is based are realistic.

Throughout your work you will need to have access to technology – in particular a graphic calculator. You should show that you can use this effectively to calculate gradients (differentiation) and find areas beneath curves (integration).

For example, in **Chapter 3** you will use the model $v = \frac{1}{16}(t - 8)^3 + 32$ to model the speed, $v\,\mathrm{ms}^{-1}$, of an aircraft along a runway at take-off t seconds after it starts from rest.

You can use your graphic calculator to plot a graph of the function.

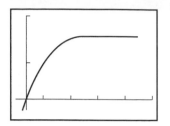

You can use this to find the gradient at any point – the acceleration of the aircraft numerically.

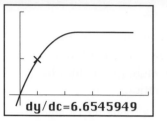

dy/dc=6.6545949

You can also find the area under the graph of the function numerically – the distance travelled numerically.

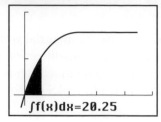

∫f(x)dx=20.25

On some occasions you may find a spreadsheet or graph plotting software on a computer useful. See the section 'Using technology' for some ideas and advice.

The activities of each chapter introduce you to the mathematical content of the unit *Modelling with calculus*. Each chapter introduction gives some ideas that you might wish to explore when producing your coursework portfolio.

Features of the chapters include:

When you are working on an activity that has this symbol your teacher may have a sheet that will help you – for example there may be a ready-scaled graph for you to use.

Practice sheet

Where you see this symbol your teacher may have a sheet of examples that you can work through to practise the mathematical techniques that you have just learned.

Excel Activity

This icon indicates that there is an Excel activity available that the authors have developed to help you understand or practise a particular mathematical technique.

Nuffield resource

This box indicates that there is an additional activity available on the Nuffield website – http://www.fsmq.org/resources/index.asp – that your teacher might ask you to do.

This symbol indicates that a question is difficult.

At the end of each chapter there are the following sections:

- Revision summary
  – giving the key mathematical points you will have learned
- Preparing for assessment
  – giving advice about how to develop your coursework portfolio and some practice exam questions to work through.

There are two comprehension articles in the book. Although the written examination papers for this unit do not include a comprehension section these introduce some interesting applications of calculus and will give you some practice in preparing for the first paper of the *Applying mathematics* examination as well as allowing you to revise aspects of calculus.

Discussion point
You should discuss these with your teacher and other students wherever possible – they introduce some important mathematical ideas as well as prompting you to think carefully about the use of mathematical models. They often provide good pointers as to the sorts of questions you should be asking when writing up your own work for your coursework portfolio.

1 Introduction to Calculus

As you are about to start using this book to study how to use calculus to help you make sense of mathematical models, you will probably be wondering what this important branch of mathematics known as calculus is all about. It is an area of mathematics which developed slowly with some of the first ideas being explored by Greek mathematicians such as Archimedes. However, it was not until relatively recently that the way in which we now use calculus was developed by, amongst others, Sir Isaac Newton. Newton's contributions to both science and mathematics have been very important in allowing us to make sense of the world about us – the development of Newton's ideas of gravity, force, motion and calculus were developed in parallel and it is not surprising that when students first look at ideas of gravity they are asked to think about motion, where the key ideas of calculus may begin to make sense.

For example, consider how your speed would vary with time if you were brave enough to do a bungee jump.

Here is a graph showing what this might look like plotted against time.

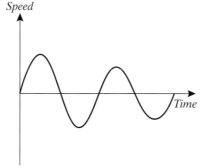

You can use a graph like this to help you make sense of different aspects of the motion, for example:

- when your speed is zero (what is happening to you then?);
- when your speed is increasing, i.e. when you are accelerating – the gradient of the graph tells you about this;
- when your speed is decreasing, i.e. when you are decelerating – again, the gradient of the graph tells you about this;
- how far you have travelled – the area under the graph tells you this.

In this chapter you will start to explore these important ideas on which calculus is based.

1.1 Interpreting gradients

Top Thrill Dragster

Every year, theme parks seek to build bigger, faster and more daring rides. Below is a description of the Top Thrill Dragster at Cedar Point (a top American theme park) which when built for the 2003 season was the world's tallest and fastest.

Riders begin their epic journey by securing themselves into ultra-cool trains that resemble top fuel dragsters. The train then moves into a 'starting line' position, where it is hydraulically launched forward, reaching speeds of 120 mph in approximately 4 seconds. The train then zooms straight up the 420-foot-tall hill on track that rotates 90 degrees, crests the coaster's apex and then free-falls back to Earth, reaching a speed of 120 mph for the second time. As the train races more than 400 feet to the ground, the track twists an unbelievable 270 degrees – what a rush! Riders then return to the station to begin regaling their friends with stories of the greatest ride of their lives.

Activity 1.1A

Read the description of a ride on the Top Thrill Dragster and sketch graphs of how you think

a the height
b the speed

of a passenger will vary with time.

On your graph mark any values of speed, height or time that you know.

Top Thrill Dragster

Growth and decay

Ferris wheel   Sunrise

Pirate ship

First roller coaster EVER to top 400 feet.

First coaster EVER to reach speeds of 120 mph.

First 'strata-coaster' built on planet Earth.

Growth and decay

Activity 1.1B

1 This graph shows how the temperature, $T°C$, of a cup of tea varies with the time, t seconds, after being poured. $T_0°C$ is the temperature of the tea when it is first poured. $T_S°C$ is the (surrounding) temperature of the room in which the cup of tea is poured.

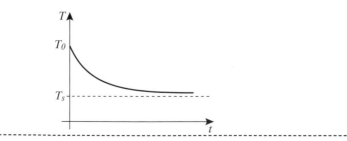

a Make a sketch of this graph and on it mark the sections where the cup of tea is cooling

  i most quickly

  ii most slowly.

b **i** Write a sentence or two to explain how the rate of cooling changes with time.

  ii Interpret what you have written in terms of the temperature of the cup of tea and the room.

2 This graph shows an exponential model of the area of a slice of bread covered by mould, A cm^2, t days after the loaf is baked.

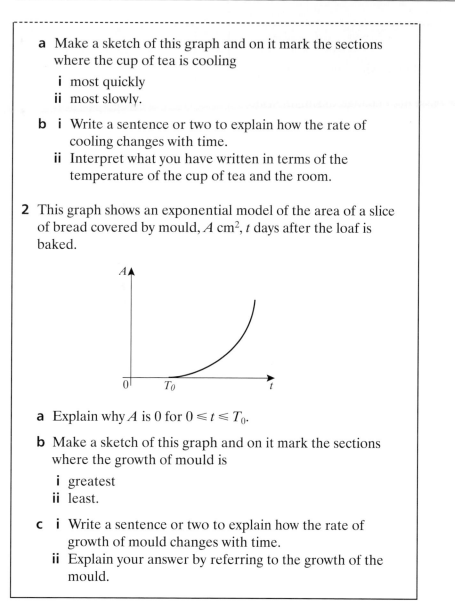

a Explain why A is 0 for $0 \leqslant t \leqslant T_0$.

b Make a sketch of this graph and on it mark the sections where the growth of mould is

  i greatest

  ii least.

c **i** Write a sentence or two to explain how the rate of growth of mould changes with time.

  ii Explain your answer by referring to the growth of the mould.

Ferris wheel

In **Chapter 5** of *Algebra and Graphs* you met the idea of plotting the height of a passenger on a Ferris wheel giving rise to a sine wave. The graph below shows the height of a passenger on one complete ride.

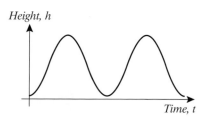

Activity 1.1C

1 How many revolutions does the Ferris wheel make during this particular ride?

2 How does the height of the passenger change during the ride? Make a copy of the graph and indicate on your copy the sections of the graph for which
  a the height of the passenger is increasing,
  b the height is decreasing,
  c the height is neither increasing nor decreasing.

Sunrise

Activity 1.1D

This graph shows sunrise time plotted against day number, n (on 1 January, $n = 0$).

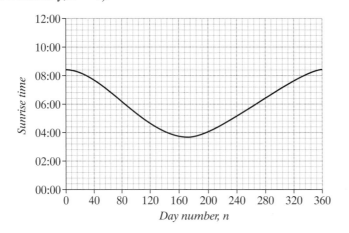

Make a sketch of this graph and on it mark
  a 21 June ($n = 172$),
  b where the rate of change of sunrise time is greatest and explain what this means from one day to the next,
  c where the rate of change of sunrise time is least and explain what this means from one day to the next.

Pirate ship

The graph shows a sketch of how the height of a passenger on a Pirate ship fairground ride might vary with time.

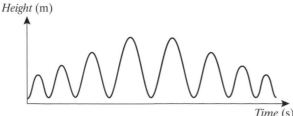

Activity 1.1E

1 Which of the graphs, **A** or **B**, could be a sketch graph of the passenger's speed against time on the Pirate ship?
Give a reason for your choice.

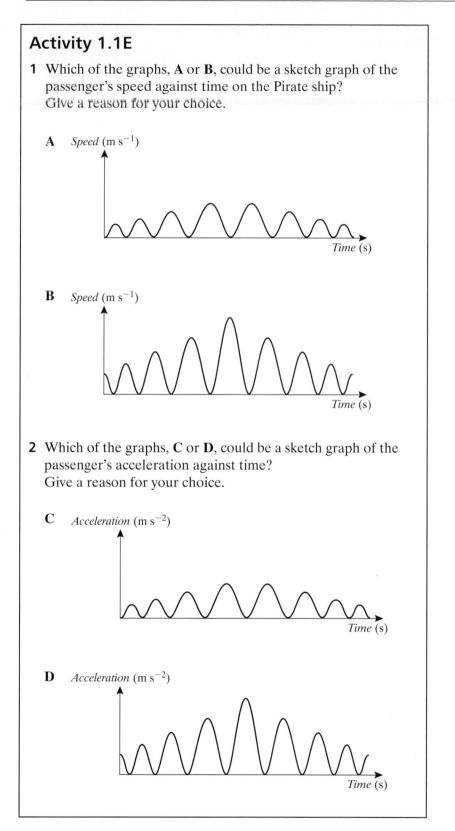

A   *Speed* (m s^{-1})

Time (s)

B   *Speed* (m s^{-1})

Time (s)

2 Which of the graphs, **C** or **D**, could be a sketch graph of the passenger's acceleration against time?
Give a reason for your choice.

C   *Acceleration* (m s^{-2})

Time (s)

D   *Acceleration* (m s^{-2})

Time (s)

1.2 Measuring gradients

Gradients of straight lines

Straight line graphs have the same gradient throughout, whereas graphs of curves such as that describing the height of a passenger on a pirate ship fairground ride have variable gradients.

Here is a straight line graph that you can use to convert between miles and kilometres. The graph was drawn using the fact that 8 kilometres is approximately 5 miles, so the graph goes through the point (8, 5). Of course, 0 kilometres is 0 miles, so the graph also goes through the origin.

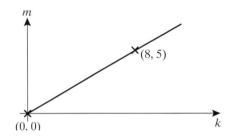

m is the number of miles equivalent to k kilometres

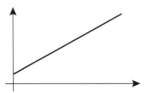

Gradients of straight lines
Gradients of curves
Sketching graphs of gradient functions
Filling containers

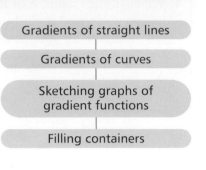

Straight line graph

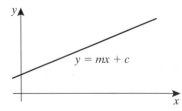

Graph of the height of a passenger on a Pirate ship fairground ride

---

Activity 1.2A

1 What is the gradient of this graph?

2 What is the equation of the graph in terms of k and m? What is the connection between the equation of the graph and its gradient?

3 A general equation of a straight line graph through the origin is $y = mx$. What is the gradient of this line?

The gradient of a graph tells you how y increases or decreases as x increases. In a straight line graph with a gradient of 3, for example, y goes up by 3 units every time x increases by 1 unit. In the conversion graph from kilometres to miles, for every increase of 1 kilometre there is an increase of 0.625 miles.

The general equation of a straight line graph is $y = mx + c$.

- Its gradient is m.
- The y co-ordinate of the point where the line cuts the y-axis is c.

The value of y increases by m units for every 1 unit increase in x. If m is positive, the graph slopes uphill from left to right. If m is negative, the graph slopes downhill. If m is zero, the graph is parallel to the x-axis, sloping neither up nor down.

Discussion point

Are conversion graphs always straight lines that go through the origin?

Discussion point

What would be different if the conversion graph had the number of miles on the horizontal axis and the number of kilometres on the vertical axis?

$y = mx + c$ graph

Activity 1.2B

Here are some situations that you can model using straight line graphs; you may have met them in *Algebra and Graphs*. For each situation, sketch a graph and find its gradient. For each, write a sentence explaining what the gradient tells you about the real situation.

1 A plumber charges £25 for a call-out plus £20 per hour.

2 Sam borrows £120 from his father and pays back the loan at £18 per week.

3 A car joins a motorway at a speed of 25 ms^{-1} and accelerates at a rate of 0.5 ms^{-2}.

4 After a 20 cm candle is lit, it burns at a steady rate of 1.6 cm per hour.

5 A joint of meat is taken from a freezer at a temperature of $-18°C$ and defrosts at a rate of 1.5°C per hour.

Discussion point
What is it about these situations that makes them suitable for modelling with straight line graphs?

Gradients of curves

Gradients of curved graphs vary: the gradient of the graph is different at neighbouring values along the horizontal axis. As you saw when interpreting the graph of the height of a passenger on a Pirate ship fairground ride, parts of the graph have positive gradients, parts have negative gradients and there are points where the gradient is zero.

Activity 1.2C

1 Identify the parts of the height of a passenger on a Pirate ship fairground ride graph with positive gradient, negative gradient and zero gradient.

2 Compare your answers with your answers to **Activity 1.1A**.

Discussion point
What is happening to the height of the passenger when the gradient of the graph is positive? negative? zero?

The answers to the discussion point are the essence of differential calculus, which you will explore further in **Chapter 2**. If you know the gradient of a function, you can identify important features of the function such as its maximum and minimum values and when it is increasing and decreasing.

Differentiation allows you to calculate gradients exactly but there is a simpler, if time-consuming, method of finding gradients even if you know nothing about differentiation.

In the margin is a graph of an exponential function. You can use such functions to model situations such as population growth, or how money grows when put into a bank or building society account. You worked with functions like this in *Algebra and Graphs*.

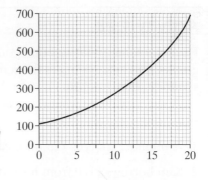

Activity 1.2D

Resource
Sheet
1.2D

The graph below shows the growth of a colony of *E. coli* bacteria. Here the number of bacteria doubles every minute.

1 a Write a sentence or two to describe how the gradient of this graph changes as time, *t* minutes, increases.

b Explain what this tells you about the growth of the colony of *E. coli*.

2 a On a full-page copy of the exponential graph, draw tangents to the curve at the points when $t = 40$, $t = 80$ and $t = 120$.

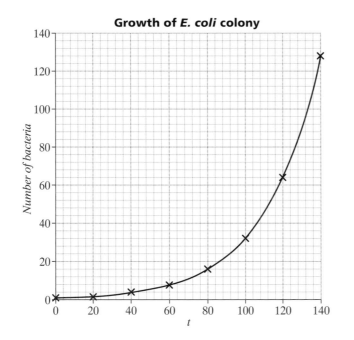

Note: A tangent to a curve at a particular point is a straight line that just touches the curve at that point. The gradient of the tangent is the same as the gradient of the curve at that point.

You will see why this statement is true in later sections of this book.

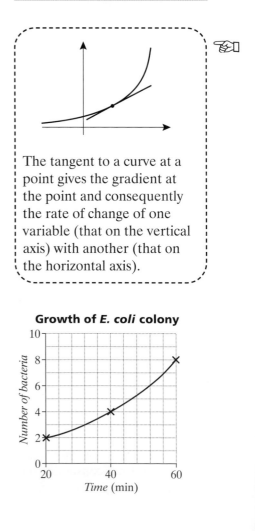

The tangent to a curve at a point gives the gradient at the point and consequently the rate of change of one variable (that on the vertical axis) with another (that on the horizontal axis).

b Calculate the gradient of each of the tangents. What happens to the gradient of the tangents (and therefore the curve) as time increases?

c A small part of the curve is reproduced here. On a copy of this part of the graph, draw a chord joining the points on the curve where $t = 40$ and $t = 41$. Calculate the gradient of this chord. How does it compare with the gradient of the curve (i.e. the gradient of the tangent) when $t = 40$?

Sketching graphs of gradient functions

Suppose a Ferris wheel has radius 10 metres and rotates once every 5 minutes. This information has been used to label the axes of the graph below, which shows how the height of a passenger changes as time increases.

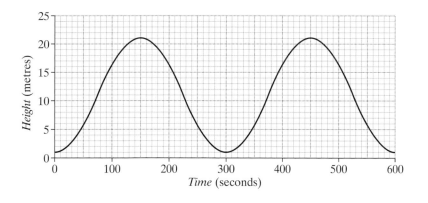

Activity 1.2E

Resource Sheet 1.2E

1   Show that the gradient of a tangent to the curve at the point where $t = 75$ is approximately 0.2. This means that after 75 seconds, the height of a passenger is increasing at $0.2 \, \text{ms}^{-1}$.

2   a   Use your answer to **question 1** to write down the rate of change of a passenger's height after 225 seconds, 375 seconds and 525 seconds – you can use the symmetries of the graph to help you. (Remember to use a negative sign to indicate when the height is decreasing.)

    b   What is the rate of change of a passenger's height after 0 seconds, 150 seconds, 300 seconds, 450 seconds and 600 seconds?

    c   Use the values you have found so far to assist you to sketch a graph of how the gradient of the height–time graph varies with time – a gradient graph. Do this on a copy of the set of axes shown.

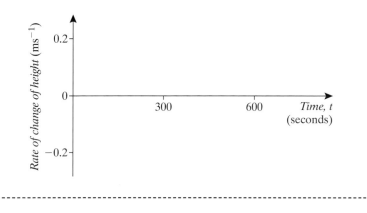

Discussion point

What features of the graph show that the height of the passenger is changing most rapidly after 90 s and 210 s?

Graphs showing how the gradient of a function varies with time are sometimes known as **graphs of gradient functions**.

9

d In words describe what the gradient graph tells you about the motion of a passenger on the Ferris wheel.

e Compare the gradient graph with the height graph. What are the similarities and differences?

3 Without calculating any *values* of gradients, sketch graphs of gradient functions for the theme park rides that give rise to the graphs below.

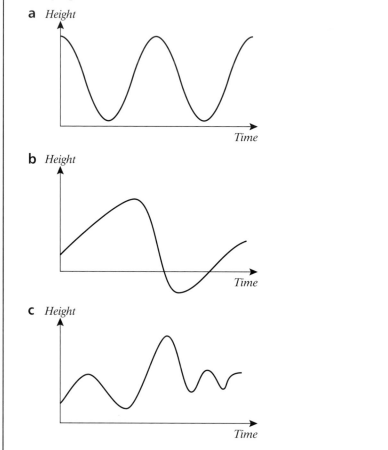

a *Height*

Time

b *Height*

Time

c *Height*

Time

Filling containers

Imagine a container being filled with water at a steady rate. How will the depth of water in the container increase? For a container with a fixed cross-section, such as a cylinder, the height will increase at a steady rate because the same amount of water will enter the container for each unit of time. So the graph of depth of water against time is a straight line.

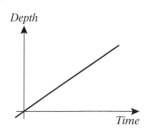

Depth

Time

Activity 1.2F

1 The diagram shows the graphs of water depth against time for three different cylindrical containers that were filled at the same steady rate. Which graph belongs with which container? Explain how you made your decisions.

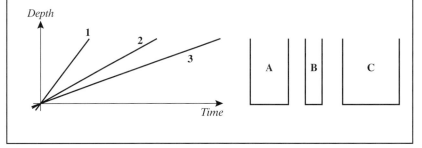

Discussion point

How would the graphs differ if the water flowed at
- a faster steady rate?
- a slower steady rate?
- different steady rates for each container?

If the area of the cross-section of the container is not fixed, the depth of the water will not increase steadily if the water flows at a steady rate.

For example, the container shown in the margin has a cross-section that increases as the depth of water increases, so the rate at which the depth increases will decrease as time goes on.

Discussion point

Can you explain this statement so that another student will understand?

Discussion point

Why should the gradient of a suitable graph never be negative?

Activity 1.2F (continued)

2 Which of these graphs gives the best picture of the depth against time for the container in the margin? Explain your decision.

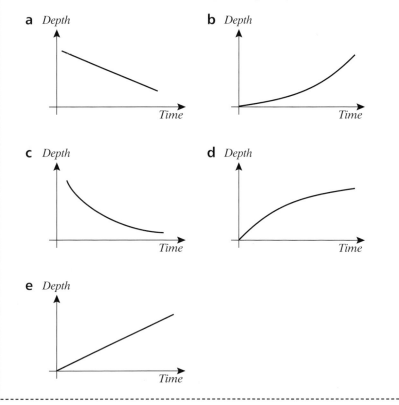

3 Match each graph with one of the containers and sketch a graph for the container left over.

Mug   Vase   Bottle

Bottle of ink   Conical flask

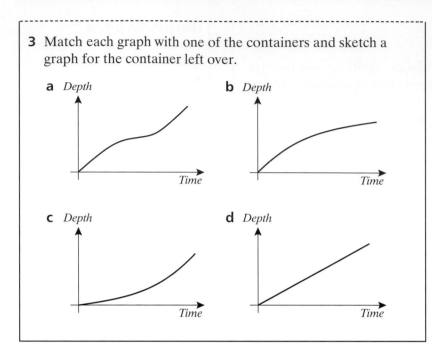

a *Depth*

Time

b *Depth*

Time

c *Depth*

Time

d *Depth*

Time

1.3 Areas under graphs

Speed–time graphs

Speed–time graphs

River cross-section

Daylight hours

You can also use calculus to help you to find areas under graphs of functions. Such areas can often give useful information about a situation. For example, the area under a graph may give the area of cross-section of a river (and hence may be used to calculate the volume of water flowing per day, perhaps). In other branches of mathematics the area under a graph may be used to calculate quantities such as the distance travelled by a car or the probability of a person's height being between certain values.

Consider the very simple model of a car travelling on a motorway at a constant speed of 60 mph (miles per hour). Its speed–time graph is shown below.

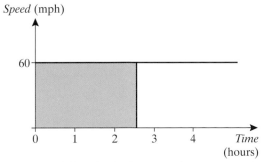

What does the area of the shaded rectangle represent?

The base of the rectangle represents 2.5 hours.

The height represents a speed of 60 miles per hour.

So the 'area' represents $2.5 \text{ hours} \times 60 \dfrac{\text{miles}}{\text{hour}} = 150 \text{ miles}$

i.e. the distance travelled by the car.

Note: Consideration of the units involved allows you to determine the units of the quantity you are calculating. Here you are multiplying quantities in miles per hour by quantities in hours so the area represents a distance in miles.

Activity 1.3A

1 a Draw a speed–time graph for a ship travelling at a constant speed of 12 mph for 6 hours.
 b Shade the part of your graph that represents the distance travelled by the ship in the 4th hour.
 c How far does the ship travel in the 4th hour?
 d How far does the ship travel in the 6th hour?
 e What distance does the ship travel in the full 6 hours?

2 a Draw a speed–time graph for a car starting from rest and accelerating steadily up to 50 ms^{-1} over 10 seconds, then maintaining a speed of 50 ms^{-1} for a further 10 seconds.
 b Use your graph to calculate the distance the car travelled whilst accelerating during the first 10 seconds.
 c Calculate the distance the car travelled during the second period of 10 seconds, whilst it was travelling at a constant speed.

3 A ship sails at a constant speed of 20 mph for 1 hour. It then slows down steadily to a speed of 15 mph over half an hour. After this, it travels at this new constant speed for a further half an hour.

   a Draw a speed–time graph to show this situation.

   b Calculate the distance travelled by the ship whilst it slowed down.

   c Calculate the distance the ship travelled whilst at a constant speed of 15 mph.

4 The table shows the depth of a river, 5 metres wide, at various distances from one bank.

Distance from bank (metres)	0	1	2	3	4	5
Depth of river (metres)	0.1	0.25	0.2	0.2	0.15	0.05

   a Draw a diagram to show this data.

   b Calculate the area of this cross-section of the river.

5 A car takes 12 seconds to accelerate steadily from rest up to constant speed, travels at this speed for 40 seconds, then slows down to a halt. It travels a total distance of 1 km in 60 seconds. What was the constant speed of the car?

Hint: Sketch a graph to help you make sense of the situation.

River cross-section

The graph below shows the cross-section of a river in Derbyshire with data of the depth of the river in the table alongside.

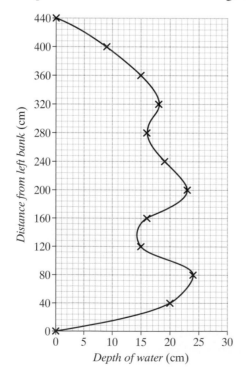

Distance from left bank (cm) (vertical axis)

Depth of water (cm) (horizontal axis)

Distance from left bank (cm)	Depth of water (cm)
0	0
40	20
80	24
120	15
160	16
200	23
240	19
280	16
320	18
360	15
400	9
440	0

Activity 1.3B

1 Use the data to calculate an estimate of the cross-sectional area of the river.

2 If the river is flowing at a rate of 0.35 m/s, calculate the flow of water in the river in cubic metres per hour.

Daylight hours

The graph below shows how the number of daylight hours varies throughout a complete year in two different cities in the UK. The table shows the data for the number of daylight hours on the first day of each month.

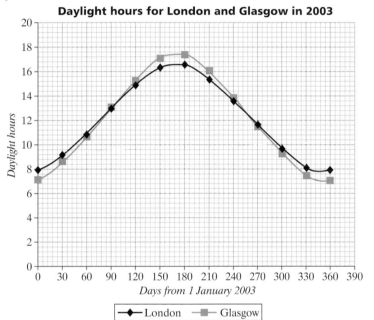

Daylight hours for London and Glasgow in 2003

Date	Daylight hours	
	London	Glasgow
01/01/03	7.92	7.12
01/02/03	9.17	8.63
01/03/03	10.88	10.68
01/04/03	12.93	13.08
01/05/03	14.83	15.33
01/06/03	16.30	17.17
01/07/03	16.57	17.48
01/08/03	15.43	16.07
01/09/03	13.58	13.85
01/10/03	11.65	11.58
01/11/03	9.68	9.25
01/12/03	8.20	7.45
01/01/04	7.92	7.08

Activity 1.3C

1 Use the data to find an estimate of the total number of daylight hours over a complete year in each city.

2 Calculate an estimate of average number of daylight hours in each city.

3 What can you deduce from the graphs and your answer to **question 2**?

For simple (and in some cases rather artificial) situations such as those described above, you can use rectangles, triangles and trapezia to calculate the relevant areas. In fact, any area can be approximated in this way, as you will see in **Chapter 3**, and sometimes this is the best (or only) way of finding areas under graphs.

Calculus, however, offers some powerful techniques for finding areas when you know a function in algebraic form. You will learn more about this in **Chapter 3**.

Discussion point

How can you tell without using the graph's key that the light coloured line represents Glasgow and the dark coloured line represents London?

1.4 Revision summary

Gradients of straight lines

This chapter introduced some key ideas of calculus, gradients of graphs and areas under graphs, that will be developed in later chapters.

The gradient of the graph of the function $y = f(x)$ gives information about the rate at which y is changing with respect to x. For example, if y is the distance travelled in time x, the gradient tells you the speed of travel (which could be constant or variable).

Straight lines have fixed gradients (or slopes).

You can calculate the gradient from a graph of a straight line as shown.

The gradient is equal to $\dfrac{\text{increase in } y}{\text{increase in } x}$.

If the line slopes downwards, the increase in y is negative and thus the gradient of the straight line is negative.

You can also calculate the gradient from the equation of the straight line. Any straight line equation can be written in the form $y = mx + c$, where m is the value of the gradient. If m is negative, the graph slopes downhill.

Gradients of curves

Curved graphs have variable gradients, as shown.

The gradient of a graph at a point is the same as the gradient of the tangent to the graph at that point.
The gradient of the tangent can be calculated as above.

The gradient function of a function $y = f(x)$ tells you what the gradient of $y = f(x)$ is for different values of x.

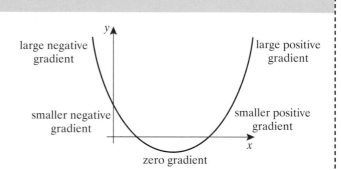

Area under graphs

The area under the graph of a function can give further information; for example, if the graph shows speed against time, the area under the graph gives the distance travelled. Other examples are finding cross-sectional areas, or calculating the total takings of a company over a year by finding the area under a graph showing monthly profits.

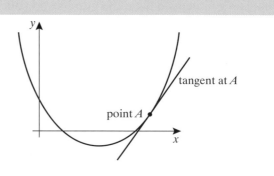

1.5 Preparing for assessment

Your coursework portfolio

In this chapter, you have met some basic ideas of calculus that will be developed further later. Some of these could provide possible portfolio activities, though you may prefer to wait until you have done later chapters.

For example, for gradients, if you have some data that produces a curved graph, you could describe what happens to the gradient of the graph as you move from left to right. Then draw tangents to the graph at appropriate points and calculate their gradients. Compare these results with your original descriptions, and say what this tells you about the original situation. What does the graph of the gradients look like? Can you find a model for it?

2 Gradient Functions

Contents

At the time that Newton developed his ideas of calculus he was also thinking about gravitation. You may have heard about how he likened the Moon orbiting the Earth to an apple falling from a tree in the garden of his house at Woolsthorpe Manor in Lincolnshire.

It is now possible to travel into space and experience weightlessness – just as Newton would have predicted. Of course it is very expensive to become a space tourist, but white knuckle theme park rides often allow you to experience zero gravity, though only for a very few seconds at a time. In fact, if you want to become a space tourist it is possible to fly in an aircraft that due to its parabolic flight allows you to experience zero-g for about 30 seconds at a time.

The Moon

A theme park ride that includes a near vertical drop allowing you to experience zero-g

The European Space Agency (ESA) uses a modified Airbus A300 for zero-g flights

In this chapter you will develop the algebra of calculus that allows you to explore, for example, the relationships between distance travelled, speed and acceleration.

Newton's Apple Tree, Woolsthorpe Manor, Grantham, Lincolnshire

2.1 Calculating gradients accurately

Car performance: 0–60 mph

Car performance 0–60 mph

Speed as a function

The graph below shows the distance travelled, *d* metres, plotted against time, *t* seconds, for a car accelerating from rest.

The table gives distance travelled every 0.1 seconds for the interval $0 \leqslant t \leqslant 1$.

However, the graph has been drawn by plotting many more points – these were recorded by a data-logger but are not given here.

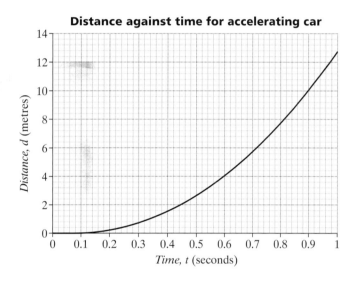

Distance against time for accelerating car

Distance, d (metres) vs *Time, t (seconds)*

Time, *t* seconds	Distance, *d* metres
0.0	0.00
0.1	0.04
0.2	0.23
0.3	0.69
0.4	1.45
0.5	2.57
0.6	4.00
0.7	5.60
0.8	7.62
0.9	10.12
1.0	12.77

Resource Sheet 2.1A

Activity 2.1A

1 On a copy of the graph, draw tangents to the curve at $t = 0.4$, $t = 0.6$ and $t = 0.8$. These tangents give the gradient of the curve and allow you to calculate how the distance travelled by the car is increasing with time, i.e. the **speed** of the car.

2 Calculate the speed of the car at $t = 0.4$, $t = 0.6$ and $t = 0.8$, using the tangents you have drawn.

Note that these are **estimates** of the speed since you have drawn the tangents by eye.

3 Write a sentence to describe how the speed of the car changes over the interval $0 \leqslant t \leqslant 1$.

If you know the distance travelled by the car, *d* metres, as a function of time, *t* seconds, you can find the speed of the car more accurately. You will see how to do this in the next activity.

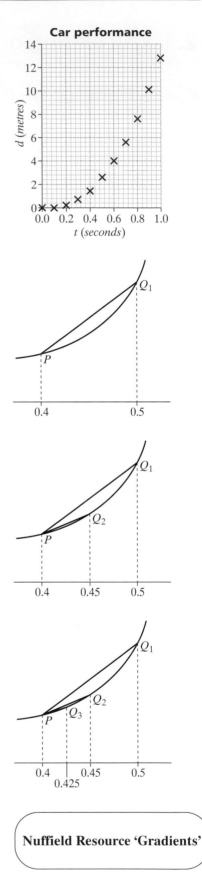

Car performance

Activity 2.1B

1 Use a graphic calculator, graph plotting software or spreadsheet to plot the data for the car given in the table so you have a graph like that shown alongside.

2 Check that the function $d = 12t^2$ reasonably closely models the data.

3 Now consider how you can find the gradient of the function at $t = 0.4$.
   a Find the distance travelled by the car predicted by the function $d = 12t^2$ when
      i $t = 0.4$ (point P)
      ii $t = 0.5$ (point Q_1).
   b Find an approximate value for the speed of the car when $t = 0.4$ by calculating the gradient of the straight line joining the points P and Q_1.
   c Find an improved approximation by finding the gradient of the line PQ_2 where Q_2 is when $t = 0.45$.
   d Find a further improved approximation by finding the gradient of the line PQ_3 where Q_3 is when $t = 0.425$.

As you use Q points that are closer and closer to P, the gradient of the line is closer and closer to the gradient of the tangent. You can use a spreadsheet to carry out the calculations quickly.

	A	B	C	D
	Point	t (seconds)	d (metres)	Gradient PQ (speed m/s)
2	P	0.4	1.92	–
3	Q_1	0.5	3	10.8
4	Q_2	0.45	2.43	10.2
5	Q_3	0.425	2.1675	9.9
6	Q_4	0.4125	2.041875	9.75

The formulae you can use in the spreadsheet cells are shown below.

	A	B	C	D
	Point	t (seconds)	d (metres)	Gradient PQ (speed m/s)
2	P	0.4	=12*B2^2	–
3	Q_1	0.5	=12*B3^2	=(C3-C$2)/(B3-B$2)
4	Q_2	=(0.4+B3)/2	=12*B4^2	=(C4-C$2)/(B4-B$2)
5	Q_3	=(0.4+B4)/2	=12*B5^2	=(C5-C$2)/(B5-B$2)
6	Q_4	=(0.4+B5)/2	=12*B6^2	=(C6-C$2)/(B6-B$2)

Nuffield Resource 'Gradients'

In the spreadsheet the gap between P and Q has been halved each time. You can see that as Q gets closer and closer to P, the gradient of PQ, that is the speed of the car, gets closer and closer to $9.6\ \mathrm{ms}^{-1}$.

Activity 2.1C

1 Repeat the method of **question 3** in **Activity 2.1B** to calculate an approximation to the speed when

a $t = 0.6$ **b** $t = 0.8$

2 Check how the values you have calculated here compare with those you found using tangents in **Activity 2.1A**.

Below is a description of the method you have been using. Discuss this with your teacher and other students if possible.

When Q is a time very close to P:

At P, $t = 0.4$, $d(0.4) = 12 \times 0.4^2 = 12 \times 0.16 = 1.92$;
At Q, $t = 0.4001$, $d(0.4001) = 12 \times 0.4001^2 = 12 \times 0.16008001$
$$= 1.92096012.$$

So the gradient of PQ is given by:

$$v = \frac{d(0.4001) - d(0.4)}{0.001} = \frac{1.92096012 - 1.92}{0.001} = 0.96012$$

In general, the gradient at $t = 0.4$ is given by

$$v = \frac{d(0.40 + h) - d(0.4)}{h},$$

where h is a small step in the horizontal direction.

The smaller the value of h, the more accurate the value of the gradient.

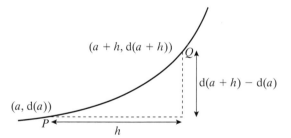

The gradient at P, where $t = a$ is given by

$$v = \frac{d(a + h) - d(a)}{h},$$

where h is a small step in the horizontal direction.

Notice that what you have been doing here is effectively zooming in on a part of the curve. You may like to try this with your graphic calculator or graph plotting software. Do this by plotting a graph of the function $d = 12t^2$ (you may have to input this as $y = 12x^2$).

Place a cursor at $x = 0.4$ (if using your graphic calculator do this by using the TRACE facility). Zoom in a number of times – the graph soon becomes almost linear. This is what you have been assuming in **Activity 2.1C**.

> Here the notation d(0.4) is used since d is a function of time t. $d(t) = 12t^2$

> **Discussion point**
> Why does a smaller value of h give a better estimate of the gradient?

> This is a very important idea used to find the gradient at a point – you will explore this further in the next few activities.

> **Discussion point**
> Can you explain how calculating the gradient using $v = \dfrac{d(a + h) - d(a)}{h}$ means that you are assuming there is a straight line between two points?

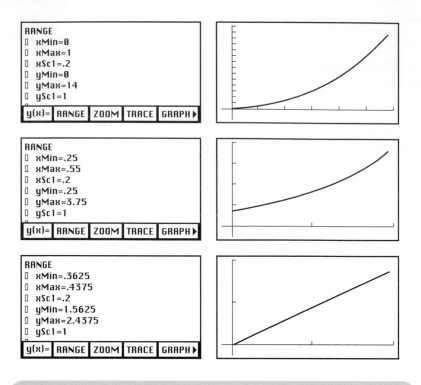

Speed as a function

In the following activity you will find a function for the speed of the car in terms of time. You will do this using the method that you have just developed.

Activity 2.1D

1 Find the speed, v ms^{-1}, of the car every 0.1 seconds so that you can complete a copy of the table below (you may wish to do this using a spreadsheet).

Find the speed using $v = \dfrac{d(a + h) - d(a)}{h}$ together with the model $d = 12t^2$.

	A	B	C	D
1	Time	Distance	Model	Speed
2	t (seconds)	x (metres)	d (metres)	v (metres per second)
3	0.0	0.00	0.00	0.012
4	0.1	0.04	0.12	2.412
5	0.2	0.23	0.48	4.812
6	0.3	0.69	1.08	7.212
7	0.4	1.45	1.92	9.612
8	0.5	2.57	3.00	12.012
9	0.6	4.00	4.32	14.412
10	0.7	5.60	5.88	16.812
11	0.8	7.62	7.68	19.212
12	0.9	10.12	9.72	21.612
13	1.0	12.77	12.00	24.012

Hint: For each value of a take $h = 0.001$

In this cell the formula is '$=12*A3 \char94 2$'.

In this cell the formula is '$=(12*(A3+0.001) \char94 2 - 12*A3 \char94 2)/0.001$'.

Discussion point

Can you explain why the formula in cell D3 is '$=(12*(A3+0.001) \char94 2 - 12*A3 \char94 2)/0.001$'?

---

2 Plot a speed–time graph for the accelerating car (with speed, v ms^{-1}, on the vertical axis and time, t s, on the horizontal axis).

3 Find the speed, v ms^{-1}, of the car as a function of time, t s.

4 Use your graph and function to write a sentence to describe how the speed of the car varies with time.

In the previous activity you started with **distance** travelled as a function of time and found **speed** as a function of time using the gradients of tangents to the graph of the original function.

The function describing speed as a function of time is sometimes known as the gradient function since it gives the gradient of the original function as a function of time.

You should have graphs like these shown here. It is useful to draw one under the other with the same scale on the time axis, so that it is possible to make sense of the features of each graph in terms of the other. For example, you could say that, over the first second, *'The speed of the car is initially zero and increases linearly with time, so that after 1 second it is travelling at 24 ms^{-1}.'*

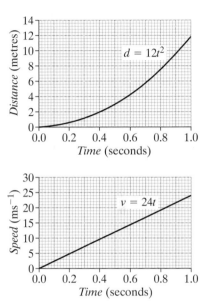

2.2 Gradient functions – differentiation

The gradient of x^n

In the next activity you will begin to explore gradient functions in general so that eventually you will be able to find these functions immediately if you are given an original function.

The function you are asked to investigate, $f(x) = x^2$, is worked through below as an example.

A spreadsheet has been used to calculate values for $f(x) = x^2$ and the gradient of the tangents using gradient $= \dfrac{f(a + 0.001) - f(a)}{0.001}$, where $a = -5, -4, -3, \ldots 3, 4, 5$.

The spreadsheet below shows the formula in each cell. The spreadsheet facility 'fill down' has been used here.

	A	B	C
1	x	f(x)	gradient of tangent
2	–5	=A2^2	=((A2+0.001)^2-A2^2)/0.001
3	=A2+1	=A3^2	=((A3+0.001)^2-A3^2)/0.001
4	=A3+1	=A4^2	=((A4+0.001)^2-A4^2)/0.001
5	=A4+1	=A5^2	=((A5+0.001)^2-A5^2)/0.001
6	=A5+1	=A6^2	=((A6+0.001)^2-A6^2)/0.001
7	=A6+1	=A7^2	=((A7+0.001)^2-A7^2)/0.001
8	=A7+1	=A8^2	=((A8+0.001)^2-A8^2)/0.001
9	=A8+1	=A9^2	=((A9+0.001)^2-A9^2)/0.001
10	=A9+1	=A10^2	=((A10+0.001)^2-A10^2)/0.001
11	=A10+1	=A11^2	=((A11+0.001)^2-A11^2)/0.001
12	=A11+1	=A12^2	=((A12+0.001)^2-A12^2)/0.001

	A	B	C
1	x	f(x)	gradient of tangent
2	-5	25	-9.999
3	-4	16	-7.999
4	-3	9	-5.999
5	-2	4	-3.999
6	-1	1	-1.999
7	0	0	0.001
8	1	1	2.001
9	2	4	4.001
10	3	9	6.001
11	4	16	8.001
12	5	25	10.001

The gradient x^n

Newton and Leibnitz

Some rules for differentiation

The graph below shows plots of the original function, $f(x) = x^2$, together with the values of the gradients which are joined to show the graph of the gradient function.

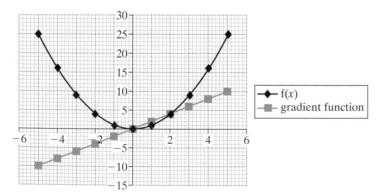

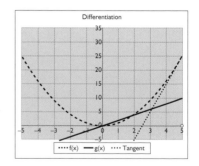

The gradient function, $g(x)$, for $f(x) = x^2$ is $g(x) = 2x$: it is a straight line of gradient 2 that passes through the origin.

Excel
Activity

Resource
Sheet
2.2A

Activity 2.2A

In this activity use a spreadsheet together with each of the functions $f(x) = x^2$, $f(x) = x^3$, $f(x) = x^4$, $f(x) = x^5$, $f(x) = x^{-1} = \frac{1}{x}$ and $f(x) = x^{\frac{1}{2}} = \sqrt{x}$.

For each function, you should:

a plot a graph of the original function, $f(x)$, for $-5 \leqslant x \leqslant 5$;

b calculate the gradients of the tangents to $f(x)$ at $x = -5, -4, -3, \ldots 3, 4, 5$;

c plot a graph of the gradients of the tangents against x, for $-5 \leqslant x \leqslant 5$;

d deduce the gradient function, $g(x)$.

Now summarise your answers in a copy of the table below.

Original function, f(x)	Gradient function, g(x)
$f(x) = x^2$	
$f(x) = x^3$	
$f(x) = x^4$	
$f(x) = x^5$	
$f(x) = x^{-1} = \dfrac{1}{x}$	
$f(x) = x^{\frac{1}{2}} = \sqrt{x}$	

As an alternative to spreadsheet software you can use graph plotting software such as Autograph, or your teacher may have a ready-built dynamic spreadsheet.

Check that you agree that:

> If the original function is $f(x) = x^n$, then the gradient function, $g(x)$, is given by $g(x) = nx^{n-1}$.

☞

This is a very important result!

Activity 2.2B

The result above means that, if $f(x) = x^{-2}$, then $g(x) = -2x^{-3}$.

Check that this is true by drawing the graphs of $f(x)$ and the gradients of tangents to the curve. Check that these points lie on the graph of $g(x) = -2x^{-3}$.

Newton and Leibnitz

Discussion point
What else do you know about
Newton and Leibnitz?

The mathematics you have been working on in the activities so far in this chapter forms the basis of a very important branch of mathematics – calculus. This was originally worked on independently by two mathematicians about three hundred years ago: Leibnitz and Newton.

Finding the gradient function of an algebraic function f(x) is commonly called **differentiation**. The gradient function is often referred to as the **derived function** or the **derivative** of the original function.

Because the gradient function is so clearly linked to the original function, the notation f'(x) is used rather than g(x) for the derived function. When talking about this we say 'f dashed of x'.

An alternative notation is also used.

If $y = f(x)$, then the gradient function is referred to as $\dfrac{dy}{dx}$.

When talking about this we say 'dee y by dee x'.

So, using the two different notations,

if $y = x^2$, then $\dfrac{dy}{dx} = 2x$ (Newton's notation)

or if $f(x) = x^2$, then (Leibnitz' notation) $f'(x) = 2x$.

This process is called **differentiating with respect to x**.

Activity 2.2C

> If $f(x) = x^n$ then $f'(x) = nx^{n-1}$.

Choose a value of n that you have not yet worked with.
Predict $f'(x)$ for your function $f(x)$.

Check that you are correct by using the spreadsheet method of this section.

Some rules for differentiation

You have just developed a rule for differentiating a function, f(x), with respect to x, when $f(x) = x^n$.

What if $h(x) = f(x) + a$, where a is a constant?
What if $h(x) = af(x)$, where a is a constant?

To answer these questions, think back to the transformations of functions that you studied in **Chapter 5** of *Algebra and Graphs*.

In later sections of this book you will investigate differentiating other important functions based on $f(x) = e^x$ and $f(x) = \sin(x)$ or $f(x) = \cos(x)$.

$h(x) = f(x) + a$ is a translation of $f(x)$ by a units in the direction of the vertical axis. The gradient of the function for any x-value is not changed by this transformation so $h'(x) = f'(x)$. You can see this illustrated in the graphs below.

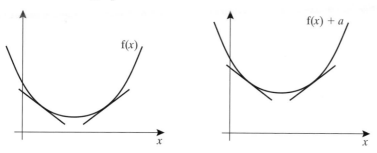

$h(x) = af(x)$ is a stretch, scale factor a, in the direction of the vertical axis. The gradient of the function at any x-value is also stretched by a scale factor a, so $h'(x) = af'(x)$. You can see this illustrated in the graphs below.

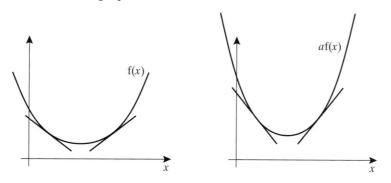

These rules allow you to find the gradient function or derivative of functions such as $d = 12t^2$, which you used to model the motion of a car accelerating from rest.

The graph of $d = 12t^2$ is the graph of $y = t^2$ stretched by a factor of 12, so the gradient is 12 times the gradient of $y = t^2$.

Therefore the derived function is $24t$.

Activity 2.2D

In this activity check that

a if $h(x) = f(x) + a$ then $h'(x) = f'(x)$,
b if $h(x) = af(x)$ then $h'(x) = af'(x)$.

1 Choose a function $f(x)$ (for example, try $f(x) = x^2$).
2 Plot $h(x) = f(x) + 2$ ($a = 2$).
3 Find and plot the gradient function $h'(x)$.
4 Plot $g(x) = 2f(x)$ ($a = 2$).
5 Find and plot the gradient function $g'(x)$.

Choose another function $f(x)$ and another value of a and repeat the investigation you carried out above. Make sure that your work confirms the rules that have been suggested.

What if f(x) is the sum or difference of two functions? That is, what if f(x) = g(x) $\pm$ h(x), e.g. f(x) = $x^2 + x$?

If you are plotting a graph of f(x) you can plot a graph of g(x) = x^2 and and h(x) = x. add the y-values of each to get the new graph of f(x).

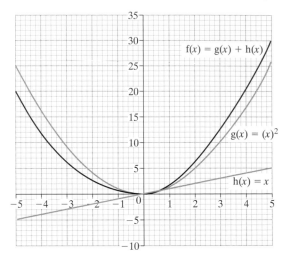

Discussion point
Are you convinced by this? Can you produce a convincing argument?

You might deduce that the gradient of f(x) is the sum of the gradients of g(x) and h(x), i.e. f$'$(x) = g$'$(x) + h$'$(x).

In the next activity you will explore whether this is true.

As an alternative method, your teacher may have a spreadsheet or graph plotting software that dynamically plots the gradient function.

Activity 2.2E

Excel Activity

1 Investigate whether f$'$(x) = g$'$(x) + h$'$(x) for the case where f(x) = $x^2 + x$. Do this, using the spreadsheet method used earlier, for $-5 \leqslant x \leqslant 5$.

	A	B	C
1	x	f(x)	gradient of tangent
2	-5	20	-8.999
3	-4	12	-6.999
4	-3	6	-4.999
5	-2	2	-2.999
6	-1	0	-0.999
7	0	0	1.001
8	1	2	3.001
9	2	6	5.001
10	3	12	7.001
11	4	20	9.001
12	5	30	11.001

	A	B	C
1	x	f(x)	gradient of tangent
2	–5	=A2^2+A2	=((A2+0.001)^2+(A2+0.001)-B2)/0.001
3	=A2+1	=A3^2+A3	=((A3+0.001)^2+(A2+0.001)-B3)/0.001
4	=A3+1	=A4^2+A4	=((A4+0.001)^2+(A2+0.001)-B4)/0.001
5	=A4+1	=A5^2+A5	=((A5+0.001)^2+(A2+0.001)-B5)/0.001
6	=A5+1	=A6^2+A6	=((A6+0.001)^2+(A2+0.001)-B6)/0.001
7	=A6+1	=A7^2+A7	=((A7+0.001)^2+(A2+0.001)-B7)/0.001
8	=A7+1	=A8^2+A8	=((A8+0.001)^2+(A2+0.001)-B8)/0.001
9	=A8+1	=A9^2+A9	=((A9+0.001)^2+(A2+0.001)-B9)/0.001
10	=A9+1	=A10^2+A10	=((A10+0.001)^2+(A2+0.001)-B10)/0.001
11	=A10+1	=A11^2+A11	=((A11+0.001)^2+(A2+0.001)-B11)/0.001
12	=A11+1	=A12^2+A12	=((A12+0.001)^2+(A2+0.001)-B12)/0.001

2 If f(x) = g(x) + h(x), then f$'$(x) = g$'$(x) + h$'$(x).
Explore, using the method you used above, whether this rule of differentiation is true for the following functions. (Deduce what you expect the solution to be and check that you are correct.)

a f(x) = $x^2 + \dfrac{x^3}{3}$ **b** f(x) = $\dfrac{x^2}{2} - x$ **c** f(x) = $x(x - 1)$ (Multiply out the bracket first.)

d f(x) = $x^2 + 2x + 1$ **e** f(x) = $\dfrac{x^4}{4} + 2$ **f** f(t) = $10t - 5t^2$

2.3 Applying differentiation

Skydiver

In the previous section you learnt how to calculate the derivatives of some functions. The derivative of a function gives the rate at which the function is changing. This can be applied to, for example, finding speeds or growth rates.

A simple model (Model 1) of the distance, d metres, fallen in time t seconds by a free-fall skydiver is:

$$d(t) = 4.9t^2$$

Skydiver

Seedlings

Disease

A packaging problem

Maximum and minimum problems

Activity 2.3A

Sketch a graph of Model 1. Use your sketch to write a sentence or two to describe how the distance fallen by the skydiver changes with time.

The derived function of $d(t) = 4.9t^2$ is $d'(t) = 9.8t$. This gives the rate of change of distance with time, which is speed. You can use this to calculate estimates of the speed of the skydiver at any time.

For example, the speed after 5 seconds of free-fall, according to this model, is 49 metres per second.

Discussion point
Why are the values that you calculate only estimates?

Discussion point
How realistic do you think the model $d(t) = 4.9t^2$ is for the falling skydiver?

Activity 2.3B

1 Write a sentence or two to describe what happens to the speed of the skydiver according to Model 1.

2 A different model (Model 2) for the distance travelled by a skydiver is $d(t) = 4.9t^2 - 0.1t^3$. Sketch a graph of this function (or use a graph drawing program).

3 How does the graph of this function differ from the graph of $d(t) = 4.9t^2$? How does this affect the gradient?

4 Find the derived function giving the speed of the skydiver according to the new model.

5 Make a table to show the speeds predicted by the two models over the first ten seconds of motion.

6 Write a sentence or two in which you compare the two models. Which model do you think is more realistic? Explain your answer.

Time seconds	Speed Model 1 (metres per second)	Speed Model 2 (metres per second)
0		
1		
2		
3		
4		
5		
6		
7		
8		
9		
10		

29

Seedlings

You can model the height of a seedling, h mm, t days after it is planted using this quadratic function.

$$h = 2.5 + 2.8t - 0.04t^2$$

Activity 2.3C

1 a Find the gradient function of $h = 2.5 + 2.8t - 0.04t^2$.

b The gradient function gives the rate of change of the height of the seedling t days after it is planted. It is measured in mm/day (millimetres per day).

Use this to calculate how fast the seedling is growing 10 days after being planted.

2 Sketch a graph of the gradient function for $0 \leqslant t \leqslant 40$.

a What does this indicate about the height of the seedling 35 days after being planted?

b Explain why this quadratic model is not appropriate for the whole of the seedling's growth.

Discussion point

What other functions could be used to model the growth of a seedling?

Disease

Infections such as colds can spread amongst workers or children in a school. The general pattern is that people infect each other so that the number of people infected increases rapidly until everyone who is going to catch the disease has caught it and people begin to recover. The number of people with the disease then decreases until everyone is better. This pattern can be modelled by a quadratic function.

The graph shows an example of what may happen.

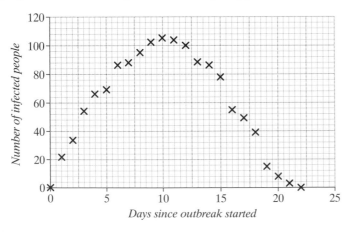

Days since outbreak started

It shows the number of people infected with a cold virus after the outbreak started.

No. of days since outbreak	No. of cases
0	0
1	22
2	34
3	54
4	67
5	69
6	86
7	88
8	95
9	102
10	105
11	103
12	100
13	89
14	86
15	78
16	55
17	49
18	39
19	15
20	8
21	3
22	0

Activity 2.3D

1 Check that the quadratic function $y = 22x - x^2$ models the data well by plotting a graph of the data and superimposing a graph of the function.

2 a Find the gradient function of $y = 22x - x^2$.

   b Explain what this function tells you about the situation it models.

   c What is the greatest value of the gradient for $0 \leqslant x \leqslant 22$? When is the cold spreading most rapidly, according to this model?

   d When is the number of cases decreasing most rapidly, according to the model?

   e When is the number of cases neither increasing nor decreasing, according to this model?

   f Compare your answers with the original data in the graph and comment.

3 Use the gradient function to find the gradient twenty two days after the start of the outbreak. What does this tell you?

A packaging problem

Suppose a packaging manufacturer wants to make trays from square sheets of card by removing square corners and folding as in the diagram.

What is the maximum volume of such a tray? You may have worked on problems like this for GCSE. You will answer it using a calculus method in the next activity.

Activity 2.3E

1 Suppose that the original sheet of card is 50 cm by 50 cm and the squares removed from each corner are of side length x cm.

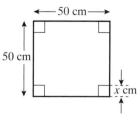

Show that the volume, V cm^3, of the tray is given by:

$$V = x(50 - 2x)^2 = 4x^3 - 200x^2 + 2500x$$

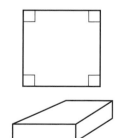

Discussion point
The following graphs below show the volume function $V(x)$ and its gradient function $V'(x)$ plotted against x.

2 Draw a graph of V plotted against x for $0 \leqslant x \leqslant 25$.

3 Use your graph to find

   a the value of x for which the volume is at its maximum

   b the value of this maximum volume.

4 What is the gradient of the graph when the volume is at its maximum? You can use the answer to this question to find accurate values of x and V at this maximum point.

5 Show that $\dfrac{\mathrm{d}V}{\mathrm{d}x} = 12x^2 - 400x + 2500$.

(This gives the gradient function for $V(x)$.)

6 At the maximum point the gradient of $V(x)$ is zero. Find the values of x for which

$$\frac{\mathrm{d}V}{\mathrm{d}x} = 12x^2 - 400x + 2500 = 0.$$

Explain your two answers.

7 Find the maximum value of the volume of the tray.

8 Compare your answers with the values you got from your graph in **question 3**.

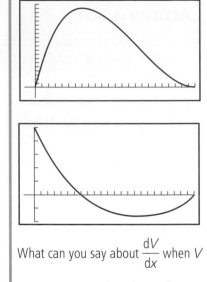

What can you say about $\dfrac{\mathrm{d}V}{\mathrm{d}x}$ when V is a maximum? What about when V is increasing or decreasing?

Note: To answer **question 6** you will have to solve a quadratic equation.
$12x^2 - 400x + 2500 = 0$ or
$3x^2 - 100x + 625 = 0$

You should use factorisation or the formula

$$x = \frac{-b \pm \sqrt{b^2 - 4ac}}{2a} \quad \text{to do}$$

this. See **Chapter 2** in *Algebra and Graphs*.

Maximum and minimum problems

In the previous activity you used calculus to find where a gradient function has a value of zero. This occurs at important features – in the case above where the volume of the packaging tray was a maximum. The technique above can therefore often be used to determine important features. The following gives more examples of this.

Activity 2.3F

1 The height, h mm, of a seedling t days after it is planted may be modelled by $h = 2.5 + 2.8t - 0.04t^2$. You may like to refer to the work you have done on this before moving on.

   a Draw a graph of h against t.

   b Find $\dfrac{\mathrm{d}h}{\mathrm{d}t}$.

   c Find the rate of growth of the seedling
     i 5 days   **ii** 25 days
    after it is planted.
    Interpret your answers in terms of the rate of growth of the seedling and its height – refer to your graph.

   d Find t and h when $\dfrac{\mathrm{d}h}{\mathrm{d}t} = 0$.

    Explain what this tells you – refer to your graph.

Day (n)	Height (h mm)
5	18
10	28
15	38
20	43
25	45

2 The table gives the sunrise and sunset times in London between 30 April and 8 August. The times are given in hours and minutes, Greenwich Mean Time.

Day n (0 = 30 April)	Sunrise time t_r (GMT)	Sunset time t_s (GMT)
0	05:33	20:23
10	05:15	20:39
20	05:01	20:54
30	04:50	21:07
40	04:44	21:16
50	04:43	21:21
60	04:47	21:21
70	04:55	21:16
80	05:07	21:06
90	05:20	20:52
100	05:36	20:35

The graph below shows sunrise time, t_r, and sunset time, t_s, plotted against n, the number of days after 30 April.

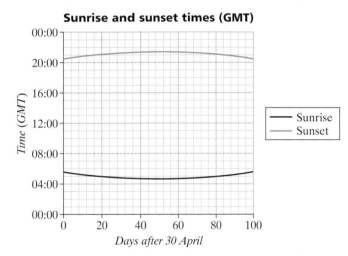

Sunrise and sunset times (GMT)

Days after 30 April

Sunrise
Sunset

The functions $t_r = 0.0003n^2 - 0.03n + 5.4$ and $t_s = -0.00035n^2 + 0.035n + 20.3$ can be used to model the data.

a Find **i** $\dfrac{dt_r}{dn}$ and **ii** $\dfrac{dt_s}{dn}$.

b Find:
  i the number of days after 30 April, and hence the date, when sunrise is earliest, i.e., when $\dfrac{dt_r}{dn} = 0$
  ii the time of sunrise when it is earliest.

c Find:
  i the number of days after 30 April, and hence the date, when sunset is latest
  ii the time of sunset when it is latest.

Discussion point
Are these good models?

Checkpoint
Check your answers by referring to the graph above.

2.4 Revision summary

Finding gradients numerically

The gradient of the graph of $y = \mathrm{f}(x)$ at a point P is approximated as the gradient of the chord PQ.

As the point Q moves closer to P, the gradient of PQ gets closer to the gradient of $y = \mathrm{f}(x)$ at P.

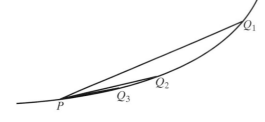

If the value of x at P is a and the value of x at Q is $a + h$, then the gradient of the chord PQ is $\dfrac{\mathrm{f}(a + h) - \mathrm{f}(a)}{h}$. The smaller h is, the closer this is to the gradient of $y = \mathrm{f}(x)$ at P.

Finding gradients by differentiation

Results using the formula above lead to the general result that the gradient function $\mathrm{f}'(x)$ of $\mathrm{f}(x) = x^n$ is $\mathrm{f}'(x) = nx^{n-1}$ and, more generally, if $\mathrm{f}(x) = kx^n$, then $\mathrm{f}'(x) = knx^{n-1}$, and if $\mathrm{f}(x) = \mathrm{g}(x) + \mathrm{h}(x)$ then $\mathrm{f}'(x) = \mathrm{g}'(x) + \mathrm{h}'(x)$.

In alternative notation, this becomes:

if $y = x^n$, $\dfrac{dy}{dx} = nx^{n-1}$, if $y = kx^n$, $\dfrac{dy}{dx} = knx^{n-1}$, and if $\mathrm{y}(x) = \mathrm{g}(x) + \mathrm{h}(x)$, $\dfrac{dy}{dx} = \dfrac{dg}{dx} + \dfrac{dh}{dx}$.

$\mathrm{f}'(x)$ and $\dfrac{dy}{dx}$ are the differentials of $\mathrm{f}(x)$ and y with respect to x.

Finding gradients by differentiation

The gradient function for a function made up of the sum of two or more simple functions is the sum of the separate gradient functions.

For example, if $y = 5x^3 - 2x^2 + 8x$, $\dfrac{dy}{dx} = 15x^2 - 4x + 8$.

The finding of gradients by calculus can be applied to problems such as finding the speed at a particular time by using the gradient function of the distance travelled. Maximising and minimising problems can also be solved by finding when the value of the gradient function is zero.

2.5 Preparing for assessment

Your coursework portfolio

In **Chapter 2** you have learnt one of the most important methods of calculus, differentiation.

For portfolio work on this chapter, look at some of the work in **Section 2.3** 'Applying differentiation'. Can you find data for situations like some of these? Perhaps you could use a data-logger to collect some speed–time data.

You need to model your data using an algebraic function that you can differentiate. Make sure you use the correct notation for all your work and show that you can do the necessary algebraic manipulations.

What does the gradient function tell you about the situation you are investigating – can you find out where the function is increasing most rapidly, or most slowly, or not increasing at all? Can you solve a maximising or minimising problem?

You could compare your results obtained by calculus with results obtained by drawing gradients by hand. Which method do you think is better?

Practice exam questions

Emergency stop

Data

1 A car accelerates to a speed of 30 miles per hour before doing an emergency stop. The sketch graph shows the distance travelled by the car, d feet, plotted against the time, t seconds, after the car started to move.

The graph of the distance travelled by the car, d feet, plotted against the time, t seconds, after the car started to move is given in more detail on the Resource Sheet.

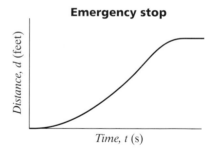
Emergency stop

Question

Resource Sheet 2.5

a   i Find the gradient of the graph at the point where $t = 4$ by drawing a tangent to the graph.
    ii Hence find the car's speed at this time, giving your answer in miles per hour. (**Note:** 1 mile = 5280 feet)

b   i What are the co-ordinates of t at the points on the graph where the gradient is zero?
    ii What does this tell you about the real situation?
    iii Estimate the value of t when the car is travelling at the greatest speed.

c   The data can be modelled by the function
    $d = 4 - 10.5t + 8.2t^2 - 0.47t^3$.
    i Find $d'(t)$.
    ii Calculate the percentage difference between the value of $d'(t)$ when $t = 4$ and the gradient you found in **part a i**.
    iii Find the values of d and $d'(t)$ predicted by this model when $t = 0$ and explain why these values are not appropriate in the real situation.
    iv Calculate the times at which the model predicts that the speed of the car will be zero.

Water tank

Data

2 Water is emptied from a water tank using a tap at its base. The depth of water in the tank, d cm, is measured at 10 second intervals.

The data collected is given in the table.

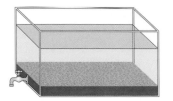

The water tank data has been plotted in the diagram below together with the model

$$d(t) = \frac{(t - 150)^2}{1000} + 1$$

Time, t (s)	Depth, d (cm)
0	23.0
10	20.2
20	17.7
30	15.2
40	12.9
50	10.8
60	8.9
70	7.1
80	5.7
90	4.5
100	3.4
110	2.5
120	1.8
130	1.4
140	1.2
150	1.1
160	1.1

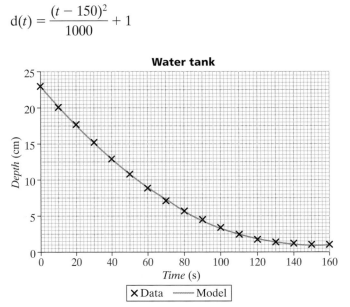

Water tank

× Data —— Model

a **i** Calculate d(80).

ii Find the percentage error when this value is compared with the actual depth after 80 seconds.

b **i** What is the minimum value of d(t)? When does this occur?

ii Sketch the graph of d(t) for $0 \leqslant t \leqslant 300$. Show clearly the co-ordinates of the minimum point and any points at which the curve meets the axes.

iii Explain why this function does not provide a good model of the situation for large values of t.

c **i** Show that the model can be written as
d(t) = $0.001t^2 - 0.3t + 23.5$.

ii Hence, find the value of d$'$(80).

3 Areas under Curves

▶ Contents

In this chapter you will extend the ideas you first met in **Chapter 1** about how the area under a graph can give you important information about situations.

For example, you have seen how the area under a velocity–time graph can let you find distance travelled.

The speed–time data and graph here, for example, are for an aircraft accelerating down a runway at take-off. The distance travelled by the aircraft can be found using the area under the graph. It is possible to find this area approximately by splitting it up into rectangles for example. As these diagrams show, the more (i.e. thinner) rectangles, you use, the more closely the area is likely to be to the actual area.

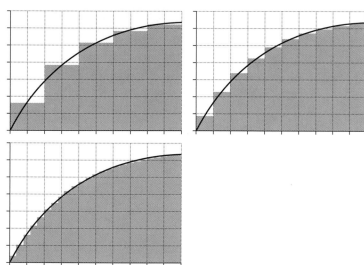

t (s)	v (ms⁻¹)
0	0
1	11.8
2	18.2
3	23.5
4	27.6
5	29.4
6	30.9
7	31.8

In this chapter you will learn how to calculate estimates of such areas and learn about **integration**, which allows you to calculate areas accurately.

These ideas can be extended beyond finding areas to calculate, for example, volumes that may be formed by rotating curves about an axis. For example, you could calculate the height to which a wine glass must be filled so that it is exactly half full – although such problems are beyond the scope of this course.

3.1 Calculating areas accurately

The trapezium method

Geographers and environmentalists sometimes need to find the cross-sectional area of a river, so that they can calculate the volume of the water flow.

This table gives the depth of a small river, in centimetres, measured at 1 metre intervals across the river at six different places.

The places chosen are bends or **meanders** of the river.

The trapezium method

Car performance data

A **meander** is a curve or winding of a stream of river.

Meander	River depths (cm) at various recording stations (1 metre intervals)							
	0	1	2	3	4	5	6	7
A	0	2	10	19	34	42	0	0
B	0	8	17	21	19	15	2	0
C	0	15	20	21	17	0	0	0
D	0	26	30	41	32	16	0	0
E	0	36	37	29	21	20	0	0
F	0	2	27	51	43	24	20	0

The data for Meander A has been used to draw this diagram, which is a picture of the cross-section of the river.

Note that the scales on the two axes are very different!

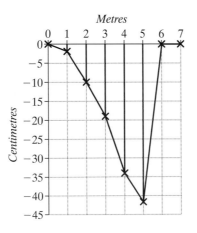

Discussion point

How could the picture of the cross-section be improved?

Discussion point

Why is the area calculated by this method only an estimate? How could you improve the accuracy of your answer?

You can split up the cross-section into triangles and trapezia so that you can estimate the area of the cross-section.

The area of this cross-section is therefore given approximately by:

$$\left[\begin{array}{l} \frac{1}{2} \times 1 \times 0.02 + \frac{1}{2} \times 1 \times (0.02 + 0.10) + \\ \quad \frac{1}{2} \times 1 \times (0.10 + 0.19) + \frac{1}{2} \times 1 \times (0.19 + 0.34) + \\ \quad\quad \frac{1}{2} \times 1 \times (0.34 + 0.42) + \frac{1}{2} \times 1 \times 0.42 \end{array} \right] m^2$$

$$= [0.01 + 0.06 + 0.145 + 0.265 + 0.38 + 0.21]\, m^2$$
$$= 1.07\, m^2$$

This method is known as the **trapezium method** even though one or more of the trapezia can become triangles if one side has zero length.

Discussion point

Could you explain this calculation to someone else?

Note that the depths in centimetres have been converted to metres here.

Activity 3.1A

1 **a** Use the trapezium method to find the area of the cross-section of the river at Meander B.

   b At Meander B, the river flows at a rate of approximately 0.1 metres per second. What volume of water flows past Meander B in an hour?

2 Find the meander that has the greatest cross-sectional area.

3 Use the trapezium method to find the approximate area of this windsurf sail.

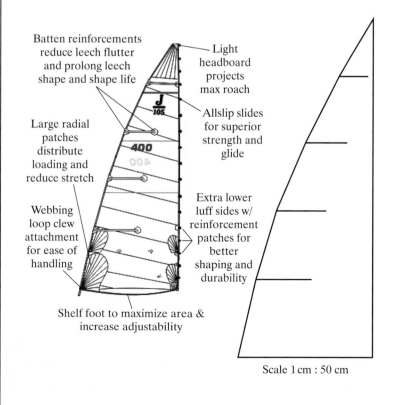

Batten reinforcements reduce leech flutter and prolong leech shape and shape life

Light headboard projects max roach

Large radial patches distribute loading and reduce stretch

Allslip slides for superior strength and glide

Webbing loop clew attachment for ease of handling

Extra lower luff sides w/ reinforcement patches for better shaping and durability

Shelf foot to maximize area & increase adjustability

Scale 1 cm : 50 cm

Car performance data

Here is a graph of the car data you used in **Section 1.3** of *Algebra and Graphs* – notice that the graph gives the speed of the car in metres per second.

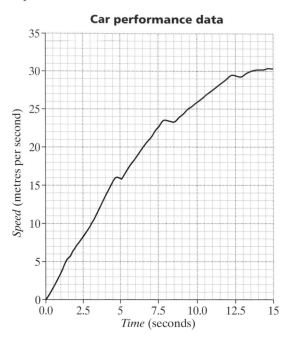

Car performance data

The area under this speed–time graph gives the distance travelled by the car. You need to be careful with units – in this particular case, the units on the horizontal axis are seconds; the units on the vertical axis are metres per second. Therefore the units for the area under the graph will be:

$$\text{seconds} \times \frac{\text{metres}}{\text{seconds}}, \text{ i.e. metres.}$$

Time, (seconds)	Speed, (mph)
0.00	0.00
0.50	2.80
1.00	6.90
1.50	11.50
2.00	14.40
2.50	17.90
3.00	21.10
3.50	25.20
4.00	29.60
4.50	33.90
5.00	35.30
5.50	37.50
6.00	40.60
6.50	43.80
7.00	46.80
7.50	49.80
8.00	52.20
8.50	51.70
9.00	53.60
9.50	55.60
10.00	57.20
10.50	59.20
11.00	60.90
11.50	62.60
12.00	64.50
12.50	65.50
13.00	65.20
13.50	66.80
14.00	67.20
14.50	67.40
15.00	67.50
15.50	66.70
16.00	65.40

Discussion point

How do you convert values in miles per hour into metres per second (ms^{-1})?

What are the units of the area under a speed–time graph with the horizontal axis in hours and the vertical axis in miles per hour?

Activity 3.1B

1 The area under this speed–time graph has been split into six 'strips' (a right-angled triangle and five trapezia). Use these to show that the area under the graph is approximately 290 (i.e. that the distance travelled by this car in the 15 seconds shown in the graph is approximately 290 metres).

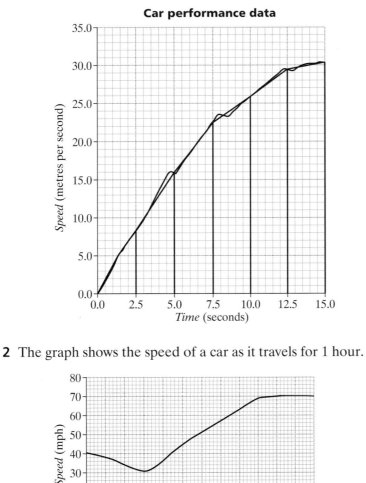

2 The graph shows the speed of a car as it travels for 1 hour.

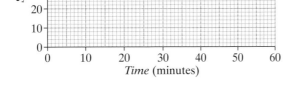

Estimate the distance travelled by the car during this time

a using 1 'strip'
b using 4 'strips'

Watch the units!

Which answer is likely to be the more accurate? Why?

3.2 Numerical methods for finding areas under graphs

The trapezium rule

Excel Activity

The trapezium rule
|
Mid-ordinate rule
|
Calculating areas

In the previous section you used trapezia to approximate areas under graphs. This is an example of a numerical method, which is not exact but, depending on the data available, can be made very accurate by increasing the number of trapezia used. In this section you will formalise this method.

Here is the river cross-section data again.

Using trapezia, the area of the river cross-section for Meander A is:

$$\left[\begin{array}{c} 1 \times \frac{1}{2}(0 + 0.02) + 1 \times \frac{1}{2}(0.02 + 0.10) + \\ 1 \times \frac{1}{2}(0.10 + 0.19) + 1 \times \frac{1}{2}(0.19 + 0.34) + \\ 1 \times \frac{1}{2}(0.34 + 0.42) + 1 \times \frac{1}{2}(0.42 + 0) \end{array} \right] \text{m}^2$$

$$= [0.01 + 0.06 + 0.145 + 0.265 + 0.38 + 0.21] \text{ m}^2$$
$$= 1.07 \text{ m}^2$$

To generalise this method, use the notation f_n to represent the depth of the river (in metres), n metres across the river.

The area is therefore:

$$A = \left[\begin{array}{c} 1 \times \frac{1}{2}(f_0 + f_1) + 1 \times \frac{1}{2}(f_1 + f_2) \\ + 1 \times \frac{1}{2}(f_2 + f_3) + 1 \times \frac{1}{2}(f_3 + f_4) \\ 1 \times \frac{1}{2}(f_4 + f_5) + 1 \times \frac{1}{2}(f_5 + f_6) \end{array} \right] \text{m}^2$$

This simplifies to:

$$A = 1 \times \tfrac{1}{2}(f_0 + 2f_1 + 2f_2 + 2f_3 + 2f_4 + 2f_5 + f_6)$$
$$= \tfrac{1}{2}(f_0 + f_6) + (f_1 + f_2 + f_3 + f_4 + f_5)$$

River depths (cm) at various recording stations (1 metre intervals)

Meander	0	1	2	3	4	5	6	7
A	0	2	10	19	34	42	0	0
B	0	8	17	21	19	15	2	0
C	0	15	20	21	17	0	0	0
D	0	26	30	41	32	16	0	0
E	0	36	37	29	21	20	0	0
F	0	2	27	51	43	24	20	0

Discussion point

Can you explain where each of the terms $1 \times \frac{1}{2}(0 + 0.02)$ and $1 \times \frac{1}{2}(0.02 + 0.10)$ come from in this expression? Why are the values 1 and $\frac{1}{2}$ included in each term?

Discussion point

Can you relate terms such as $1 \times \frac{1}{2}(f_0 + f_1)$ and $1 \times \frac{1}{2}(f_1 + f_2)$ to the numerical terms in the expression above?

Discussion point

Can you carry out the algebraic simplification necessary to give this? Why are the terms f_0 and f_6 added once only whilst the terms f_1, f_2, f_3, f_4 and f_5 are added twice?

Activity 3.2A

1 Use the data for Meander D with the formula above to calculate the area of the cross-section of the river at this point.

2 How would you adapt the formula for

a Meander C

b Meander F?

In general, if you have a set of values $f_0 \ldots f_n$ corresponding to a set of evenly spaced x-values $x_0 \ldots x_n$, the area under the graph of the points (x_n, f_n) is

☞ $A = \frac{1}{2}h[f_0 + 2(f_1 + \ldots + f_{n-1}) + f_n]$ The trapezium rule

where h is the width of each trapezium, i.e. the difference between each x-value and the next.

Activity 3.2B

This table shows the speed of a single-scull boat during one rowing stroke.

Time (s)	0	0.2	0.4	0.6	0.8	1	1.2	1.4	1.6
Speed (ms⁻¹)	4.5	3.5	3.8	4.7	5.7	6.2	6	5.4	4.5

Use the trapezium rule formula to find the distance travelled by the boat during the stroke.

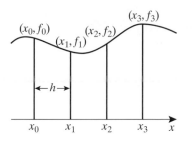

Mid-ordinate rule

Another method you can use to find areas under graphs is by using rectangles. Here is the car performance graph again. A series of rectangles have been superimposed on the graph. You can use these to find approximately the area under the graph.

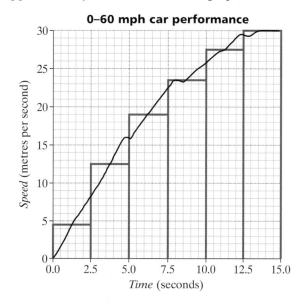

The height of each rectangle is the y co-ordinate of the graph in the middle of each $2\frac{1}{2}$ second time-interval. This is why this method is often known as the mid-ordinate rule.

The x and y co-ordinates of a point are also known as its **abscissa** and its **ordinate**.

Activity 3.2C

1 a Calculate the areas of the six rectangles in the diagram to estimate the distance travelled by the car in the first 15 seconds.

b Compare your answer with your answer to the question in **Activity 3.1C**. Which do you think is the better estimate?

2 a Use the mid-ordinate rule to estimate the area under the graph of $y = x^2$ from $x = 0$ to $x = 6$
   i using 3 rectangles
   ii using 6 rectangles.

b Which of your answers to **part a** gives the better estimate? Explain your answer.

3 You can use the function $v = 1.4 \sin 225(t + 0.93)° + 4.8$ to model the speed of the single-scull rowing boat, where v ms^{-1} is the speed of the boat after t seconds.

a Draw a graph of the data together with the function $v = 1.4 \sin 225(t + 0.93)° + 4.8$.

b Use the model to calculate the speed of the boat when $t = 0.1, 0.3, 0.5$, etc. Hence estimate, using the mid-ordinate rule, the distance travelled by the boat over the 1.6 seconds of the stroke.

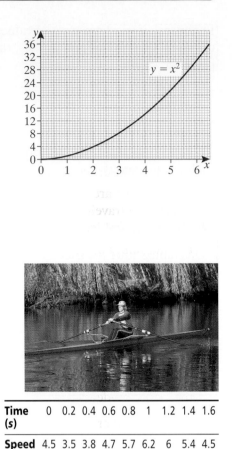

$y = x^2$

Time (s)	0	0.2	0.4	0.6	0.8	1	1.2	1.4	1.6
Speed (ms^{-1})	4.5	3.5	3.8	4.7	5.7	6.2	6	5.4	4.5

There are other numerical methods for finding areas under curves; one you may meet is called Simpson's rule. Here, parts of the graph are approximated by quadratic functions, and the areas under those quadratic graphs are calculated. This is obviously a complicated procedure but there is a formula which does all the thinking for you!

With all numerical methods, you get a better result by using strips of smaller width.

Discussion point
Is this always true?

Calculating areas

In the following activity there are a number of practical situations in which you are asked to calculate the area under a graph.

Activity 3.2D

1 The speed, v ms^{-1}, of an aircraft t seconds after it starts from rest and accelerates along a runway at take-off can be modelled by $v = \frac{1}{16}(t - 8)^3 + 32$ for $0 \leqslant t \leqslant 8$.

a Draw up a table giving v for the aircraft at 1 second intervals.

t	0	1	2	3	4	5	6	7	8
v									

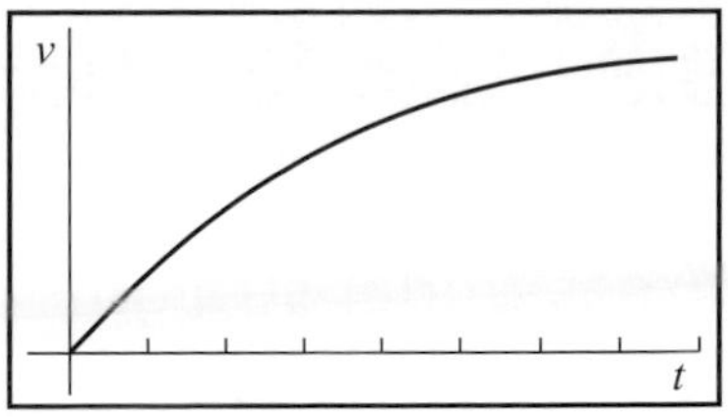

b Use

i the trapezium rule

ii the mid-ordinate rule

to find the area under a graph of v plotted against t, i.e. the distance travelled along the runway by the plane in the first 8 seconds of its motion.

c Find values of v for every half-second, i.e. at $t = 0.5, 1.5, 2.5, 3.5, 4.5, 5.5, 6.5$ and 7.5.

Use your new data to recalculate the distance travelled by the plane again using both the trapezium and mid-ordinate rules.

Comment on your answers.

2 The cross-section of a model aeroplane wing is the shape of the area bounded by the graphs of $y = 50 + \dfrac{3x}{2} - \dfrac{x^2}{20}$ and $y = 50 - x$, where x and y are measured in centimetres.

a Plot graphs of the above functions on your graphic calculator.

b Use a numerical method, with strip widths of 10 cm, to find the area enclosed by the graph of $y = 50 + \dfrac{3x}{2} - \dfrac{x^2}{20}$ and the x-axis for $0 \leqslant x \leqslant 50$.

c Find the area of the cross-section of the model aeroplane wing by subtracting the area enclosed by $y = 50 - x$ and the x-axis for $0 \leqslant x \leqslant 50$ from your answer to **part b**.

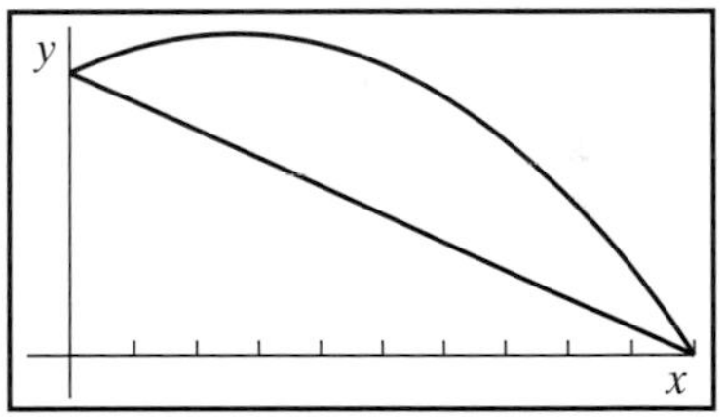

You might like to do these questions using a spreadsheet.

Discussion point

Which answer do you think is most accurate?

What are the reasons for your answers?

3.3 Area functions

Areas under straight line graphs

Consider a skydiver who falls from rest (that is, starts with zero speed). If we ignore air resistance, free-falling objects have constant acceleration of approximately 10 metres per second per second (ms^{-2}), as shown in the graph below. The graph has the equation $a = 10$.

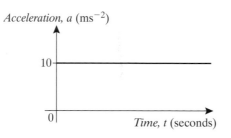

Acceleration, a (ms^{-2})

Time, t (seconds)

Activity 3.3A

a What will the increase in speed of the skydiver be in

   i the first second of motion;
   ii the first 2 seconds of motion;
   iii the first 5 seconds of motion;
   iv the first t seconds of motion?

   Note that because the speed of the skydiver is initially zero your answers here therefore give the speed of the skydiver.

b Make sure you understand how the function $v(t) = 10t$ gives the area under the acceleration–time graph and consequently the increase in speed of the skydiver. In this case (because the speed of the skydiver is zero when $t = 0$, $v(t) = 10t$ gives the speed of the skydiver.

   Sketch a graph of this function.

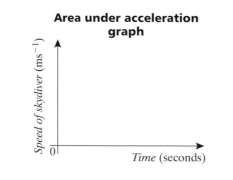

Area under acceleration graph

Speed of skydiver (ms^{-1})

Time (seconds)

c What does the area under this graph represent?

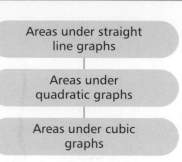

Areas under straight line graphs

Areas under quadratic graphs

Areas under cubic graphs

Discussion point

The area under this graph gives the increase in speed. In what units will this be measured?

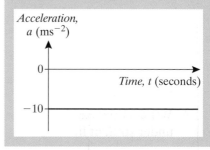

Note: Acceleration is a quantity that needs to take account of magnitude and direction. In this case the skydiver accelerates downwards. If you were to measure the upward direction as positive then $a = -10$ and the graph corresponding to this is shown below.

Acceleration, a (ms^{-2})

Time, t (seconds)

Discussion point

Acceleration on the Moon is approximately $\frac{1}{6}$ of that on the Earth. How would this affect a graph of speed of a skydiver near the surface of the Moon?

Activity 3.3B

Consider a simplified model of a car starting from rest and accelerating steadily for 5 seconds until it reaches a speed of 15 ms^{-1}. This gives a speed–time graph that is a straight line.

1 a Use the area under the straight line graph to find the distance travelled by this car during the first 5 seconds of its motion.

   b How far does the car travel in the final 2 seconds of this motion (i.e. from $t = 3$ to $t = 5$)?

2 Suppose the car accelerates at the same rate as before for t seconds.

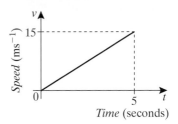

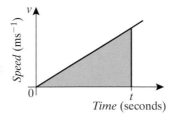

   a Explain why the equation of the straight line speed–time graph is $v = 3t$, where $v \text{ ms}^{-1}$ represents the speed of the car after t seconds.

   b By finding the shaded area, show that the car travels $x = \frac{1}{2} \times t \times 3t = \frac{3}{2}t^2$ metres in the first t seconds.

   c How far does the car travel in the final 2 seconds, that is from $t = 3$ to $t = 5$? Explain how you can use the formula $x = \frac{3}{2}t^2$ to calculate this.

3 a Find a general formula for the area under the straight line $y = mx$ from the origin to x.

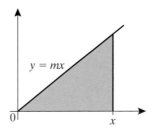

   b Check your formula by using it to answer **1a**.

4 Write a brief explanation that shows that the area from 0 to x under straight lines of the form $y = c$ is given by cx.

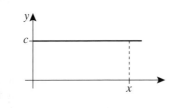

Discussion point

Do you know any other method that you can use to calculate the distance travelled?

Discussion point

How will your formula be different for graphs of the form $y = mx + c$?

Areas under quadratic graphs

You can find the area under a straight line graph easily and exactly using trapezia and triangles or the formulae you have just developed.

To find the area under the graphs of more complex functions, you need to go back to using approximating trapezia again.

The simplest of all quadratic graphs is $y = x^2$.

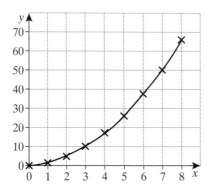

You can find the heights of the trapezia using the equation $y = x^2$.

x	y	Area under graph between this x-value and the previous one	Area under curve from 0 up to x
0	0	0	0
1	1	0.5	0.5
2	4	2.5	3
3	9	6.5	9.5
4	16	12.5	22
5	25	20.5	42.5
6	36		
7	49		
8	64		

Discussion points

Can you explain how the value of 2.5 gives the area under the graph from $x = 1$ to $x = 2$?

Are the areas in the last column of the table under- or over-estimates of the actual area under the curve?

Activity 3.3C

Resource Sheet 3.3C

1 Complete the table above by calculating the values for $x = 6$, 7 and 8. You could use a spreadsheet to do this.

2 a Plot a graph showing the values in the final column of the table plotted against x.

   b Find a function, $A(x)$ (the area function), that fits these data points.

3 Use the results you have so far to help you find the area under the graph of $y = x^2 + 2$ from

   a 0 to 1   **b** 0 to 2   **c** 0 to 3   **d** 0 to 4   **e** 0 to 5.

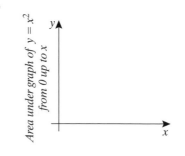

4 What is the connection between the area under the graph of $y = x^2$ from 0 to x and the area under the graph of $y = x^2 + c$ from 0 to x?

5 a Draw up a table like the one you used for **question 1** to help you find the area under the graph of $y = 3x^2$ from

   i 0 to 1   **ii** 0 to 2   **iii** 0 to 3   **iv** 0 to 4   **v** 0 to 5.

b Set up a spreadsheet to do the same thing but use many more strips to give a more accurate answer.

6 What is the connection between the area under the graph of $y = x^2$ from 0 to x and the area under the graph of $y = mx^2$ from 0 to x?

7 Collect together results from this section so far to fill in the area function column in the table below.

Function, f(x)	Area function, A(x)	Derivative of A(x)
$y = c$		
$y = mx$		
$y = x^2$		
$y = mx^2$		
$y = mx^2 + c$		

8 Complete the table by filling in the final column of the table. Write down what you notice about your results.

Remember that the functions in the second column may not be exact because you used trapezia to approximate the areas under the curves.

How can you use what you have noticed to find A(x) if you know f(x)?

Test your rules out on the functions you have used so far.

You should now have the following results.

Function, f(x)	Area function, A(x)	Derivative of A(x)
$y = c$	$A = cx$	$\dfrac{dA}{dx} = c$
$y = mx + c$	$A = \dfrac{mx^2}{2} + cx$	$\dfrac{dA}{dx} = mx + c$
$y = x^2$	$A = \dfrac{x^3}{3}$	$\dfrac{dA}{dx} = x^2$
$y = mx^2 + c$	$A = \dfrac{mx^3}{3} + cx$	$\dfrac{dA}{dx} = mx^2 + c$

Activity 3.3D

1 Check that these results are consistent with yours and reconcile any discrepancies.

2 Use the rules demonstrated in the table above to find area functions for:

a $y = x^2 + 3$

b $y = 5x - 4$

c $y = \frac{1}{2}x^2 - 10$

> **Nuffield Resource**
> 'That's a lot of rock'

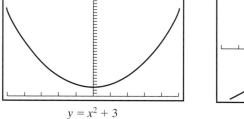

$y = x^2 + 3$

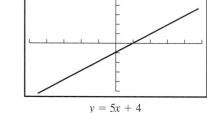

$y = 5x + 4$

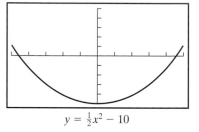

$y = \frac{1}{2}x^2 - 10$

Areas under cubic graphs

In the previous Activity you explored the areas under the graphs of some simple polynomial functions, and the derivatives of the area functions you found. This should have led you to make some observations, such as:

- the function for the area under the graph of a function that is a power of x is based on x raised to a power that is one greater than the original power – for example, the area function for a quadratic graph is a cubic;
- the derivative of the area function is the function itself.

These general rules can help you to calculate the area function for any function based on x raised to a power.

The simplest cubic function is $y = x^3$.

The derivative of the area function must be x^3, so the area function involves x^4.

> **Discussion point**
> Does this make sense?
>
> Can you express it algebraically?

Activity 3.3E

1 a What is the derivative of x^4?

b What do you have to do to this to obtain x^3?

c So what is the area function for $y = x^3$?

2 Work out the area functions for these functions:

a $y = 2x^3$ b $y = 4x^3$ c $y = \frac{1}{2}x^3$ d $y = ax^3$

3 Here are sketches of the graph of $y = x^3$.
Calculate the shaded areas.

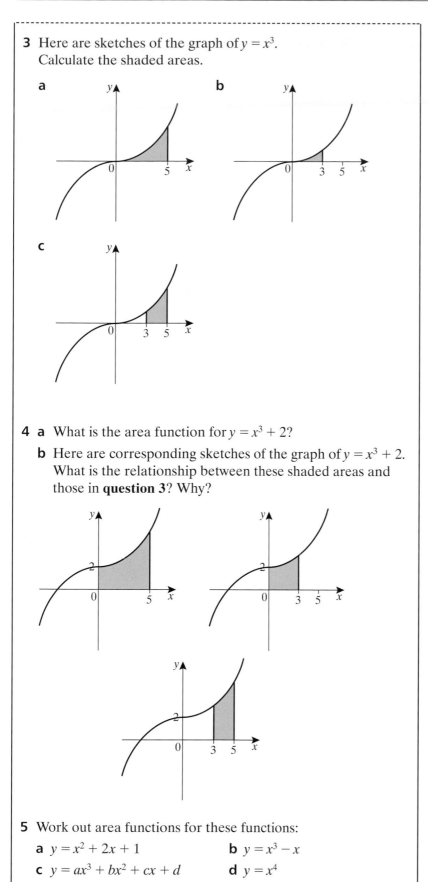

a

b

c

4 a What is the area function for $y = x^3 + 2$?

b Here are corresponding sketches of the graph of $y = x^3 + 2$.
What is the relationship between these shaded areas and
those in **question 3**? Why?

5 Work out area functions for these functions:

a $y = x^2 + 2x + 1$ **b** $y = x^3 - x$

c $y = ax^3 + bx^2 + cx + d$ **d** $y = x^4$

3.4 Integrating polynomial functions

Straight line graphs

Straight line graphs

Areas under higher order polynomial graphs

So far you have met one main branch of calculus: differentiation.

Finding areas beneath graphs of functions is the basis of the other main area of calculus – integration. In this section you will practise finding areas under graphs and learn the notation of integration.

In the previous section, you found that the area function for any straight line $y = mx + c$ is $A = \dfrac{mx^2}{2} + cx$.

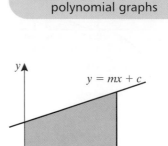

This 'area function' gives the area shaded in the diagram, from 0 to x.

If you want to find the area from, for example, $x = a$ to $x = b$, you find the area from 0 to b and subtract the area from 0 to a.

So, for the straight line $y = 3x + 1$, the area function is $A = \dfrac{3x^2}{2} + x$.

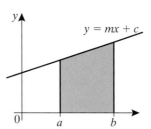

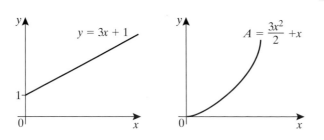

To find the area under $y = 3x + 1$ between $x = 2$ and $x = 4$, find the value of the area function for $x = 4$ and subtract the value for $x = 2$.

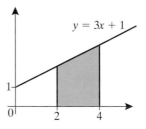

So the area under $y = 3x + 1$ between $x = 2$ and $x = 4$ is:

$$\left(\frac{3 \times 4^2}{2} + 4\right) - \left(\frac{3 \times 2^2}{2} + 2\right)$$

$$= (24 + 4) - (6 - 2)$$

$$= 20$$

Activity 3.4A

1 Show that the answer of 20 above is correct by calculating the area of the shaded trapezium.

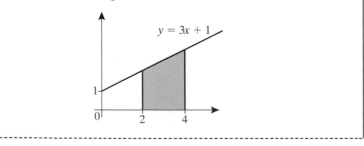

2 Find the area under the graph of $y = 2x + 3$ between $x = 1$ and $x = 3$ (shown shaded in the diagram below).

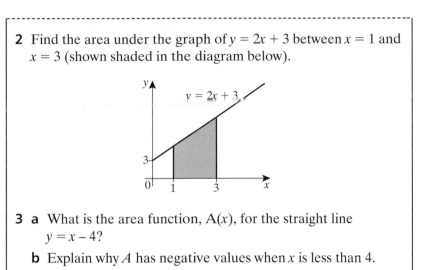

3 a What is the area function, $A(x)$, for the straight line $y = x - 4$?

b Explain why A has negative values when x is less than 4.

c i Draw a diagram and use it to calculate the area 'under' $y = x - 4$ between $x = 2$ and $x = 6$.

ii Show that using the area function gives the same result.

It is helpful to use some notation to indicate what you are doing when you are calculating areas under graphs.

The area under the line $y = 3x + 1$ between $x = 2$ and $x = 4$ is written as

$$\int_2^4 (3x + 1)dx.$$

This is read as 'the integral of $3x + 1$ with respect to x from $x = 2$ to $x = 4$'.

This is expanded so that the calculation done earlier is written like this:

$$\text{Area} = \int_2^4 (3x + 1)dx = \left[\frac{3x^2}{2} + x \right]_2^4$$

$$= \left(\frac{3 \times 4^2}{2} + 4 \right) - \left(\frac{3 \times 2^2}{2} + 2 \right)$$

$$= (24 + 4) - (6 + 2)$$

$$= 20$$

This is important notation that is used throughout calculus.

Activity 3.4B

1 Work out the following integrals. Write out your answers in full showing clearly the correct notation.

a $\int_1^6 (3x + 1)dx$

b $\int_2^6 (x - 4)dx$

c $\int_0^4 (5 - x)dx$

d $\int_2^4 \left(\frac{x}{3} - 2 \right)dx$

2 Express each shaded area using integration notation. Calculate the area showing your working out in full.

a

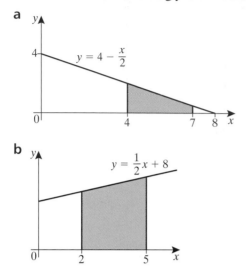

b

3 Check your answers to **question 2** using area calculations.

4 Elastic strings, when stretched, store energy that can be used, for example to fire arrows or lift a trampolinist high into the air.

a The force needed to stretch a string increases as the extension of the string increases; it can be modelled as $F = kx$, where F newtons is the force, x metres is the extension of the string and k is a constant depending on the characteristics of the string.

The energy in the string can be calculated by integration:

$$E = \int_0^x F \, dx = \int_0^x kx \, dx, \text{ where } E \text{ is measured in joules.}$$

For a particular string, $k = 10$.
  i Show that the energy stored in this string when it is extended by 0.2 metres from its natural length is 0.2 joules.
  ii Calculate the energy stored in the string when it is extended by 0.4 metres from its natural length.
  iii Hence calculate the energy stored in the string when the extension is increased from 0.2 metres to 0.4 metres.

b When an archer stretches a bow to shoot an arrow, energy is stored in the system until the archer releases the string, when the energy is transferred to the arrow, causing it to fly through the air.

For a simple bow, the force required to stretch the bowstring to a distance of 0.7 m from its original position is modelled as the straight line graph shown in the margin. The area under the line represents the potential energy stored in the bow system. Use integration to calculate this energy in newton-metres (or joules).

Discussion point
Which method do you prefer, integration or area calculations? Why?

Why will area calculations only give exact answers for straight line graphs?

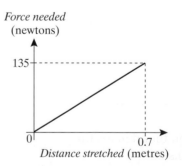

Discussion point
You will find that the energy stored in this string is more than doubled when its extension is doubled. Does this match what you would expect? Try doing this with an elastic string.

Force needed (newtons)

135

0   0.7
Distance stretched (metres)

Discussion point
If you are studying science, can you use your knowledge of potential and kinetic energy to find the speed of the arrow as it is fired?

Areas under higher order polynomial graphs

The simplest quadratic is $y = x^2$. Its area function is $A = \dfrac{x^3}{3}$.

The simplest cubic is $y = x^3$. Its area function is $A = \dfrac{x^4}{4}$.

In general, the area function for any power of x is one degree higher than the original power of x.

So the area functions for straight line graphs are quadratics and area functions for quadratics are cubics.

Activity 3.4C

1 a Find the area under the graph of $y = x^2$ between $x = 5$ and $x = 6$.

  b Evaluate $\displaystyle\int_3^5 x^2\, dx$.

2 Use integration to find the shaded area between the graphs of $y = x$ and $y = x^2$.

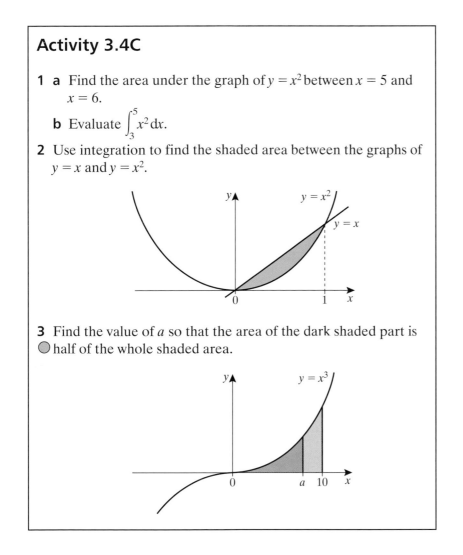

3 Find the value of a so that the area of the dark shaded part is half of the whole shaded area.

You found in **Section 3.3** that, if a function is multiplied by a constant, the area function is also multiplied by that constant.

For example, the area function for x^2 is $\dfrac{x^3}{3}$, so the area function for $5x^2$ is $\dfrac{5x^3}{3}$.

In integration notation: $\displaystyle\int_0^x (5x^2)\, dx = \left[\dfrac{5x^3}{3}\right]_0^x$

Activity 3.4D

1 Work out the integrals from 0 to x of:

a $3x^2$ **b** $-x^2$ **c** $\frac{1}{3}x^2$

d $2x^3$ **e** $4x^3$ **f** $-\frac{1}{2}x^3$

2 Draw a sketch to show the area under the curve $\frac{1}{2}x^3$ from $x = 2$ to $x = 4$.

Use integration to evaluate this area.

3 Evaluate these integrals.

a $\displaystyle\int_1^6 \left(\frac{x^2}{3}\right) dx$ **b** $\displaystyle\int_1^2 (12x^2) dx$ **c** $\displaystyle\int_3^5 (-5x^2) dx$

You also found in **Section 3.3** that the area function for a function consisting of the sum of several terms is the sum of the area functions of the terms.

For example,
the area function for $3x^2$ is x^3,

the area function for $5x$ is $\dfrac{5x^2}{2}$,

the area function for 4 is $4x$.

So the area function for $3x^2 + 5x + 4$ is $x^3 + \dfrac{5x^2}{2} + 4x$.

In general, the area function for $ax^2 + bx + c$ is $\dfrac{ax^3}{3} + \dfrac{bx^2}{2} + cx$.

Using integration notation,

$$\int_0^x (ax^2 + bx + c)dx = \left[\frac{ax^3}{3} + \frac{bx^2}{2} + cx\right]_0^x$$

Discussion point

Can you explain this using sketches of the graphs?

Activity 3.4E

1 Evaluate

a $\displaystyle\int_2^3 (3x^2 - 2x)dx$ **b** $\displaystyle\int_2^5 \left(\frac{x^2}{3} - x + 5\right)dx$ **c** $\displaystyle\int_0^3 (3x - x^2)dx$

2 a Show that the line $y = x$ and the curve $y = \dfrac{-x^2}{5} + 2x - \dfrac{4}{5}$ intersect at the points where $x = 1$ and $x = 4$.

b Draw a sketch to show the area enclosed between the line and the curve.

c Calculate this area.

The area function for a function of the form ax^n, where n is a positive integer, is $\dfrac{ax^{n+1}}{n+1}$, i.e. $\displaystyle\int (ax^n)\,dx = \left[\dfrac{ax^{n+1}}{n+1}\right]$

Notice that the power of x increases by one and the resulting function is divided by the new power. You can now integrate a wide range of polynomial functions.

Activity 3.4F

1 Evaluate these integrals.

   a $\displaystyle\int_1^2 (x^3 - 2x + 2)\,dx$ **b** $\displaystyle\int_0^3 (x^4)\,dx$

2 The speed of a shuttlecock falling from rest for 2 seconds can be modelled by the quadratic function $v = 5t - \dfrac{5t^2}{4}$.
   a Sketch a graph to show this.
   b Use integration to find the distance travelled by the shuttlecock during these 2 seconds of motion.

3 In **Activity 3.4B** you looked at the energy needed to stretch a simple bow. The force needed to stretch a compound bow varies in a different way. The graph in the margin shows the relationship between the distance stretched and the force needed for a particular bow. This can be modelled by the quadratic function $F = 735x(0.7 - x)$. Find the energy stored in the stretched bow and string.

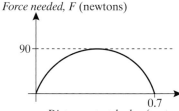

Force needed, F (newtons)

90

0.7
Distance stretched, x (metres)

4 The diagram shows a simplified cross-section of an aeroplane wing, with measurements in metres.

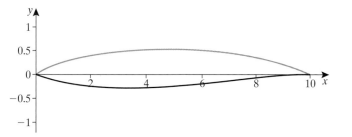

The lower profile of this section of the wing is modelled by the part of the cubic curve $y = -0.002x(10 - x)^2$ for which $0 \leqslant x \leqslant 10$. The upper part of the profile is modelled by a quadratic curve with its maximum point at $(5, 0.5)$.
   a Find the equation of the quadratic curve that models the upper part of the profile.
   b Integrate this function between $x = 0$ and $x = 10$ to find the area between the upper profile and the x-axis.
   c Integrate the cubic function between the same x-values to find the area between the lower profile and the x-axis. Why is this area negative?
   d Hence find the total area of the cross-section of the aeroplane wing at this point.

Discussion point
Why do aeroplane wings have this shape?

You might want to draw these functions on your graphic calculator.

3.5 Applying integration

Car performance

Here is the car performance data that you looked at in **Section 3.1**. In that section, you approximated the area under the graph with trapezia to find its area.

Another way of finding the area is to model the graph with a simple function and then find the area function.

A possible quadratic to model the car data is $v = 4t - \dfrac{2t^2}{15}$, where

t seconds is the time and v ms^{-1} is the speed of the car.

> Resource Sheet 3.5A

Activity 3.5A

1 On a copy of a graph of the car performance data, draw the
  graph of $v = 4t - \dfrac{2t^2}{15}$.

2 Show that the area function for this quadratic is
  $A(t) = 2t^2 - \dfrac{2t^3}{45}$.

3 Use this area function to calculate the distance travelled by the car during the 15 seconds of acceleration.

4 Is this an under-estimate or an over-estimate of the distance travelled? Explain your answer.

5 Compare your answer with that obtained in **Section 3.1**.

Carbon dioxide

Ecosystems in lakes and rivers are affected by the concentration of carbon dioxide (CO_2) in the water. During the day plants use CO_2 in photosynthesis and during the night they give out CO_2 by respiration. Animals always give out CO_2 by respiration (there is no photosynthesis in animals).

If you know the rates of production of CO_2 by plants and animals over a period of time, you can determine the total amount of CO_2 produced in that period.

The table in the margin shows the rate of production of CO_2 at various times of day.

You will notice that some of the rates of production are negative, as plants remove CO_2 from water during the day.

Car performance

Carbon dioxide

More problems

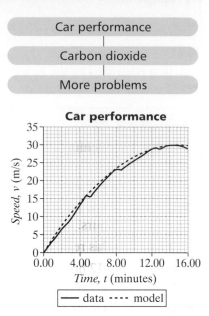
Car performance

— data ···· model

Discussion point
Can you find a quadratic to fit the car data graph better?

Discussion point
Which method do you prefer and why?

Number of hours after dawn	Rate of production of carbon dioxide (mmols per litre per hour)
0	0.010
1	−0.042
2	−0.044
3	−0.041
4	−0.039
5	−0.038
6	−0.035
7	−0.030
8	−0.026
9	−0.023
10	−0.020
11	−0.008
12	0.000
13	0.054
14	0.045
15	0.040
16	0.035
17	0.030
18	0.027
19	0.023
20	0.020
21	0.015
22	0.012
23	0.005

Activity 3.5B

1 Draw a graph of the data in the table and explain its shape.

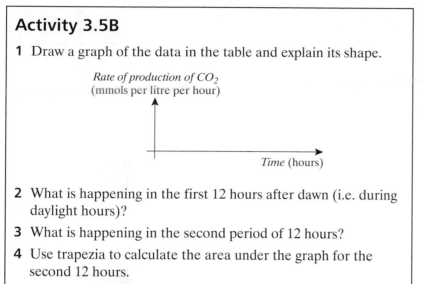

Rate of production of CO_2
(mmols per litre per hour)

Time (hours)

2 What is happening in the first 12 hours after dawn (i.e. during daylight hours)?

3 What is happening in the second period of 12 hours?

4 Use trapezia to calculate the area under the graph for the second 12 hours.

   What does this represent and what units is it measured in?

5 For the first 12 hours, the area 'under' the graph is negative. What does this tell you?

6 Use trapezia to calculate this negative area.

7 Is the amount of CO_2 in the lake more or less at the end of the 24-hour period than at the beginning, according to your estimates of the areas?

Discussion point

How can you use the rate of production data to find the amount of CO_2 produced?

In what units will the amount of CO_2 be measured?

What would be the effect on the amount of CO_2 in the lake or river if the rate of production were always positive?

Note: A millimole (mmol) is a chemical measure of the mass related to the substance under consideration, in this case CO_2. A mole is the molecular weight of the substance in grams, which in the case of CO_2 is approximately 44 grams. So a millimole of CO_2 is approximately 0.044 g.

More problems

In this section you will look back to two problems you met in **Activity 3.2**. You can now tackle these using integration methods.

Activity 3.5C

1 The speed, v ms^{-1}, of an aircraft t seconds after it starts from rest and accelerates along a runway at take-off can be modelled by $v = \frac{1}{16}(t-8)^3 + 32$ for $0 \leqslant t \leqslant 8$.

   a Show that $v = \frac{t^3}{16} - \frac{3}{2}t^2 + 12t$ for $0 \leqslant t \leqslant 8$.

   b Use integration to show that the distance, x metres, of the aircraft t seconds after starting its take-off is given by $x = \frac{t^4}{64} - \frac{t^3}{2} + 6t^2$.

   c Hence find the total distance travelled by the aircraft in the first 8 seconds of its motion.

   d Plot a graph of x against t. Is this what you would expect for an aircraft at take-off?

Discussion point

When might it be better to use numerical methods?

When might it be better to use integration?

2 The cross-section of a model aeroplane wing is the shape of the area bounded by the graphs of $y = 50 + \dfrac{3x}{2} - \dfrac{x^2}{20}$ and $y = 50 - x$, where x and y are measured in centimetres.

   a Use integration to find the area under each graph for $0 \leqslant t \leqslant 50$.

   b Hence find the area of the cross-section of the model aeroplane wing.

   c Check that this is given directly by integrating the function:

   $$f(x) = \left(50 + \frac{3x}{2} - \frac{x^2}{20}\right) - (50 - x)$$

   $$= \frac{5x}{2} - \frac{x^2}{20}$$

Note: $f(x)$ gives the area under the linear graph subtracted from the area under the quadratic graph directly.

3.6 Integration as the reverse of differentiation

Area functions and derivatives

In **Section 3.3**, you found formulae for the areas under the graphs of some functions. You produced a table like this.

Area functions and derivatives

Indefinite integration

Function, f(x)	Area function, A(x)	Derivative of A(x)
$y = c$	$A = cx$	$\dfrac{dA}{dx} = c$
$y = mx + c$	$A = \dfrac{mx^2}{2} + cx$	$\dfrac{dA}{dx} = mx + c$
$y = x^2$	$A = \dfrac{x^3}{3}$	$\dfrac{dA}{dx} = x^2$
$y = mx^2 + c$	$A = \dfrac{mx^3}{3} + cx$	$\dfrac{dA}{dx} = mx^2 + c$

This shows that the derivative of an area function is the same as the original function.

As you now know that the area function can be found by integration, this indicates that differentiation may be the inverse of integration.

Activity 3.6A

Find the original functions for these area functions using differentiation.

1 $A(x) = x^2 + 2x$

2 $A(x) = 6x - \frac{1}{3}x^3$

3 $A(x) = -3x$

The next activity demonstrates an important point about using integration to reverse differentiation.

Activity 3.6B

1 a Find the gradient functions for:
  i $y = 5x^2 + 2x$
  ii $y = 5x^2 + 2x + 3$
  iii $y = 5x^2 + 2x - 4$

  b Comment on your answers.

2 Draw a diagram to show that the functions $y = x^2$, $y = x^2 + 5$ and $y = x^2 - 4$ all have the same gradient function.

Indefinite integration

The previous activity shows that the gradient of a function is not affected by the constant term – only the terms involving the variable (x in this case) make a difference.

So all these functions, $y = x^2 + 2x$, $y = x^2 + 2x - 1$, $y = x^2 + 2x + 10$ and $y = 5 + 2x + x^2$ have the same derivative (or gradient function).

When you differentiate, the constant disappears, as the differential of any constant is zero.

So when you do the opposite of differentiating, integrating, you have to remember to add a constant.

Using integration notation you write

$$\int (2x + 2)\,dx = x^2 + 2x + c, \text{ where } c \text{ is a constant.}$$

This is called an 'indefinite' integral.

Activity 3.6C

Find these indefinite integrals.

a $\int (x^2 + 3)\,dx$ **b** $\int (5x + 3)\,dx$ **c** $\int (4x^3)\,dx$

Sometimes you can find the value of the constant of integration. For example, if you know that a quadratic graph has a gradient function $x + 1$ and goes through the point $(1, 5)$, you can find its equation.

First, integrate the gradient function to give $y = \dfrac{x^2}{2} + x + c$.

The curve goes through the point $(1, 5)$, so when $x = 1$, $y = 5$.

Putting these x- and y-values into the equation $y = \dfrac{x^2}{2} + x + c$ gives
$5 = \dfrac{1}{2} + 1 + c, \therefore c = \dfrac{7}{2}$.

So the equation of the quadratic function is $y = \dfrac{x^2}{2} + x + \dfrac{7}{2}$.

Activity 3.6D

1 Find the quadratic function whose gradient function is $4x - 1$ and that goes through the point $(0, 2)$.
2 A straight line has a gradient of 5 and goes through the point $(2, 5)$. What is the equation of the line?
3 'Just Chat' charges 8 pence per minute for calls (i.e. the gradient of the cost in pounds against calltime graph is 0.08). 'Just Chat' charges £12 per month for line rental. Find the equation of the cost–calltime graph for 'Just Chat'.
4 When a temperature increases by 1°C, it increases by $\frac{9}{5}$°F. This means that the gradient of the conversion graph for changing Celsius to Fahrenheit temperatures is $\frac{9}{5}$.
   32°F is equivalent to 0°C. Use integration to find the equation of the Celsius–Fahrenheit conversion graph.

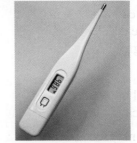

The integrals you did in **Activity 3.4B** for example, which were definite integrals, didn't have constants of integration.
The following section illustrates:

The definite integral $\int_2^5 (x^3 + 2x + 1)\mathrm{d}x$ can be used to find the area under the cubic curve $y = x^3 + 2x + 1$ between $x = 2$ and $x = 5$.

You worked it out like this:

$$\int_2^5 (x^3 + 2x + 1)\mathrm{d}x \quad = \left[\frac{x^4}{4} + x^2 + x\right]_2^5$$

$$= \left[\frac{625}{4} + 25 + 5\right] - \left[\frac{16}{4} + 4 + 2\right]$$

$$= \frac{609}{4} + 24 = 176.25$$

Now try it with a constant of integration:

$$\int_2^5 (x^3 + 2x + 1)\mathrm{d}x \quad = \left[\frac{x^4}{4} + x^2 + x + c\right]_2^5$$

$$= \left[\frac{625}{4} + 25 + 5 + c\right] - \left[\frac{16}{4} + 4 + 2 + c\right]$$

$$= \frac{609}{4} + 24 = 176.25$$

You can see that the constant, c, appears in both terms and therefore cancels out. This will always happen with definite integrals (those that have limits between which you calculate the value of the integral).

Activity 3.6E

1 Find these indefinite integrals.

   a $\int (x^2 + 3)\mathrm{d}x$ **b** $\int (x^5 - 2)\mathrm{d}x$ **c** $\int (2 + 3x - x^2)\mathrm{d}x$

2 Evaluate these definite integrals.

   a $\int_3^5 (4x^3)\mathrm{d}x$ **b** $\int_0^1 (5x)\mathrm{d}x$ **c** $\int_0^3 (x^2 - 2x)\mathrm{d}x$

3 At the beginning of the last century, there was a plague carried by rats in Bombay. The number of cases per week for the first 15 weeks of the outbreak can be modelled by the quadratic function $y = 3x^2$.

   Integrate this function between 0 and 15 to estimate the total number of cases during the first 15 weeks.

You can model a skydiver as having constant acceleration, a ms^{-2}. Since acceleration is the rate of change of velocity, v ms^{-1}, you can integrate acceleration with respect to time to find velocity,

i.e. $v = \int a\, \mathrm{d}t = at + c$.

c will be zero if the object is falling from rest, but if it has an initial velocity of u ms^{-1} (i.e. when $t = 0$, $v = u$) then c is u, $\therefore v = u + at$.

You may recognise this formula from your work in science.

Discussion point

Why is this not a very realistic model?

Activity 3.6F

1 a Start with the formula $v = u + at$ and integrate again to find a formula for the distance, x metres, travelled. In this case, the usual assumption is that the distance travelled at the start is zero, so the constant of integration is also zero.

b Use your formula to find the distance fallen in the fifth second by a skydiver free-falling with an inital speed of $3 \, \text{ms}^{-1}$. Free-fall acceleration is approximately $10 \, \text{ms}^{-2}$.

c On the Moon, the acceleration due to the Moon's gravity is approximately $\frac{1}{6}$ of the value of the acceleration due to gravity on the Earth. In the unlikely event of a skydiver free-falling with an initial speed of $3 \, \text{ms}^{-1}$ on the Moon, find the distance she would fall in the fifth second.

How does this compare with your answer to **part b**? Is it what you would expect?

2 Explain why this integration

$$\int_4^5 (3 + 10t) \, \mathrm{d}t$$

also gives the distance travelled by the skydiver in the fifth second. Evaluate the integral and check that it gives the same answer as **question 1**.

Near the Earth's surface, the acceleration due to gravity is approximately $10 \, \text{ms}^{-2}$.

3.7 Revision summary

Finding areas under graphs numerically

You can calculate the area under a graph approximately by dividing it into strips and finding the total area of the strips by the trapezium rule, the mid-ordinate rule or Simpson's rule.

In each case, the estimate is more accurate if you use more strips.

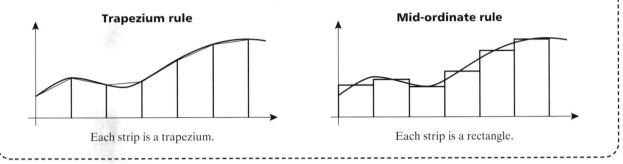

Trapezium rule	**Mid-ordinate rule**
Each strip is a trapezium.	Each strip is a rectangle.

Area functions

Area functions giving an algebraic formulae for the areas under curves can be deduced from the numerical answers.

The derivative of the area function is the equation of the curve itself.

For example, the function $f(x) = x^3 + 3x^2 - x$ has an area function $A(x) = \dfrac{x^4}{4} + x^3 - \dfrac{x^2}{2}$ and

$$\frac{d}{dx}(A(x)) = \frac{d}{dx}\left(\frac{x^4}{4} + x^3 - \frac{x^2}{2}\right) = x^3 + 3x^2 - x = f(x).$$

So area functions can be found by integration, which is the opposite of differentiation.
The area function $A(x)$ gives the area under the graph from 0 to x.

To find the area between the lines $x = a$ and $x = b$, subtract the value of the area function when $x = a$ from the value of the area function when $x = b$.

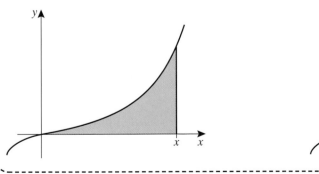

Finding areas under graphs by integration

This chapter develops from the informal work on areas under graphs using approximate numerical methods to the use of integration to calculate such areas.

The numerical work leads to the important basic result that the function for the area under the graph of $y = kx^n$ is $\dfrac{kx^{n+1}}{n+1}$.

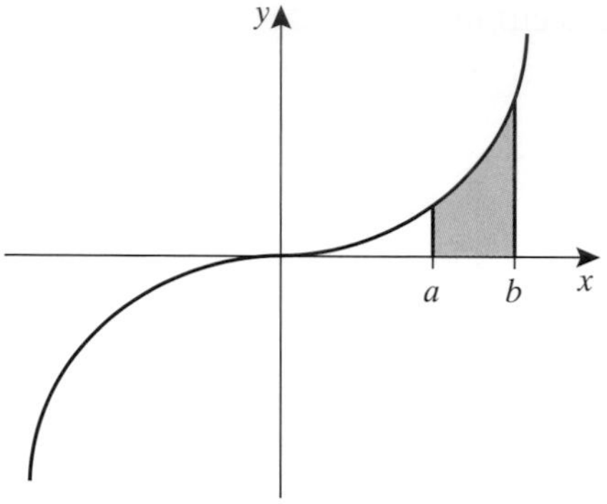

So the area under the graph between $x = a$ and $x = b$ (shaded in the diagram) is $\dfrac{kb^{n+1}}{n+1} - \dfrac{ka^{n+1}}{n+1}$

In calculus notation, this is written as $\displaystyle\int kx^n \mathrm{d}x = \left[\dfrac{kx^{n+1}}{n+1}\right]_a^b = \dfrac{kb^{n+1}}{n+1} - \dfrac{ka^{n+1}}{n+1}$.

As for differentiation, the area function of a sum of functions is the sum of the area functions.

So, for example, $\displaystyle\int_b^a (3x^2 - 12x + 2)\mathrm{d}x = [x^3 - 6x^2 + 2x]_a^b$.

3.8 Preparing for assessment

Your coursework portfolio

Portfolio work relevant to this chapter is about finding the areas under graphs of data, using both numerical methods and formal integration.

Your data could involve a rate such as speed so that the area under the graph tells you something else about the situation (in the case of speed, the distance travelled).

Other examples could be the rate of production of natural gases such as carbon dioxide, rate of oil flow along a pipe line, etc.

Another possibility is to use some data about the shape of something, such as the sail or the river profile in **Section 3.1**, so that you can work out the area.

Use a numerical method to find the area under your graph (you may like to look at the effect of using different methods or different numbers of strips).

You could also model your data with a mathematical function. What functions are appropriate? Are some functions better for some parts of the data than others?

You can then use your model to generate data for as many strips as you like and therefore get a more accurate estimate of the area, perhaps using a spreadsheet. This may or may not be useful, depending on how closely your model fits your data, but is an interesting point to discuss.

Integrate your function and thus obtain an exact answer for the area – but is this the exact area under the graph of your original data? Whilst doing the integration, you have the opportunity to show your ability to use integration notation correctly and to use algebra.

When you have done the mathematical manipulation, interpret your results in the light of the original situation. How good is your original model of the data? How does integration help you to understand the situation or to find out further information? How can this information be used?

Practice exam questions

Mount St. Helens

Data

Volcanoes release sulphur dioxide (SO_2), carbon dioxide (CO_2) and other gases into the atmosphere. The United States Geological Society (USGS) collects data about volcanic emissions from both the ground and air.

The table below gives data collected by the USGS at Mount St. Helens during December 1980.

Date Dec:	SO₂ flux (tonnes/day)	CO₂ flux (tonnes/day)
1	567	4100
6	811	5800
7	1344	3840
8	470	3200
12	664	5110
13	874	no data
15	966	11 870
16	831	5520
18	410	2440
19	1960	9110

Question

1 The carbon dioxide data is shown again in the table and graph below.

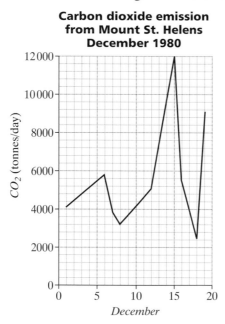

Date Dec:	CO₂ flux (tonnes/day)
1	4100
6	5800
7	3840
8	3200
12	5110
13	no data
15	11 870
16	5520
18	2440
19	9110

a   **i** On which day was the measured release of carbon dioxide the greatest?

    ii Estimate the amount of carbon dioxide released per hour on this day.

b According to the graph, between which two consecutive days did the release of carbon dioxide:

    i increase most quickly;

    ii decrease most quickly?

c Use the area of trapezia to estimate the amount of carbon dioxide released:
  i from 1 December to 8 December;
  ii from 12 December to 19 December.

d Which of the estimates that you have found in **part c** do you think is more accurate?

Give a reason for your answer.

Hydrograph

Data

This hydrograph shows the river runoff during and after a storm. The river runoff was estimated in cubic metres per second (m^3s^{-1}) from measurements taken at a gauging station in a nearby river.

Baseflow is the expected runoff that would have occurred if there had been no storm. This hydrograph uses the simplest method of estimating baseflow that assumes it is constant and equal to the runoff just before the storm began.

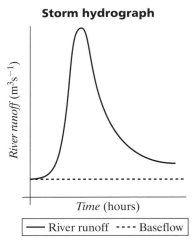

Storm hydrograph

Question

2 The hydrograph and the data from which it was drawn are given below.

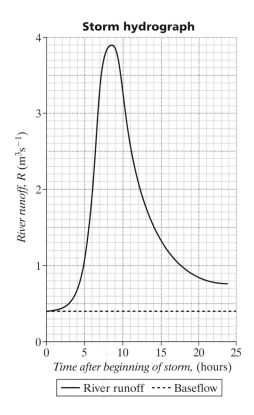

Storm hydrograph

Time, t (hours)	River runoff, R (m^3s^{-1})
0	0.40
1	0.42
2	0.45
3	0.49
4	0.61
5	0.92
6	1.83
7	2.96
8	3.82
9	3.85
10	3.23
11	2.54
12	2.10
13	1.75
14	1.51
15	1.28
16	1.12
17	1.01
18	0.94
19	0.85
20	0.81
21	0.78
22	0.76
23	0.75
24	0.74

a Use the hydrograph to estimate:
  i the maximum river runoff;
  ii the time when the river runoff was at its maximum;
  iii the time when the river runoff was increasing most rapidly;
  iv the time when the river runoff was decreasing most rapidly.

b Express the maximum river runoff as a percentage of the baseflow.

c Use the trapezium rule with strips of width 1 hour to estimate the volume of water that flows down the river during the
12-hour period between $t = 5$ and $t = 17$.

d **i** Use the mid-ordinate rule with strips of width 2 hours to estimate the volume of water that flows down the river over the 24-hour period shown in the hydrograph.
ii Find the normal volume of water that would flow down the river during this 24-hour period as predicted by the baseflow line.
iii Use your answers to **parts d i** and **d ii** to estimate the percentage increase in river runoff due to the storm during this 24-hour period.

4 Differentiation Techniques

Naturally occurring data, such as the heights of adults, when collected and plotted as a graph often give rise to a 'bell-shaped' normal distribution.

The function that can be used to model this type of distribution is based on $f(x) = e^{-x^2}$. You can see that it has very interesting features. In this chapter you will learn differentiation techniques that will allow you to investigate and make sense of functions based on exponential functions and other functions such as trignometrical functions.

For example, consider what happens to a sound wave as it dies away after a drum beat.

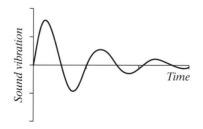

This wave based on $x = \sin \omega t$ decays so you may suspect that it is based on a function of the form $x = e^{-t} \sin \omega t$.

You will learn how to differentiate relatively complex functions like this towards the end of this chapter.

4.1 Using gradients to identify key features of functions

Maximum and minimum points

In **Chapter 2** you looked at how you can use the gradient of a function to deduce important features of the graph of that function.

In this section you will build on this to learn the techniques for identifying key features of functions and how these can be used to solve problems.

Activity 4.1A

The diagram shows the graph of the function $y = x^2 - 5$ and its gradient function, $y = 2x$, for $-10 \leqslant x \leqslant 10$.

Graph of $y = x^2 - 5$ and its gradient function

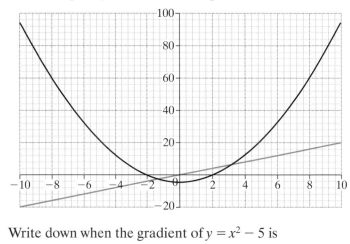

1 Write down when the gradient of $y = x^2 - 5$ is

   a negative   **b** zero   **c** positive.

2 Describe how you can deduce your answers to **question 1** from the graph of the gradient function.

The function $y = x^2 - 5$ has a **minimum point** when $x = 0$. At a minimum point, the gradient of the function is zero. To the left of the minimum, the gradient is negative and to the right of the minimum, the gradient is positive. So the gradient **increases** as you pass through a minimum point from left to right.

You can identify the nature of stationary points (i.e. whether they are maximum or minimum points or points of inflection) without having to draw a graph; the method is shown below.

For $y = x^2 - 5$, calculus gives the gradient function $\dfrac{dy}{dx} = 2x$. This is zero when $x = 0$, so the function $y = x^2 - 5$ has a stationary point when $x = 0$.

When $x = 0, y = -5$, so the co-ordinates of the stationary point are $(0, -5)$.

Maximum and minimum points

|

Points of inflection

Sometimes it is useful to have the graph of a gradient function immediately below the graph of the original function so you can match up how the key features on each are linked.

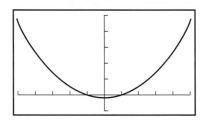

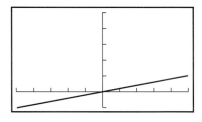

Discussion points
How can you tell which graph is which?
Does every quadratic graph have a linear gradient function? Explain your answer.

Any point on a curve where the gradient is zero, i.e. when $\dfrac{dy}{dx} = 0$, is called a **stationary point**. For $y = x^2 - 5$, the stationary point is a minimum. The two other types of stationary point are **maximum points**, which you have already met, and **points of inflection**. You will learn about points of inflection later in this chapter.

Choose a value of x a little less than zero, say -0.1, to check the sign of the gradient to the left of the stationary point.

When $x = -0.1$, $\frac{dy}{dx} = 2 \times (-0.1) = -0.2$, which is negative.

Choose a value of x a little more than zero, say 0.1, to check the sign of the gradient to the right of the stationary point.

When $x = 0.1$, $\frac{dy}{dx} = 2 \times 0.1 = 0.2$, which is positive.

So this stationary point is a minimum. (The gradient is negative, then zero, then positive.)

For a maximum point, the gradient is positive to the left, zero at the point, and negative to the right. The gradient **decreases** as x increases through a maximum point.

Maxima and minima are called **turning points**, for obvious reasons.

Activity 4.1B

1 For the function $y = x^2 - 2x$, find:

   a the gradient function, $\frac{dy}{dx}$;

   b where $\frac{dy}{dx} = 0$ (i.e. where there is a stationary point);

   c whether the stationary point is a maximum or minimum point.

2 Show that the function $y = 10 - x^2$ has a maximum point and find its co-ordinates.

3 Find the minimum value of the function $y = x^2 - 3x + 2$.

4 A farmer has 100 m of fencing to enclose a rectangular field. What are the possible measurements for the length and width of the field? Which measurements will enable the farmer to enclose the biggest area?

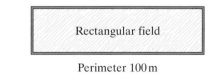

Rectangular field

Perimeter 100 m

So far you have considered quadratic functions, which have only one stationary point.

Cubic functions can have both a maximum point and a minimum point.

The gradient functions for cubics are quadratic functions, which can be zero for

- two values
- one value
- no values.

Discussion point

Every quadratic function has one stationery point. Can you explain why? How can you tell whether it will be a maximum or at minimum?

A minimum point

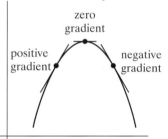

negative gradient

positive gradient

zero gradient

A maximum point

zero gradient

positive gradient

negative gradient

Checkpoint

Check your answers by drawing your graph of the function using your graphic calculator.

Discussion point

Why is this statement true?

Discussion point

Can you explain this by sketching some graphs?

Discussion point

Can you link these ideas to different types of cubics?

Activity 4.1C

1 a Find the gradient function of the cubic function
   $y = 2x^3 + 3x^2 - 12x$.

   b Show that $\dfrac{dy}{dx}$ is zero when $x^2 + x - 2 = 0$.

   c Hence, show that $y = 2x^3 + 3x^2 - 12x$ has stationary points when $x = 1$ and $x = -2$.

   d Find whether each of these stationary points is a maximum or a minimum.

2 a Find the x co-ordinates of the turning points of the cubic function $y = x^3 - x^2 - 2$.

   b Identify whether each turning point is a maximum or a minimum.

3 Find any maximum or minimum points, stating clearly which is which, for the function $y = 3x - x^3$.

4 The graph in the margin shows information about the value of the pound against the euro for 10 weeks in the middle of 2001. The data is shown as dots and a cubic model as a curve.

   a Comment on how well the model fits the data.

   b Explain why a cubic model would not be an appropriate long-term model of the value of the pound against the euro.

   c The cubic model is $y = \dfrac{x^3}{1000} - \dfrac{13x^2}{1000} + \dfrac{35x}{1000} + 1.63$.

   Differentiate this to find estimates of the maximum and minimum values of the pound against the euro for this period according to the model.

Checkpoint

Check your answers by using your graphic calculator to draw graphs of each function.

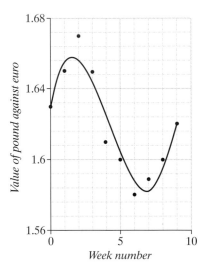

Value of pound against euro

Week number

Discussion point

How does the maximum and minimum values predicted by the model compare with the data values?

Points of inflection

Imagine a vase, such as the symmetrical one shown here, being filled by water poured at a constant rate. Sketch what you think a graph of depth of water against time will look like.

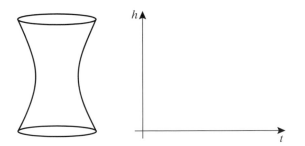

Write a sentence or two about what happens to the rate of change of depth of water with time by considering the gradient of your graph.

At the narrowest point of the vase, the rate of change of depth of water is greatest. On either side of this, the rate of change is positive, increasing just before this point and decreasing afterwards. This is known as a **point of inflection**.

The cubic graph of $y = x^3$ is shown in the margin. This function does not have a maximum point or a minimum point – but it does have a stationary point, as the gradient is zero at the origin.

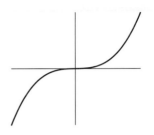

For $y = x^3$, $\dfrac{dy}{dx} = 3x^2$, which is 0 when $x = 0$.

So there is a stationary point when $x = 0$.

When $x = -0.1$, $\dfrac{dy}{dx} = 3 \times (-0.1)^2 = 0.03$, which is positive.

When $x = 0.1$, $\dfrac{dy}{dx} = 3 \times 0.1^2 = 0.03$, which is positive.

To the left of this stationary point, the gradient is positive and to the right it is also positive. A stationary point that has a gradient of the same sign to the left and to the right is a **point of inflection**.

Note: The equation $3x^2 = 0$ is a quadratic and really has two solutions, but they are both the same, $x = 0$.
It is as if the maximum and the minimum points of the cubic function have moved so close together that they are both in the same place. Can you picture this?

Activity 4.1D

1. **a** Show that the function $y = x^3 + 6x^2 + 12x$ has a stationary point when $x = -2$.

    b Show that this is a point of inflection.

2. **a** Show that the gradient of the function

    $y = \dfrac{x^3}{3} - 5x^2 + 25x - 8$ is given by $\dfrac{dy}{dx} = (x - 5)^2$.

    b When $x = 5$, $\dfrac{dy}{dx} = 0$.

    Determine what is happening to the function

    $y = \dfrac{x^3}{3} - 5x^2 + 25x - 8$ at this point. Illustrate your answer

    by drawing a sketch graph (use your graphic calculator to help you.)

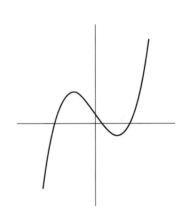

4.2 Differentiating functions of functions

The chain rule

In **Chapter 2** you met rules for differentiating polynomials. You can use these rules to differentiate functions such as $y = (3x - 5)^2$ and $y = (x^2 + 1)^3$ if you first expand the brackets. However, expanding the brackets in such functions becomes very difficult if the power is high. This section introduces the chain rule, which provides a much quicker method of differentiating functions of this type – and many others.

You can expand the brackets in $y = (3x - 5)^2$ as follows:

$$y = (3x - 5)^2 = (3x - 5)(3x - 5) = 9x^2 - 15x - 15x + 25$$
$$\Rightarrow \quad y = 9x^2 - 30x + 25$$

Differentiating this gives:

$$\frac{dy}{dx} = 18x - 30 = 6(3x - 5)$$

Factorising the result shows more clearly the relationship between the original function $y = (3x - 5)^2$ and its derivative $\frac{dy}{dx} = 6(3x - 5)$.

Complete the following activity to find the derivatives of more functions of this type.

Activity 4.2A

For each of the following functions:

- expand the brackets;
- find the derivative;
- factorise the result;
- compare the result with the original function.

1 $y = (6x + 1)^2$	**2** $y = (7x - 3)^2$	**3** $y = (x^2 + 5)^2$
4 $y = (1 - x^3)^2$	**5** $y = (6x + 1)^3$	**6** $y = (7x - 3)^3$
7 $y = (x^2 + 5)^3$	**8** $y = (1 - x^3)^3$	

Have you spotted the relationship between each function and its derivative?

If not, consider the quadratic functions and their derivatives again as set out in the table below.

Function	Derivative
$(6x + 1)^2$	$12(6x + 1) = 2(6x + 1) \times 6$
$(7x - 3)^2$	$14(7x - 3) = 2(7x - 3) \times 7$
$(x^2 + 5)^2$	$4x(x^2 + 5) = 2(x^2 + 5) \times 2x$
$(1 - x^3)^2$	$-6x^2(1 - x^3) = 2(1 - x^3) \times (-3x^2)$

The chain rule

Helium balloons

Other related rates of change

If possible share this work with other students and pool your results.

Multiply the expanded forms from **questions 1** to **4** by an extra bracket to find the cubics for **questions 5** to **8**, e.g. $(6x + 1)^3$
$= (6x+1)^2 \, (6x +1)$
$= (36x^2+12x+1) \, (6x+1).$

In each case the result is:
$2 \times$ term in brackets $\times$ derivative of term in brackets

Activity 4.2B

For the cubic functions (**questions 5** to **8** in **Activity 4.2A**) show that the derivative can be expressed as:

$$3 \times \text{bracket squared} \times \text{derivative of bracket}$$

These examples illustrate the **chain rule** which can be stated as:

If y is a function of u and u is a function of x then:

$$\frac{dy}{dx} = \frac{dy}{du} \times \frac{du}{dx}$$

☞

y is said to be a **composite** function.

(If $y = (6x + 1)^2$, for example, $u = 6x + 1$ and $y = u^2$.)
You can use this rule to differentiate a wide variety of functions. Later in this chapter you will use it to differentiate some trigonometric and exponential functions. For the time being you will use it for functions that can be written in brackets.

For example, you can write $y = \dfrac{1}{\sqrt{3x^2 + 2}}$ as $y = (3x^2 + 2)^{-\frac{1}{2}}$.

This is a function of a function:

$$y = u^{-\frac{1}{2}} \quad \text{where} \quad u = 3x^2 + 2$$

$$\frac{dy}{du} = -\frac{1}{2}u^{-\frac{3}{2}} \quad \text{and} \quad \frac{du}{dx} = 6x$$

Using the chain rule:

$$\frac{dy}{dx} = -\frac{1}{2}(3x^2 + 2)^{-\frac{3}{2}} \times 6x$$

$$= -3x(3x^2 + 2)^{-\frac{3}{2}}$$

$$= -\frac{3x}{\sqrt{(3x^2 + 2)^3}}$$

This is called the chain rule because it can be extended to a 'chain' of functions,

e.g. $\dfrac{dy}{dx} = \dfrac{dy}{du} \times \dfrac{du}{dv} \times \dfrac{dv}{dw} \times \dfrac{dw}{dx}$.

If possible do this in your head as follows:

Derivative of $(\text{bracket})^{-\frac{1}{2}}$ is: $-\frac{1}{2}(\text{bracket})^{-\frac{3}{2}} \times$ derivative of bracket

It is usual to give the answer in the same form as the question – here as a square root rather than a fractional power.

Activity 4.2C

1   Use the chain rule to differentiate:

  a $y = (5x - 2)^4$ **b** $y = (x^2 + 3)^5$ **c** $y = (5 + 2x^3)^3$

  d $h = \dfrac{1}{9t - 4}$ **e** $v = \sqrt{t^4 - 1}$ **f** $y = \dfrac{1}{(5 - 3x)^2}$

2   Projections of the population of a town suggest that in t years from now the population (in thousands) will be given by the function $p(t) = 25 - \dfrac{7}{t + 1}$.

  a   **i**   Calculate $p(0)$ and explain your result in terms of the real situation.
      ii   Sketch a graph of $p(t)$.
      iii   Describe what happens to the population as $t \to \infty$.

Discussion point
Why would the function
$q(t) = 25 - \dfrac{7}{t}$ (where t is the time in years from now) not be a suitable model for the population (in thousands) of a town?

b **i** Find $p'(t)$.

    ii Calculate $p'(0)$ and explain your result in terms of the real situation.

    iii Sketch a graph of $p'(t)$ against t.

    iv Describe in real terms what happens to $p'(t)$ as $t \to \infty$.

3 The total sales of a particular CD can be modelled by the function $y = 9t + \dfrac{5}{3}\left(1 - \dfrac{t}{5}\right)^3$ where y is the total number sold, in thousands, t weeks after the CD is released.

a Find $\dfrac{dy}{dt}$.

b Sketch a graph of $\dfrac{dy}{dt}$ against t.

c Describe the main features of the graph and explain them in terms of the real situation.

4 When a new painter is employed to paint the outside walls of a factory, the amount of paint, V litres, he uses in the first t hours can be modelled using $V = 4(0.5t + 1)^{\frac{3}{2}} - 4$.

a Find $\dfrac{dV}{dt}$.

b Calculate the values of V and $\dfrac{dV}{dt}$ when

    i $t = 0$ **ii** $t = 6$

    and explain what each result tells you about the real situation.

c **i** Draw sketches of V and $\dfrac{dV}{dt}$ against t.

    ii Explain in real terms what each graph predicts. Do you think the model is realistic? Explain your reasoning.

> You could sketch the graphs by using:
> - a graphic calculator
> - graph plotting software
> - a spreadsheet
> - transformations of basic curves that you know.

Helium balloons

Balloons are often filled with helium to make them float in the air. Large balloons can be used to carry people or equipment whilst small balloons filled with helium are often found at parties and fairs.

When a balloon is filled with helium, how quickly does its size increase? How are the rates of increase of its radius and surface area related to the rate at which it is filled with helium? How long would it take to fill a large balloon with helium? Questions such as these can be answered by using differentiation and the chain rule.

The formulae relating the surface area, $S\,\text{m}^2$, and volume, $V\,\text{m}^3$, of a sphere to its radius are:

$$S = 4\pi r^2 \quad \text{and} \quad V = \frac{4}{3}\pi r^3$$

Differentiating with respect to r gives:

$$\frac{dS}{dr} = 8\pi r \quad \text{and} \quad \frac{dV}{dr} = 4\pi r^2$$

Applying the chain rule allows us to find relationships between the rates at which the radius, surface area and volume increase with respect to time as the balloon is filled:

$$\frac{dS}{dt} = \frac{dS}{dr} \times \frac{dr}{dt} \quad \text{and} \quad \frac{dV}{dt} = \frac{dV}{dr} \times \frac{dr}{dt}$$

$$\Rightarrow \quad \frac{dS}{dt} = 8\pi r \times \frac{dr}{dt} \quad \text{and} \quad \frac{dV}{dt} = 4\pi r^2 \times \frac{dr}{dt}$$

> Both S and V are functions of r and r is a function of t.

Suppose we know that helium is pumped into the balloon at a constant rate of 2 litres per second. This is the rate of change of volume with time. Writing this in terms of m^3 per second:

$$\frac{dV}{dt} = 0.002$$

> It is important to be consistent in the use of units. Here it is best to work in terms of metres and seconds. Since 1 m^3 = 1000 litres and 1 litre = 0.001 m^3, 2 litres/s = 0.002 m^3/s.

Substituting this value into the formula for $\frac{dV}{dt}$ gives:

$$4\pi r^2 \times \frac{dr}{dt} = 0.002 \quad \Rightarrow \quad \frac{dr}{dt} = \frac{0.0005}{\pi r^2}$$

This shows how the rate at which the radius increases depends on the size of the balloon at that instant.

For example, when $r = 0.2$ $\quad \dfrac{dr}{dt} = \dfrac{0.0005}{\pi \times 0.2^2} = 0.003\,97$

but when $r = 0.4$ $\quad \dfrac{dr}{dt} = \dfrac{0.0005}{\pi \times 0.4^2} = 0.000\,995$

Discussion points

What does a graph of $\frac{dr}{dt}$ against r look like?
What does the graph predict:
- when r is very small;
- when r is very large?

Is the model realistic?

This means that when the radius of the balloon is 20 cm, it is increasing at a rate of approximately 4 mm per second, whereas when the radius is 40 cm it is only increasing at a rate of about 1 mm per second.

Activity 4.2D

1 For the balloon described above:

    a Find the rate at which the radius is increasing when:
        i $r = 0.1$ **ii** $r = 0.3$ **iii** $r = 0.5$

    b Find the rate at which the surface area, S m^2, is increasing when:
        i $r = 0.1$ **ii** $r = 0.3$ **iii** $r = 0.5$

    c **i** Find $\dfrac{dS}{dt}$ in terms of r.

        ii Draw a sketch of $\dfrac{dS}{dt}$ against r and explain what it shows in real terms.

> The results you will need from the working above are:
> $$\frac{dr}{dt} = \frac{0.0005}{\pi r^2} \text{ and}$$
> $$\frac{dS}{dt} = 8\pi r \times \frac{dr}{dt}$$

79

2 A spherical balloon is inflated so that its radius increases at a constant rate of 0.2 cm per second.

   a Find formulae in terms of r for:

     i $\dfrac{dS}{dt}$ **ii** $\dfrac{dV}{dt}$

   b Find the values of $\dfrac{dS}{dt}$ and $\dfrac{dV}{dt}$ when $r = 10$ and explain your results in terms of the real situation.

   c **i** Sketch graphs of $\dfrac{dr}{dt}, \dfrac{dS}{dt}$ and $\dfrac{dV}{dt}$ plotted against r.

     ii Explain what your graphs show in terms of the real situation.

     iii Do you think the model is realistic? Explain your answer.

3 Helium is leaking from a large spherical balloon at a rate given by $\dfrac{dV}{dt} = -0.01r$ where r is in metres and $\dfrac{dV}{dt}$ is in m³ per minute.

   a Find formulae in terms of r for:

     i $\dfrac{dr}{dt}$ **ii** $\dfrac{dS}{dt}$

   b Find the values of $\dfrac{dV}{dt}, \dfrac{dr}{dt}$ and $\dfrac{dS}{dt}$ when $r = 2$ and explain your results in terms of the real situation.

   c **i** Sketch graphs of $\dfrac{dV}{dt}, \dfrac{dr}{dt}$ and $\dfrac{dS}{dt}$ against r.

     ii Explain what your graphs show in real terms.

> Don't forget to use your graphic calculator or computer software to help you sketch graphs.

> In this case the rate of change of volume with time is *negative* because the volume of the balloon is *decreasing* as time goes by.

Other related rates of change

Activity 4.2E includes a range of other situations in which the chain rule can be used to find relationships between rates of change.

Activity 4.2E

1 Oil leaks from a pipe and forms a circular stain of radius r mm on the floor.

   a In one model of this situation it is assumed that the radius increases at a constant rate of 3 mm per second $\left(\text{i.e. } \dfrac{dr}{dt} = 3\right)$.

     i Find a formula in terms of r for $\dfrac{dA}{dt}$, the rate at which the area of the circular stain, A mm², increases with the time, t seconds.

     ii Sketch graphs of $\dfrac{dr}{dt}$ and $\dfrac{dA}{dt}$ against r and explain what the graphs show in terms of the real situation.

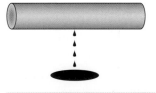

> Hint: $A = \pi r^2$ so you can easily find $\dfrac{dA}{dr}$.

b In a second model of this situation the rate of increase of r is modelled by $\dfrac{\mathrm{d}r}{\mathrm{d}t} = \dfrac{10}{r}$.

   i Find $\dfrac{\mathrm{d}A}{\mathrm{d}t}$, the rate at which the area of the circular stain, A mm², increases with the time t seconds.

   ii Sketch graphs of $\dfrac{\mathrm{d}r}{\mathrm{d}t}$ against r and $\dfrac{\mathrm{d}A}{\mathrm{d}t}$ against r and explain what your graphs show in terms of the real situation.

c Which of the two models do you think is more realistic? Explain your choice.

2 The pressure of a gas, P (measured in cm of mercury), is related to its volume, V cm³, by the formula $PV = 8000$.

  a Sketch a graph of P against V and explain what it shows in real terms.

  b **i** Show that $\dfrac{\mathrm{d}P}{\mathrm{d}V} = -\dfrac{8000}{V^2}$.

     ii Find the value of $\dfrac{\mathrm{d}P}{\mathrm{d}V}$ when $V = 10$ and explain what your answer means in real terms.

  c The volume of the gas is increased at a constant rate of 10 cm³ per second $\left(\text{i.e. } \dfrac{\mathrm{d}V}{\mathrm{d}t} = 10 \text{ cm}^3\right)$.

    i Find an expression in terms of V for $\dfrac{\mathrm{d}P}{\mathrm{d}t}$.

    ii Find the value of $\dfrac{\mathrm{d}P}{\mathrm{d}t}$ when $V = 10$ and explain what your answer means in real terms.

3 An ice cube has sides of length l mm.

  a Find formulae for
    i the volume, V mm³,
    ii the surface area, S mm², of the ice cube in terms of l.

  b Find:
    i $\dfrac{\mathrm{d}V}{\mathrm{d}l}$ **ii** $\dfrac{\mathrm{d}S}{\mathrm{d}l}$

  c The ice cube is melting so that the length of each side *decreases* at a constant rate of 0.1 mm per second $\left(\text{i.e. } \dfrac{\mathrm{d}l}{\mathrm{d}t} = -0.1\right)$.

    Find:
    i $\dfrac{\mathrm{d}V}{\mathrm{d}t}$

    ii $\dfrac{\mathrm{d}S}{\mathrm{d}t}$ in terms of l (where t seconds is the time).

  d Find the values of $\dfrac{\mathrm{d}V}{\mathrm{d}t}$ and $\dfrac{\mathrm{d}S}{\mathrm{d}t}$ when $l = 20$ and explain each of your answers.

l mm

e **i** Sketch graphs of $\dfrac{dV}{dt}$ and $\dfrac{dS}{dt}$ against l.

    ii Explain what each graph shows in real terms.

4 A hemispherical bowl has a radius of 10 cm.
The bowl is being filled with water at a constant rate of 5 cm³ per second.
When the depth of water in the bowl is h cm its volume is given by:

$$V = 10\pi h^2 - \frac{\pi h^3}{3}$$

a Find expressions for

    i $\dfrac{dV}{dt}$ **ii** $\dfrac{dh}{dt}$ in terms of h.

b Find the rate at which the depth is increasing when the depth of water in the bowl is

    i 1 cm   **ii** 5 cm.

c **i** Use your graphic calculator to sketch a graph of $\dfrac{dh}{dt}$ against h.

    ii For what values of h does the graph give a realistic model of the real situation? Explain your answer.

4.3 Differentiating trigonometric functions

Radians

So far in this course angles have been measured in degrees. You have been familiar with degrees since primary school. The ancient Babylonians introduced this method of measuring angles thousands of years ago. There is, however, another way of measuring angles that is much more useful when studying advanced mathematics, especially calculus.

The basic unit of this system is called a **radian**.

> A radian is the angle subtended at the centre of a circle by an arc that is equal in length to the radius.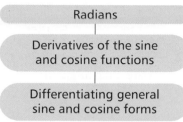

One radian can be abbreviated to 1 rad or 1^c.

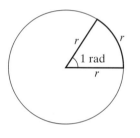

An angle of 2 radians at the centre corresponds to an arc of length $2r$ and an angle of 3 radians corresponds to an arc of length $3r$, etc.

The circumference of a circle is $2\pi r$, so a complete revolution must be equivalent to 2π radians, giving the relationship:

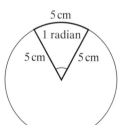

$$2\pi \text{ radians} = 360° \quad \Rightarrow \quad \pi \text{ radians} = 180°$$

So, to convert between the two systems you can use:

$$1 \text{ rad} = \frac{180°}{\pi} \quad \text{or} \quad 1° = \frac{\pi}{180} \text{ rad}$$

Angles measured in radians are often given in terms of π with the units omitted.

For example: $90° = 90 \times \dfrac{\pi}{180} = \dfrac{\pi}{2}$

It is useful to know:

Degrees	0	30	45	60	90	180	270	360
Radians	0	$\dfrac{\pi}{6}$	$\dfrac{\pi}{4}$	$\dfrac{\pi}{3}$	$\dfrac{\pi}{2}$	π	$\dfrac{3\pi}{2}$	2π

Radians
|
Derivatives of the sine and cosine functions
|
Differentiating general sine and cosine forms

The Babylonians thought that the length of a solar year was 360 days and this is why they divided a complete revolution into 360 degrees. They also divided a degree into 60 'minutes' and a minute into 60 'seconds'. Some navigators still give latitudes and longitudes in degrees, minutes and seconds today.

This may seem a strange idea at first. To get a better idea of what this means, draw a circle with radius 5 cm. Colour a 5 cm length of the circumference (an arc). Now draw radii from the end points of this arc to the centre of the circle. The angle enclosed by these radii is 1 radian.

Check that 1 radian is a bit less than 60°.

> Learn π radians = 180°

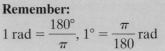

Activity 4.3A

1 Write these angles in radians in terms of π:

    a $120°$ **b** $135°$ **c** $150°$ **d** $720°$

2 These angles are all given in radians.
Write each angle in degrees:

    a $\dfrac{5\pi}{6}$ **b** $\dfrac{5\pi}{4}$ **c** 3π **d** 5π

3 **a** Write each of these angles in degrees, correct to the nearest degree:

    i 0.25 rad
    ii 1.3 rads
    iii 2.543 rads

    b Write each of these angles in radians, giving your answers correct to 3 significant figures:

    i $80°$
    ii $236°$
    iii $400°$

4 Change the angle setting on your calculator to radians. Copy and complete the following table to give the sine and cosine of angles between 0 and 6 radians.

x (rads)	0	1	2	3	4	5	6
sin x							
cos x							

5 **a** When a Ferris wheel rotates at a rate of $3°$ per second, the angle it turns through in t seconds is $3t$ degrees. If the radius of the wheel is 10 metres and a pod is at the same level as the centre of the wheel and moving upwards when $t = 0$, then its height, h metres, above the centre of the wheel t seconds later is given by $h = 10 \sin 3t°$. (See **Section 5.3** of *Algebra and Graphs*.)

Show that in terms of radians, $h = 10 \sin\left(\dfrac{\pi}{60}t\right)$.

    b Use this formula and the radians setting on your calculator to complete the following table for the height of the pod at intervals of 10 seconds during 2 minutes of the ride.

t	0	10	20	30	40	50	60	70	80	90	100	110	120
h													

    c On graph paper draw a graph of h against t.

    d Describe in words what happens to the pod during this time.

Note that angles given in terms of π should be written as improper fractions rather than mixed numbers,

e.g. $\dfrac{3\pi}{2}$ rather than $1\frac{1}{2}\pi$.

Remember:

$1 \text{ rad} = \dfrac{180°}{\pi}$, $1° = \dfrac{\pi}{180} \text{ rad}$

Find out if your calculator has an in-built function to convert angles between degrees and radians. If so, use it to check your answers to **parts a** and **b**.

Checkpoint

Check your answers to **4** by converting the angles to degrees and finding the sine and cosine of the angles using the degrees setting on your calculator.

Checkpoint

Use your graphic calculator to draw a graph of the function

$h = 10 \sin\left(\dfrac{\pi}{60}t\right)$ for $0 \leqslant t \leqslant 120$.

Note that you will have to enter this into your graphic calculator as Y=10SIN((π/60)X).

Derivatives of the sine and cosine functions

Variables that follow cyclic patterns can often be modelled using trigonometric functions. In this section you will learn how to differentiate trigonometric functions and this will allow you to find the rates of change of trigonometric variables. For example, you will be able to find the rate at which a tide is rising or falling and the rate at which you gain or lose height when you ride on a Ferris wheel.

The derivative of a function gives the gradient function. In the following activities, you will use this idea to deduce the derivatives of the sine and cosine functions.

Activity 4.3B

Resource Sheet 4.3B

The graph of $y = \sin x$ is shown below where the angle, x, is measured in radians.

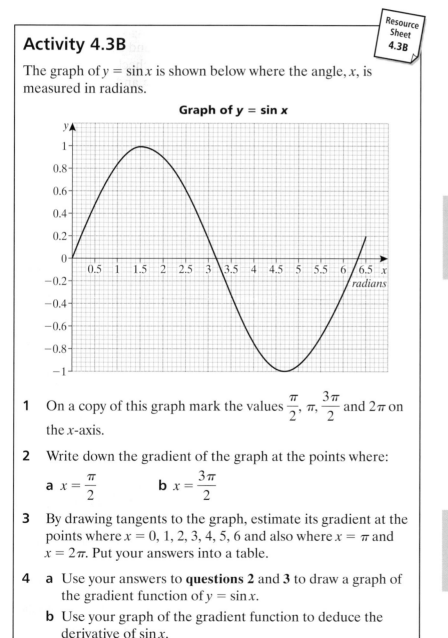

Graph of $y = \sin x$

Check that the values for $\sin x$ that you found in **question 4** of **Activity 4.3A** give points on this curve.

1 On a copy of this graph mark the values $\dfrac{\pi}{2}$, π, $\dfrac{3\pi}{2}$ and 2π on the x-axis.

2 Write down the gradient of the graph at the points where:

   a $x = \dfrac{\pi}{2}$ **b** $x = \dfrac{3\pi}{2}$

3 By drawing tangents to the graph, estimate its gradient at the points where $x = 0, 1, 2, 3, 4, 5, 6$ and also where $x = \pi$ and $x = 2\pi$. Put your answers into a table.

4 **a** Use your answers to **questions 2** and **3** to draw a graph of the gradient function of $y = \sin x$.

   b Use your graph of the gradient function to deduce the derivative of $\sin x$.

If possible, share the work for **question 3** with other students and pool your results.

85

Your graph should have suggested that the derivative of $y = \sin x$ is given by $\dfrac{dx}{dy} = \cos x$, but drawing tangents is not a very accurate method of finding the gradient of a curve.

The next activity should give a much more convincing result.

Activity 4.3C

The spreadsheet shown below has been set up to calculate values of $f(x) = \sin x$ and the gradient of (very short) chords using

$$\text{gradient} = \frac{f(a + 0.001) - f(a)}{0.001}$$

as you did in **Chapter 2**.

The increment used in this case is 0.001. You can change this by altering the content of cell F1.

	A	B	C	D	E	F
1	x	f(x) = sin x	gradient of chord		increment =	0.001
2	0	=SIN(A2)	=(SIN(A2+$F$1)–SIN(A2))/$F$1			
3	=A2+0.1	=SIN(A3)	=(SIN(A3+$F$1)–SIN(A3))/$F$1			
4	=A3+0.1	=SIN(A4)	=(SIN(A4+$F$1)–SIN(A4))/$F$1			
5	=A4+0.1	=SIN(A5)	=(SIN(A5+$F$1)–SIN(A5))/$F$1			
6	=A5+0.1	=SIN(A6)	=(SIN(A6+$F$1)–SIN(A6))/$F$1			
7	=A6+0.1	=SIN(A7)	=(SIN(A7+$F$1)–SIN(A7))/$F$1			
8	=A7+0.1	=SIN(A8)	=(SIN(A8+$F$1)–SIN(A8))/$F$1			
9	=A8+0.1	=SIN(A9)	=(SIN(A9+$F$1)–SIN(A9))/$F$1			
10	=A9+0.1	=SIN(A10)	=(SIN(A10+$F$1)–SIN(A10))/$F$1			
11	=A10+0.1	=SIN(A11)	=(SIN(A11+$F$1)–SIN(A11))/$F$1			
12	=A11+0.1	=SIN(A12)	=(SIN(A12+$F$1)–SIN(A12))/$F$1			
13	=A12+0.1	=SIN(A13)	=(SIN(A13+$F$1)–SIN(A13))/$F$1			
14	=A13+0.1	=SIN(A14)	=(SIN(A14+$F$1)–SIN(A14))/$F$1			
15	=A14+0.1	=SIN(A15)	=(SIN(A15+$F$1)–SIN(A15))/$F$1			
16	=A15+0.1	=SIN(A16)	=(SIN(A16+$F$1)–SIN(A16))/$F$1			

1 **a** Set up a spreadsheet using the formulae shown above and use 'fill down' to extend the results to $x = 6.5$.

    b **i** Use the values obtained to draw a scatter graph showing both the original function, $f(x) = \sin x$, and its gradient function.

      ii Does your graph support the theory that the derivative of $\sin x$ is $\cos x$?

    c Use the spreadsheet cosine formula to calculate the values of $\cos x$ in column D and compare the results with the values in column C.

2 **a** Set up a spreadsheet to give values of the function $g(x) = \cos x$ and the gradients of chords of the graph of $g(x)$ for values of x from 0 to 6.5.

    b **i** Use the values to draw a scatter graph showing both the original function, $g(x) = \cos x$, and its gradient function.

      ii Use your graph to suggest what the derivative of $\cos x$ might be.

Discussion point
Why are the values of the gradients of the tangents more accurate for smaller values of the increment (in cell F1)?

The spreadsheet cosine formula you should use in cell D2 is '=COS(A2)'. Use 'fill down' for the others.

c Use the spreadsheet sine formula to calculate the values of $\sin x$ and compare the results with the values of the gradient function.

Differentiating general sine and cosine forms

From the previous section we now have the following results:

$$\frac{d}{dx}(\sin x) = \cos x \quad \text{and} \quad \frac{d}{dx}(\cos x) = -\sin x$$

In real contexts involving trigonometric functions the independent variable is often time, t. The function $y = A \sin \omega t$ is a sine wave with amplitude A and angular velocity ω that passes through the origin. A more general form for a sine wave that does not pass through the origin is $y = A \sin(\omega t + \alpha) + c$ where A, ω, α and c are constants.

Revise this from *Algebra and Graphs*, **Chapter 5** if necessary.

You can find the derivative of $y = \sin(\omega t + \alpha)$ using the function of a function method in the form $\dfrac{dy}{dt} = \dfrac{dy}{dx} \times \dfrac{dx}{dt}$ as follows:

Discussion point
Can you say how each of the coefficients A, ω, α and c is related to features of each of these graphs?

$$y = \sin x \quad \text{where } x = \omega t + \alpha$$

$$\Rightarrow \quad \frac{dy}{dx} = \cos x \quad \text{and} \quad \frac{dx}{dt} = \omega$$

$$\Rightarrow \quad \frac{dy}{dt} = \cos x \times \omega$$

$$\Rightarrow \quad \frac{dy}{dt} = \omega \cos(\omega t + \alpha)$$

Remember that ω and α are constants.

This method can be used to give all of the derivatives of the general forms listed below:

Function	Derivative
$\sin \omega t$	$\omega \cos \omega t$
$\cos \omega t$	$-\omega \sin \omega t$
$A \sin \omega t$	$\omega A \cos \omega t$
$A \cos \omega t$	$-\omega A \sin \omega t$
$\sin(\omega t + \alpha)$	$\omega \cos(\omega t + \alpha)$
$\cos(\omega t + \alpha)$	$-\omega \sin(\omega t + \alpha)$
$A \sin(\omega t + \alpha) + c$	$\omega A \cos(\omega t + \alpha)$
$A \cos(\omega t + \alpha) + c$	$-\omega A \sin(\omega t + \alpha)$

Activity 4.3D

1 Write down the derivative of each of the following functions.

a $y = \sin 2t$ b $y = \cos 3t$ c $y = \sin \frac{1}{2}t$

d $y = 4 \cos 5t$ e $y = 5 \sin 0.3t$ f $y = 6 \cos \frac{1}{3}t$

2 a Use the function of a function method to show that

  i the derivative of $y = \cos(\omega t + \alpha)$ is $\dfrac{dy}{dt} = -\omega \sin(\omega t + \alpha)$

  ii the derivative of $y = A\sin(\omega t + \alpha) + c$ is
  $\dfrac{dy}{dt} = \omega A \cos(\omega t + \alpha)$.

b Differentiate the following functions with respect to t:

  i $y = \sin(2t + 3)$ **ii** $y = \cos(4t - 1)$

  iii $y = \sin\left(5t - \dfrac{\pi}{6}\right)$ **iv** $y = \cos\left(\dfrac{1}{2}t + \dfrac{\pi}{3}\right)$

  v $y = 2\sin(7t + 1)$ **vi** $y = 8\cos(t - 6)$

  vii $y = 3\sin\left(2t + \dfrac{\pi}{4}\right)$ **viii** $y = 5\cos\left(4t - \dfrac{\pi}{4}\right) + 1$

  ix $y = 5\cos(3t + \pi) - 4$ **x** $y = \dfrac{1}{2}\sin(10t + 3) + 5$

In **Activity 4.3A** you showed that when a Ferris wheel of radius 10 metres rotates at a rate of 3° per second, the height, h metres, of a pod after t seconds is given by $h = 10\sin\dfrac{\pi}{60}t$.

Differentiating this function with respect to t gives the rate of change of height with time:

$$\frac{dh}{dt} = \frac{\pi}{60} \times 10\cos\frac{\pi}{60}t = \frac{\pi}{6}\cos\frac{\pi}{60}t$$

This gives the rate at which the pod is rising or falling.

So, for example, after 40 seconds:

$$\frac{dh}{dt} = \frac{\pi}{6}\cos\frac{\pi \times 40}{60} = \frac{\pi}{6}\cos\frac{2\pi}{3} = -0.26 \text{ (to 2 s.f.)}$$

After 40 seconds the pod is losing height at a rate of 0.26 metres per second.

As height is in metres and time is in seconds, the units for the rate of change of height with respect to time are metres per second.

Activity 4.3E

1 The London Eye has a radius of 67.5 metres and rotates once every 30 minutes. When $t = 0$ a pod moving upwards is at the same height as the centre of the Eye.

  a Show that $h = 67.5\sin\left(\dfrac{\pi t}{15}\right)$ gives the height h metres, of the pod (above the centre of the Eye) after t minutes.

  b Find and simplify an expression for $\dfrac{dh}{dt}$.

  c Use a spreadsheet to draw graphs of h against t and $\dfrac{dh}{dt}$ against t for one complete revolution of the Eye.

Alternatively you could draw these graphs by hand or using a graphic calculator.

d Use your graphs to find the times when $\dfrac{dh}{dt} = 0$ and describe where the pod is at these times.

e Write down the maximum and minimum values of $\dfrac{dh}{dt}$ and describe where the pod is at these times.

2 You can model a patient's blood pressure using the function $p = 90 + 30 \sin 7t$, where p mm Hg is the blood pressure at time t seconds.

   a Find $\dfrac{dp}{dt}$ and explain what information this gives.

   b Use a graphic calculator, spreadsheet or graph plotting software to draw graphs of p against t and $\dfrac{dp}{dt}$ against t for $0 \le t \le 1$.

   c Write a brief account of what is happening to the patient's blood pressure over this period.

3 The depth of water, h metres, at the entrance to a harbour t hours after midnight is given by the function

$$h(t) = 5 + 3 \cos \frac{\pi t}{6}.$$

   a Find $w'(t)$.

   b Calculate the depth of the water and rate at which the tide is rising or falling at the following times:

   i midnight

   ii 2 am

   iii 4 am

   iv 6 am

   v 8 am

   vi 10 am

   vii noon

   c Sketch the graph of $h(t)$. Indicate on this graph when you think the tide is rising most rapidly and when it is falling most rapidly.

   d Sketch the graph of $h'(t)$. Indicate on this graph where the function $h'(t)$ has a maximum value and where it has a minimum value. Compare your answers with those you gave for **part c**.

4 **a** An alternating voltage is given by $V_1 = 120 \sin \dfrac{\pi}{10} t$ where V_1 is the voltage in volts and t is the time in milliseconds. Calculate the voltage and the rate at which it is changing when:

   i $t = 2$ **ii** $t = 4$ **iii** $t = 6$

   b Repeat **part a** for the voltage $V_2 = 120 \sin\left(\dfrac{\pi}{10} t - \dfrac{2\pi}{3}\right)$.

Discussion point

The London Eye rotates at a constant speed. Why then are there times when $\dfrac{dh}{dt}$ is zero and other times when it has maximum and minimum values?

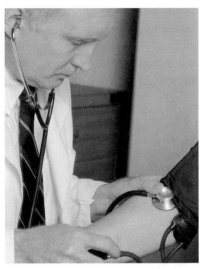

4.4 Differentiating exponential functions

The derivative of e^x

You can use exponential functions to model many real variables that grow or decay with time. Differentiating such functions gives the **rate** at which the variable is growing or decaying. For example, the derivative of the function that models the number of bacteria in a colony will give the rate at which the colony is growing and the derivative of the function that models the temperature of a hot object will give the rate at which it is cooling.

In the last section you used the gradient of the graph of $\sin x$ to find the derivative of $\sin x$. In the following activity you will use a similar method to find the derivative of the exponential function, e^x, and other functions related to it.

The derivative of e^x
|
Differentiating general exponential functions

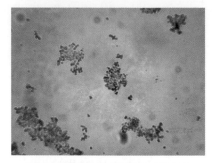

Nuffield Resource
'Exponential rates of change'

Activity 4.4A

Resource Sheet **4.4A**

Excel Activity

You can find a close approximation to the gradient of the function f(x) at $x = a$ using:

$$\text{gradient of chord} = \frac{f(a + 0.001) - f(a)}{0.001}$$

1 **a** Set up a spreadsheet like the one shown below to calculate values of f(x) = e^x and approximations to its gradient.

	A	B	C	D	E	F	
1	x	f(x) = e^x	gradient		increment =	0.001	
2	–3	=EXP(A2)	=(EXP(A2+$F$1)-EXP(A2))/$F$1				
3	=A2+0.1	=EXP(A3)	=(EXP(A3+$F$1)-EXP(A3))/$F$1				
4	=A3+0.1	=EXP(A4)	=(EXP(A4+$F$1)-EXP(A4))/$F$1				
5	=A4+0.1	=EXP(A5)	=(EXP(A5+$F$1)-EXP(A5))/$F$1				
6	=A5+0.1	=EXP(A6)	=(EXP(A6+$F$1)-EXP(A6))/$F$1				
7	=A6+0.1	=EXP(A7)	=(EXP(A7+$F$1)-EXP(A7))/$F$1				
8	=A7+0.1	=EXP(A8)	=(EXP(A8+$F$1)-EXP(A8))/$F$1				
9	=A8+0.1	=EXP(A9)	=(EXP(A9+$F$1)-EXP(A9))/$F$1				
10	=A9+0.1	=EXP(A10)	=(EXP(A10+$F$1)-EXP(A10))/$F$1				
11	=A10+0.1	=EXP(A11)	=(EXP(A11+$F$1)-EXP(A11))/$F$1				
12	=A11+0.1	=EXP(A12)	=(EXP(A12+$F$1)-EXP(A12))/$F$1				
13	=A12+0.1	=EXP(A13)	=(EXP(A13+$F$1)-EXP(A13))/$F$1				
14	=A13+0.1	=EXP(A14)	=(EXP(A14+$F$1)-EXP(A14))/$F$1				
15	=A14+0.1	=EXP(A15)	=(EXP(A15+$F$1)-EXP(A15))/$F$1				
16	=A15+0.1	=EXP(A16)	=(EXP(A16+$F$1)-EXP(A16))/$F$1				

b Use 'fill down' to extend your results to $x = 3$.

c What do you notice about the values in columns B and C?

d What does this suggest about the derivative of f(x) = e^x?

Discussion points

The spreadsheet formula in cell C2 is '=(EXP(A2+$F$1)−EXP)(A2))/$F$1'. Can you explain how this relates to the formula

$$\text{gradient} = \frac{f(a + 0.001) - f(a)}{0.001}?$$

What happens when you alter the value in cell F1?

Note: Save your spreadsheet for use later.

2 The graph of $y = e^x$ is shown below.

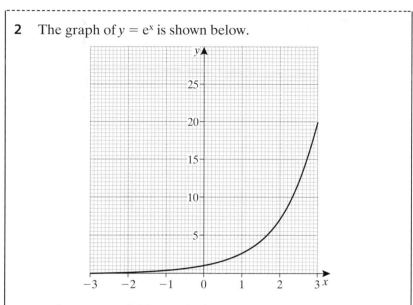

a On a copy of this graph, draw a tangent to the curve at the point where $x = 1$ and find its gradient. Compare your result with the value given on your spreadsheet for the gradient at the point where $x = 1$.

b Repeat **part a** at one other point on the graph.

> You could use your spreadsheet to produce a printed version of the graph of $y = e^x$.

3 **a** Make a copy of the spreadsheet you used for **question 1**. Alter the formulae so that this new spreadsheet gives values for $y = e^{-x}$ and its derivative.

b What is the derivative of $y = e^{-x}$?

c **i** Sketch the graphs of $y = e^x$ and $y = e^{-x}$.

   ii Use your graphs to explain your answer to **part b**.

4 **a** Make another copy of the spreadsheet you used for **question 1** and alter the formulae so that this new worksheet gives values for $y = e^{2x}$ and its derivative.

b What is the derivative of $y = e^{2x}$?

c **i** Sketch the graphs of $y = e^x$ and $y = e^{2x}$.

   ii Use your graphs to explain the answer to **part b**.

> In **question 3a** you will need to insert a negative sign in the formula in cell B2 so that it becomes '=EXP(-A2)' and negative signs and brackets in the formula in cell C2 so that it becomes '=(EXP(-(A2+$F$1))-EXP(-A2))/$F$1'. Use 'fill down' for the other cells.

Differentiating general exponential functions

After working through the previous activity, you should have these results:

$$\frac{d}{dx}(e^x) = e^x, \quad \frac{d}{dx}(e^{-x}) = -e^{-x} \quad \text{and} \quad \frac{d}{dx}(e^{2x}) = 2e^{2x}$$

In real contexts involving exponential functions the independent variable is often time, usually denoted by t. The general form for exponential growth is $y = Ae^{kt}$ and the general form for exponential decay is $y = Ae^{-kt}$, where k is a positive constant. In this next activity you will find and use the derivatives of these general forms to find rates of change.

> Revise this from **Chapter 3** of *Algebra and Graphs* if necessary.

Activity 4.4B

1 Use the function of a function method to show that

a the derivative of $y = Ae^{kt}$ is $\dfrac{dy}{dt} = kAe^{kt}$

b the derivative of $y = Ae^{-kt}$ is $\dfrac{dy}{dt} = -kAe^{-kt}$.

2 Write down the derivative of each of the following functions.

a e^{-5t} **b** $2e^{3t}$ **c** $30e^{-\frac{t}{6}}$

d $4e^{0.25t} + 6$ **e** $1 - 5e^{-4t}$ **f** $24(1 - e^{-5t})$

Remember that A and k are constants.

In **Activity 3.4C** in *Algebra and Graphs* you modelled the spread of cane toads across Australia using the function $y = 36.45 \times 1.081^t$, where y represents the area in thousands of square kilometres inhabited by cane toads t years after 1939 (so that $t = 0$ represents the year 1939, $t = 1$ the year 1940, etc.).

This function can be written as $y = 36.45e^{kt}$ where $e^k = 1.081$ and so $k = \ln 1.081 = 0.0779$ (to 3 s.f.).

Differentiating $y = 36.45e^{0.0779t}$ gives a function that models the *rate* of spread of cane toads across Australia.

$$\frac{dy}{dt} = 0.0779 \times 36.45e^{0.0779t} = 2.84e^{0.0779t}$$

You can now make predictions about the rate at which the cane toads will spread across Australia in future years.

For example, substituting $t = 66$ gives a prediction for the rate at which cane toads will spread across Australia in 2005:

$$\frac{dy}{dt} = 2.84e^{0.0779 \times 66} = 2.84e^{5.1414} = 486 \text{ (to 3 s.f.)}$$

The model predicts that in 2005 cane toads will be spreading across Australia at a rate of approximately 500 000 km^2 per year.

The models predicting the area inhabited by cane toads and the rate at which this area is increasing are shown in the graphs below.

If necessary revise solving exponential and logarithmic equations from **Section 3.5** of *Algebra and Graphs*.

Note that here you have seen the use of an important technique to express a function such as as $y = 36.45 \times 1.081^t$ as $y = 36.45e^{0.0779t}$.

Discussion point
Why does putting $t = 66$ give a prediction of the rate of increase in 2005?

Discussion point
What transformation of the first graph would give the second graph?

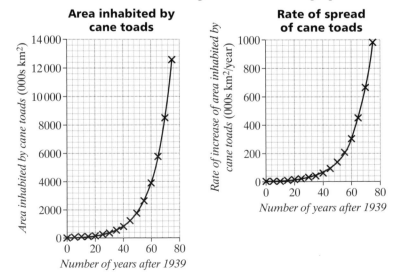

In **Activity 4.4C** you will differentiate some of the functions that you first met in *Algebra and Graphs* to model situations involving exponential growth and decay. In each case the relevant section of *Algebra and Graphs* is identified so that you can look back at this work if you wish.

Activity 4.4C

1 The function $y = 23.3e^{0.0646t}$ is a model for crude oil production since 1900, where y is the annual amount of oil produced (in megatonnes) t years after 1900.

  a Find $\dfrac{dy}{dt}$.

  b Use your answer to **part a** to predict the rate of growth in crude oil production in:

    i 1950

    ii 2000

    iii 2050

Activity 3.4A in *Algebra and Graphs.*

Discussion point
How accurate do you think the prediction for 2050 will be?

2 When a colony of *E. coli* bacteria is allowed to grow unchecked, you can model the number of bacteria after t minutes using the function $N = 2^{0.05t}$.

  a Show that this function can be written as $N = e^{0.0347t}$.

  b Write down $\dfrac{dN}{dt}$ and explain what information this gives.

  c **i** Sketch graphs of N against t and $\dfrac{dN}{dt}$ against t.

    ii What transformation of the first graph would give the second graph?

Activity 3.2A in *Algebra and Graphs.*

3 Carbon dating relies on the fact that if the mass of carbon-14 in an organism is m_0 grams when it dies, then the mass of carbon-14 in the organism t years after death can be modelled by the function $m = m_0 e^{-0.000121t}$.

  a Write down an expression in terms of m_0 and t for $\dfrac{dm}{dt}$.

  b **i** Sketch graphs of m against t and $\dfrac{dm}{dt}$ against t.

    ii What happens to m and $\dfrac{dm}{dt}$ as $t \to \infty$?
Explain your answer in terms of the real situation.

Activity 3.4E in *Algebra and Graphs.*

4 When 1 kilogram of plutonium is left to decay, the number of grams, y, remaining after t thousand years can be modelled using $y = 1000 \times 1.029^{-t}$.

  a Show that y can also be written as $1000e^{-0.0286t}$ and find an expression for $\dfrac{dy}{dt}$.

  b Find the amount of plutonium that is left and the rate at which it is decaying after

    i 1000 years   **ii** 5000 years   **iii** 1 million years.
Explain your answers in real terms.

Activity 3.2D in *Algebra and Graphs.*

Hint: You will need to use the method shown just after the previous activity to do this.

5 You can model the world's population, y billion, in year x using the function $y = 8.7 \times 10^{-12}e^{0.0136x}$.

   a Find $\dfrac{dy}{dx}$.

   b Use the model to estimate the population of the world and its rate of growth in the years:

     i 1500   **ii** 2000   **iii** 2500

6 The function $y = 2.6e^{0.48x} + 400$ can be used to model the amount of waste, y tonnes, dealt with per year by the East London Waste Authority (ELWA), where x is the number of years after 1992.

   a Find $\dfrac{dy}{dx}$.

   b Sketch graphs of y against x and $\dfrac{dy}{dx}$ against x.

   c Describe the main features of each graph in terms of the real situation.

   d How well do you think this model will predict what will happen in future years?

7 You can model the temperature of a cup of coffee using the function $\theta = 67 \times 1.018^{-t} + 19$, where $\theta°C$ is the temperature of the coffee after t minutes.

   a Show that this function can be written as

     $\theta = 67e^{-0.0178t} + 19$.

   b Find $\dfrac{d\theta}{dt}$ and explain what information this gives.

   c **i** Sketch graphs of θ against t and $\dfrac{d\theta}{dt}$ against t, showing clearly what happens as $t \to \infty$.

     ii Describe the main features of the graphs in terms of the real situation.

8 The velocity, v metres per second, of a skydiver can be modelled by the function $v = 40(1 - e^{-0.25t})$, where t is the time in seconds after jumping from an aircraft.

   a Find the values of v and $\dfrac{dv}{dt}$ when

     i $t = 0$ **ii** $t = 60$ **iii** $t = 120$

     and in each case explain what the values you find tell you about the real situation.

   b **i** Sketch graphs of v against t and $\dfrac{dv}{dt}$ against t, showing clearly what happens as $t \to \infty$.

     ii Describe what the graphs suggest will happen in the real situation.

     iii What do you think will happen to t and $\dfrac{dv}{dt}$ in practice? Sketch graphs to illustrate your answer.

Activity 3.4B in *Algebra and Graphs.*

Discussion point

Why might your answer to **part b iii** be particularly inaccurate? You might like to consider how you have modelled population growth using both exponential functions and recurrence relations in *Algebra and Graphs.*

Activity 3.4D in *Algebra and Graphs.*

Activity 3.2E in *Algebra and Graphs.*

4.5 Differentiating products

The product rule

The product rule
|
Skycoaster
|
Other applications

In **Chapter 2** of *Algebra and Graphs* you studied the way in which the height above the ground, h metres, of a Skycoaster flyer varies with the time, t seconds.
The graph of h against t is shown again below.

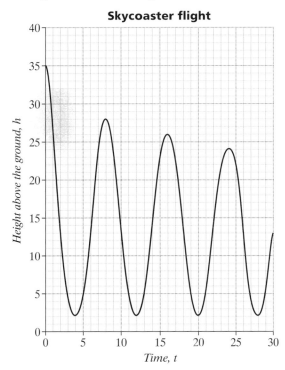

Skycoaster flight

Height above the ground, h (vertical axis)

Time, t (horizontal axis)

SKYCOASTER

This graph has cycles like a trigonometric function but the amplitude decreases as t increases. The function

$h = 14e^{-0.01t}\left(1 + \cos\dfrac{\pi t}{4}\right) + 2$ can be used to model this situation.

If you could differentiate $h = 14e^{-0.01t}\left(1 + \cos\dfrac{\pi t}{4}\right) + 2$ the result

would give a model of the rate at which the height of the rider changes with time.

This function is the **product** of an exponential function, $u = 14e^{-0.01t}$

and a trigonometric function, $v = \left(1 + \cos\dfrac{\pi t}{4}\right)$.

The **product rule**, gives a method of differentiating functions of this type.

Consider the function $y = x^2(3x + 1)$. This is the product of x^2 and $3x + 1$.

The derivative of x^2 is $2x$ and the derivative of $3x + 1$ is 3, but the derivative of $x^2(3x + 1)$ is *not* $6x$.

Use your graphic calculator to draw the graph of this function and compare it with the graph shown above. What are the similarities and differences?

Since $x^2(3x + 1) = 3x^3 + x^2$, its derivative is $9x^2 + 2x$.

This shows that if a function y is the product of functions u and v, the derivative of y is *not* the same as the product of the derivatives of u and v.

The derivative of y can be found using the product rule:

When y is a product of u and v, where both u and v are functions of x, then:

$$\frac{dy}{dx} = \frac{du}{dx} \times v + u \times \frac{dv}{dx}$$

Applying this to $y = x^2(3x + 1)$:

$$y = u \times v, \text{ where}$$
$$u = x^2 \quad \text{and} \quad v = 3x + 1$$
$$\frac{du}{dx} = 2x \quad \text{and} \quad \frac{dv}{dx} = 3$$

and the product rule gives:

$$\frac{dy}{dx} = 2x \times (3x + 1) + x^2 \times 3 = 6x^2 + 2x + 3x^2 = 9x^2 + 2x$$

which you can see is the same as the answer found earlier by expanding the brackets first.

How does this rule arise?
Suppose $y = uv$, where u and v are both functions of x. If x changes by a small amount, say δx, then u, v and y will also change by small amounts, say δu, δv and δy, where:

$$y + \delta y = (u + \delta u)(v + \delta v)$$
$$= uv + u\delta v + v\delta u + \delta u \delta v$$

Since $y = uv$ then:

$$\delta y = u\delta v + v\delta u + \delta u \delta v$$

and dividing by δx:

$$\frac{\delta y}{\delta x} = u\frac{\delta v}{\delta x} + v\frac{\delta u}{\delta x} + \frac{\delta u \delta v}{\delta x}$$

As δx, δu, δv and $\delta y \to 0$ this reduces to:

$$\frac{dy}{dx} = u\frac{dv}{dx} + v\frac{du}{dx}$$

Activity 4.5A

For each of the following functions:

- use the product rule to find the derivative;
- expand the brackets in the original function, then find the derivative;
- compare your results.

1 $y = 5x(x + 1)$ **2** $y = x^4(1 - 3x)$

3 $y = x(x^2 - 4)$ **4** $y = 2x^3(7 - x^5)$

5 $y = (2x + 5)(x + 4)$ **6** $y = (1 - 2x^2)(x^3 + 5)$

Products can also involve exponential and trigonometric functions, and functions of functions.

For example, $y = 10e^{2x}(1 - x)^3$ is a product of two functions, u and v, where:

$$u = 10e^{2x} \quad \text{and} \quad v = (1 - x)^3$$

so

$$\frac{du}{dx} = 20e^{2x} \quad \text{and} \quad \frac{dv}{dx} = -3(1 - x)^2$$

In this case both u and v are functions of functions.

Using the product rule:

$$\frac{dy}{dx} = 20e^{2x} \times (1-x)^3 + 10e^{2x} \times -3(1-x)^2$$

$$= 20e^{2x}(1-x)^3 - 30e^{2x}(1-x)^2$$

This can be simplified by taking out the common factors:

$$\frac{dy}{dx} = 10e^{2x}(1-x)^2[2(1-x) - 3]$$

$$= 10e^{2x}(1-x)^2[-1 - 2x]$$

$$= -10e^{2x}(1-x)^2(1 + 2x)$$

> Note that the product rule,
> $$\frac{dy}{dx} = \frac{du}{dx} \times v + u \times \frac{dv}{dx},$$
> can also be written in other forms, for example:
> $$(uv)' = u'v + uv'$$

Activity 4.5B

In each question simplify your answers as far as possible.

1 Use the product rule to find $\dfrac{dy}{dx}$ where:

a $y = x^4 e^x$

b $y = x^2 \cos 4x$

c $y = x^5(x^2 - 1)^3$

d $y = (x + 2)^5 e^x$

e $y = 4x\sqrt{x - 1}$

f $y = (x - 4)^4(2x - 1)^3$

g $y = x^2 e^{-x} + 5$

h $y = e^{3x} \sin x - x$

i $x^3 - e^x \cos 4x$

2 a Find the derivative of $y = \dfrac{5x}{2x + 1}$ by writing $\dfrac{5x}{2x + 1}$ as $y = 5x(2x + 1)^{-1}$ and then using the product rule.

   b Find the derivative of $y = \dfrac{4x - 1}{e^{5x}}$ by writing $\dfrac{4x - 1}{e^{5x}}$ as $y = (4x - 1)e^{-5x}$.

   c Differentiate each of the following functions:

   i $y = \dfrac{\sin x}{x^2}$ ii $h = \dfrac{e^t}{(2t - 3)^3}$ iii $v = \dfrac{t^4}{t^2 - 3}$

Skycoaster

The height, h metres, of a flyer above the ground during the first part of a Skycoaster flight can be modelled using the function

$$h = 14e^{-0.01t}\left(1 + \cos\frac{\pi t}{4}\right) + 2$$

where t seconds is the time after the ride began.

Activity 4.5C

1 Use the product rule to find $\dfrac{dh}{dt}$.

2 a Calculate the value of $\dfrac{dh}{dt}$ at each of the following times.

    i $t = 2$ **ii** $t = 6$

  b Explain what this model predicts is happening to the flyer at each of these times.

3 a Show that $\dfrac{dh}{dt}$ is equal to zero when $t = 4$.

  b Explain what this tells you about the real situation.

4 a Draw a sketch of $\dfrac{dh}{dt}$ against t. (Use a graphic calculator to help you.)

  b Describe the main features of the graph and how they relate to the real situation.

Other applications

This activity includes a range of situations in which the product rule can be used to find rates of change.

Activity 4.5D

1 A car sets off from one set of traffic lights and 15 seconds later passes another set of traffic lights. The speed of the car, v ms^{-1}, as it travels between these traffic lights is modelled by the function $v = 5te^{-0.2t}$ where t seconds is the time after the car sets off from the first set of traffic lights.

  a i Sketch a graph of v against t.

    ii Describe the main features of your graph and what they tell you about the speed of the car as it travels between the two sets of traffic lights.

  b i Show that this model suggests that the acceleration of the car is given by the function $a = e^{-0.2t}(5 - t)$.

    ii Sketch a graph of a against t.

    iii Describe the main features of this graph and how they relate to the real situation.

2 The depth of a river, h cm, over the course of a day is modelled by the function $h(t) = t^4e^{-0.5t} + 105$ where t hours is the time after midnight.

  a i Sketch the graph of the model for $0 \leqslant t \leqslant 24$.

    ii What is the maximum depth predicted by this model and at what time does it occur?

Use a graphic calculator or computer to help you sketch each graph.

When sketching graphs you should work out particular values, such as the starting value of the variable when $t = 0$.

b **i** Find h′(t) and explain what information it gives.

 ii Use your expression for h′(t) to confirm the time at which the maximum depth occurs.

 iii Sketch the graph of h′(t) for $0 \leqslant t \leqslant 24$.

 iv Identify the values of t for which h′(t) is positive and explain what this means in terms of the real context.

 v Find the maximum and minimum points on the graph of h′(t) and explain your results in terms of the real context.

3 The height of a swing above its initial position, h metres, during the first t seconds of a ride can be modelled by h(t) = 0.1t(1 + sin t).

 a Find h′(t) and explain what information it gives.

 b **i** Sketch the graphs of h(t) and h′(t) for $0 \leqslant t \leqslant 16$.

 ii Explain how the graph of h′(t) relates to the graph of h(t).

 iii Describe the main features of each graph and explain what these features tell you about the real situation.

4 The current, I amps, flowing in an electrical circuit may be modelled by the function $I = 10e^{-0.2t} \sin t$ where t milliseconds is the time.

 a **i** Sketch a graph of I against t.

 ii Describe the main features of your graph and explain how they relate to the real situation.

 b **i** Find $\dfrac{dI}{dt}$ and explain what information this gives.

 ii Sketch a graph of $\dfrac{dI}{dt}$ against t.

 iii Find the first value of t for which $\dfrac{dI}{dt} = 0$.

   Describe what is happening to I at this time.

 iv Find the value of t at the first minimum point on the graph of $\dfrac{dI}{dt}$.

   Describe what is happening to I at this time.

5 After a lake is stocked with fish, the number of fish may be modelled by the function $p = 10 + 2e^{-0.1t} \cos t$, where p is the number of fish in thousands after t months.

 a **i** Find the value of p when t = 0 and explain what this tells you about the real situation.

 ii Sketch a graph of p against t.

 iii What does the model suggest will be the smallest number of fish in the lake and when will this occur?

 iv What does the model suggest will happen to the number of fish as time passes?

b **i** Find $\dfrac{dp}{dt}$.

  ii Sketch a graph of $\dfrac{dp}{dt}$ against t.

  iii Find the first two values of t for which $\dfrac{dp}{dt} = 0$ and explain their significance in terms of the real situation.

  iv Find the greatest value of $\dfrac{dp}{dt}$ and explain its significance in terms of the real situation.

  v Find the smallest value of $\dfrac{dp}{dt}$ and explain its significance in terms of the real situation.

  vi What happens to $\dfrac{dp}{dt}$ as $t \to \infty$?

  What does this mean in real terms?

4.6 Second derivatives

Galileo

Galileo

Differentiating twice

The motion of a falling body intrigued some of the best minds over the last few hundreds of years – Newton is one you have heard about in this book. Another is Galileo. You may have read descriptions of how he dropped two objects with different masses from the top of the leaning tower of Pisa and noticed that they both hit the ground at the same time.

He suggested that the displacement, x metres, of a falling body t seconds after it is released from rest can be modelled by a function of the form $x = kt^2$ where k is a constant. You will realise if you drop something to the ground how difficult it would be to collect displacement–time data as the speed of falling objects increases very quickly.

Galileo's solution was to deflect the motion down a slope – he found data for a ball released so that it rolled down a track. You might like to carry out such an experiment yourself in **Activity 4.6B**.

Galileo Galilei (1564–1642)

Leaning tower of Pisa, Italy

Galileo was unable to use an expression such as $x = kt^2$ when he was carrying out his investigations as this algebraic notation was just being developed at the time.

Activity 4.6A

A free-falling body accelerates due to gravity. Its displacement, x metres, t seconds after being released can be modelled as $x = 5t^2$.

1 a Sketch a graph of $x = 5t^2$ for $0 \leqslant t \leqslant 5$.
 (Use a graphic calculator to help when you are sketching graphs.)

Displacement

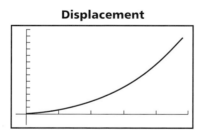

 b The velocity of the falling body is then modelled as $v = \dfrac{\mathrm{d}x}{\mathrm{d}t} = 10t$. Immediately under your displacement–time graph, sketch a velocity–time graph.

Velocity

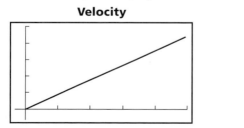

Acceleration

c The acceleration of the falling body is modelled by $\dfrac{dv}{dt} = 10$, that is the derivative of $\dfrac{dx}{dt}$. An alternative way of writing this is $\dfrac{d^2x}{dt^2}$ (spoken as 'dee two x by dee t squared'). Immediately under your velocity–time graph, sketch an acceleration–time graph.

d Write a couple of sentences about the main features of the graphs.

2 The velocity of a falling body increases at a constant rate.

a Explain how the velocity–time graph shows this.

b Explain how the acceleration–time graph shows this.

3 If a ball is thrown vertically downwards with a velocity of $10\,\text{ms}^{-1}$, its displacement, x metres, t seconds after it is released may be modelled by $x = 5t^2 + 10t$.

a Sketch a displacement–time graph for $0 \leq t \leq 5$.

b Find an expression, in terms of t, for the velocity of the ball. Immediately under your displacement–time graph, sketch a velocity–time graph.

c Find an expression, in terms of t, for the acceleration of the ball. Immediately under your velocity–time graph sketch an acceleration–time graph.

d Compare your graphs with those you sketched for **question 1**. Write a sentence or two to explain features that are the same and the features that are different for each pair of graphs.

Activity 4.6B – Optional

You will need a track, a ball, a stopwatch and a metre ruler or tape measure. You will find tape, Blu-Tack and possibly building blocks helpful.

Carry out a version of Galileo's experiment by timing how long it takes a ball to roll set distances down a slope.

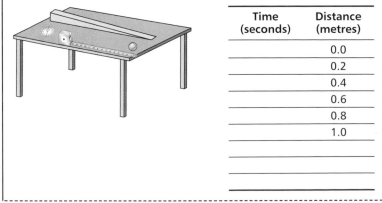

Time (seconds)	Distance (metres)
	0.0
	0.2
	0.4
	0.6
	0.8
	1.0

1   Carry out the experiment, writing your data in a copy of the table. You may like to do the experiment three times for each distance and average your results.

2   Plot a graph of your data on a graphic calculator or use graph plotting or spreadsheet software on a computer.

3   a   Find a function of the form $x = kt^2$ that is a reasonably good fit to your data.

    b   Find expressions for the velocity and acceleration of the ball.

    c   Write a brief description of what is happening.

Discussion point
The most accurate of your data points is the origin. Why?

Differentiating twice

You have already learnt how to differentiate a wide range of functions such as polynomials, exponential functions and trigonometrical functions. When you differentiate a function, you obtain the **derivative** (gradient function), which is another function. You can usually differentiate this function again to give a **second derivative** (gradient of the gradient function).

This second derivative can give you important information about the rate of change of a variable.

Consider the quadratic function $y = x^2 + 2x - 18$.

Differentiating gives $\dfrac{dy}{dx} = 2x + 2$, which is a linear function.

Differentiating again gives $\dfrac{d^2y}{dx^2} = 2$ (the second derivative), which is a positive constant.

Below are graphs of y, $\dfrac{dy}{dx}$ and $\dfrac{d^2y}{dx^2}$ plotted against x, one under the other and all together.

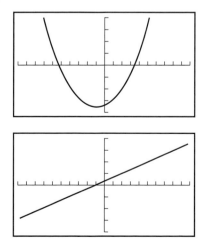

Discussion point
What functions cannot be differentiated more that once?

Note: $\dfrac{d^2y}{dx^2}$ is pronounced 'dee two y by dee x squared'.

Note: Second derivatives can be shown in alternative notation:
$$y = f(x)$$
$$\frac{dy}{dx} = f'(x)$$
$$\frac{d^2y}{dx^2} = f''(x)$$

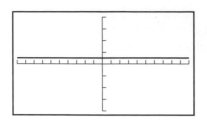

All together on one screen:

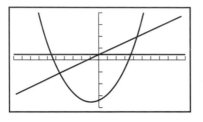

Activity 4.6C

Find the second derivatives of each of the following functions.
For each, use a graphic calculator or a computer to plot graphs of
y, $\dfrac{dy}{dx}$ and $\dfrac{d^2y}{dx^2}$.

1 **a** $y = 3x^2 + 5x$

   b $y = x^2 - 6x + 3$

   c $y = (x - 3)^2$

2 **a** $y = \sin t$

   b $y = \cos 3t$

   c $y = 2 \sin t + \sin 2t$

   d $y = \sin t^2$

3 **a** $y = e^t$

   b $y = e^{2t} + t^2$

   c $y = e^t \cos t$

4 Find the value when $x = 0$ of the second derivative of these functions.

   a $y = \cos 2x$

   b $y = e^{3x}$

Discussion point

What do you notice about y, $\dfrac{dy}{dt}$ and $\dfrac{d^2y}{dt^2}$ for $y = \sin t$?
Predict what you think will happen for $y = \cos t$. Check by differentiation and plotting graphs.

Discussion point

What do you notice about y, $\dfrac{dy}{dt}$ and $\dfrac{d^2y}{dt^2}$ for $y = e^t$?

4.7 Applications of second derivatives

Ferris wheel again

What do second derivatives tell you?
As you know, the first derivative of a function gives information about how the function is changing – whether it is increasing or decreasing and how rapidly. So the second derivative tells you how the first derivative (or gradient) is changing.

One example with which you will by now be familiar is the motion of a Ferris wheel, which you first considered in **Chapter 5** of *Algebra and Graphs*.

Consider a Ferris wheel that has a radius of 10 m and turns at 3° per second. The height, h metres, above the centre of the wheel of a pod that starts off level with the centre of the wheel after t seconds is given by $h = 10 \sin\frac{\pi}{60}t$.

Differentiating this gives:

$$\frac{dh}{dt} = 10\,\frac{\pi}{60}\cos\frac{\pi}{60}t$$

$$= \frac{\pi}{6}\cos\frac{\pi}{60}t$$

$\frac{dh}{dt}$ is the gradient of h, the rate at which h is increasing or decreasing. As h metres is the distance vertically above the centre of the wheel and t seconds is time, $\frac{dh}{dt}$ ms^{-1} is the vertical velocity of the pod (since velocity is the rate at which distance changes).

Ferris wheel again

Inflation

h plotted against time

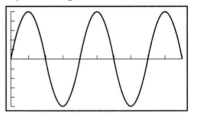

$\frac{dh}{dt}$ **plotted against time**

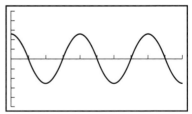

Activity 4.7A

1   Use the expression for $\frac{dh}{dt}$ to find when the pod's vertical speed is zero.
    Do your answers agree with your common-sense knowledge of the motion of the wheel?
    Look at the graphs of the motion to help you make sense of what is happening.

2   Use the expression for $\frac{dh}{dt}$ to find when the pod has the greatest vertical speed (upwards and downwards).
    Do your answers agree with common sense?
    Again, look at the graphs of the motion to help you make sense of what is happening.

How did you work out your answers to **question 2** of the last activity? You may have differentiated to find the gradient of the vertical velocity, then put the expression equal to zero to find the values of t for which the velocity had its greatest and least values.

If so, you found the second derivative of h, $\dfrac{d^2h}{dt^2}$.

$\dfrac{d^2h}{dt^2}$ ms^{-2} is the rate at which the vertical velocity changes and is therefore the vertical acceleration. Finding the values of t for which $\dfrac{d^2h}{dt^2}$ is zero tells you when the vertical velocity has its maximum and minimum values.

Discussion point
What other possible ways are there to find the maximum and minimum values of the vertical velocity?

Activity 4.7B

1. For the Ferris wheel, show that the vertical acceleration is given by $\dfrac{d^2h}{dt^2} = -\dfrac{\pi^2}{360}\sin\dfrac{\pi}{60}t$.

2. On your graphic calculator, on one screen, plot graphs of the vertical velocity and acceleration of a pod.

3. Find all the values of t for $0 \leqslant t \leqslant 360$ for which the vertical acceleration is zero. Check that these values coincide with where the pod's vertical velocity has maximum or minimum values.

Inflation

The table and graph below show how retail prices in the UK changed between 1986 and 2000, using 1986 as the base year with a retail price index of 100.

Year	Years since 1986, x	RPI, y
1986	0	100
1987	1	101.9
1988	2	106.9
1989	3	115.2
1990	4	126.1
1991	5	133.5
1992	6	138.5
1993	7	140.7
1994	8	144.1
1995	9	148.1
1996	10	152.7
1997	11	157.5
1998	12	162.9
1999	13	165.4
2000	14	170.3
2001	15	173.3
2002	16	176.2

Each month around 150 000 price quotations are collected for over 600 items which make up the retail price index (RPI) 'basket' of goods. This is a measure of price changes used in determining certain state benefits such as pensions, the value of gilts and National Savings certificates and it is also widely used in pay negotiations.

Discussion point
What does 'using 1986 as the base year with retail price index of 100' mean?

UK retail price index 1986–2002

Years since 1986

Discussion point

Describe the general features of the graph. What functions would be good models for the data? What would the second derivatives of the functions tell you?

The data can be modelled with a number of different functions; you may like to experiment with a spreadsheet to find appropriate ones.

One possibility is the quadratic function $y = 97 + 7.1x - 0.14x^2$.

For this function, the first derivative is $\dfrac{dy}{dx} = 7.1 - 0.28x$

and the second derivative is $\dfrac{d^2y}{dx^2} = -0.28$.

Discussion point

How realistic is this quadratic model? Investigate by plotting the data and function on a graphic calculator or computer.

The first derivative gives the annual change in the retail price index (i.e. the rate of inflation) and the second derivative gives the annual rate of change of the rate of inflation. This is a small negative constant, indicating that the rate of inflation is decreasing each year. This would imply that eventually (when?) the rate of inflation would become negative, so retail prices would stop increasing and start decreasing.

Discussion point

Make sure you understand what this paragraph is saying. Discuss in a group if possible.

Activity 4.7C

1   You could also model the RPI data using the linear function $y = 5x + 103$.

   a Find the first derivative of this function and say what it tells you about the rate of inflation, according to this model.

   b What is the second derivative of the linear function? What does this tell you about the rate of inflation and, therefore, about what will happen to prices according to this model?

2   Another possible model is the exponential function $y = 105e^{0.04x}$.
   Investigate what first and second derivatives of this model tell you about the retail price index.

4.8 Stationary points and points of inflection

Maxima and minima

You can use second derivatives to help you determine the nature of stationary points. For example, the quadratic function

$y = x^2 + 2x - 8$ has gradient $\dfrac{dy}{dx} = 2x + 2$, which is zero when

$x = -1$, so there is a stationary point when $x = -1$. As you learnt earlier in this chapter, you can tell whether this is a maximum, a minimum or a point of inflection by considering the sign of the gradient before and after the stationary point.

$$\frac{dy}{dx} = 2x + 2$$

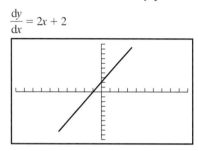

In this case, the gradient is negative before and positive after the stationary point (i.e. the gradient is **increasing**), so the stationary point is a minimum.

The graph of $\dfrac{dy}{dx}$ plotted against x can help you see this.

If the gradient had been positive before and negative after the stationary point (i.e. if the gradient were **decreasing**), the stationary point would have been a maximum.

Maxima and minima

Points of inflection

$y = x^2 + 2x - 8$

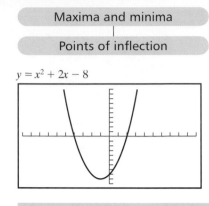

Note: At the stationary point, $\dfrac{dy}{dx} = 0$.

Discussion point
How can you tell from the function formula $y = x^2 + 2x - 8$ whether this quadratic function has a maximum or a minimum point without doing any calculus at all? Can you use a non-calculus method for other types of function?

The graphs of y and $\dfrac{dy}{dx}$ for the first function have been drawn to assist you.

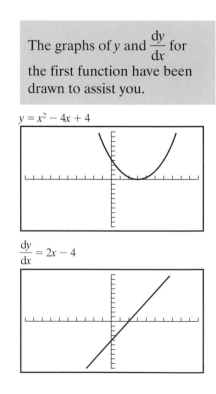

$y = x^2 - 4x + 4$

$\dfrac{dy}{dx} = 2x - 4$

Activity 4.8A

For each function below:

a find an expression for its first derivative;

b find the stationary points by finding where the first derivative $\dfrac{dy}{dx}$ is equal to zero;

c find the nature of each stationary point by considering the sign of the gradient on each side. Use graphs of y and $\dfrac{dy}{dx}$ plotted against x to help you.

1 $y = x^2 - 4x + 4$ **2** $y = 8 - 2x - x^2$

3 $y = x^3 - 2x^2 - 5x + 6$ **4** $y = \sin x$

5 $y = \cos x$

Another method of finding whether the stationary point is a maximum or a minimum is to use the second derivative, $\dfrac{d^2y}{dx^2}$.

Local minimum point

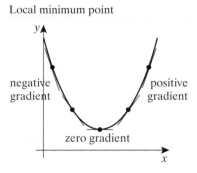

If $\dfrac{d^2y}{dx^2}$ is **positive** at the stationary point, this means that the gradient is **increasing** (from negative through zero to positive), so there is a **minimum**.

Local maximum point

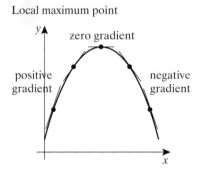

If $\dfrac{d^2y}{dx^2}$ is **negative**, the gradient is **decreasing** (from positive through zero to negative), so there is a **maximum**.

Activity 4.8B

1 Is the second derivative of $y = x^2 + 2x - 8$ positive or negative when $x = -1$?

Does this mean that the stationary point is a maximum or a minimum?

You can consider the graphs of y, $\dfrac{dy}{dx}$ and $\dfrac{d^2y}{dx^2}$ plotted against x to help you answer this.

2 a Find the co-ordinates of the turning point of the quadratic function $y = 5 + 2x - x^2$ by finding where $\dfrac{dy}{dx} = 0$.

b Use the second derivative of y to determine whether the turning point is a maximum or a minimum.

c Draw sketches of the graphs of y, $\dfrac{dy}{dx}$ and $\dfrac{d^2y}{dx^2}$.

Make sure you fully understand what each of these is telling you.

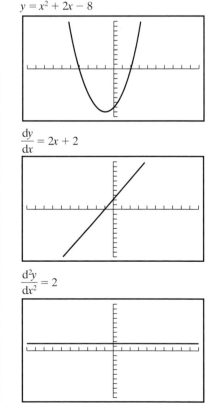

$y = x^2 + 2x - 8$

$\dfrac{dy}{dx} = 2x + 2$

$\dfrac{d^2y}{dx^2} = 2$

3 **a** Find the first and second derivatives of the cubic function $y = x^3 - 6x + 5$.

b Find the x co-ordinates of the stationary points of the function by putting $\dfrac{dy}{dx}$ equal to zero.

c Find the y co-ordinates of the stationary points and draw a sketch of the graph.

d Find $\dfrac{d^2y}{dx^2}$.

e Use the sign of the second derivative at the stationary points to determine whether the points are maxima or minima.

4 **a** Find the co-ordinates (both x and y-values) of the stationary points of the cubic function $y = x^3 + 6x^2 - 9x + 8$.

b Use the second derivative of y to determine whether the stationary points are maxima or minima.

5 **a** Show that the function $y = \cos x$ has a stationary point when $x = \pi$ $\left(\text{i.e. show that } \dfrac{dy}{dx} = 0 \text{ when } x = \pi\right)$ and use the second derivative to show that this stationary point is a minimum.

b Draw sketch graphs of y, $\dfrac{dy}{dx}$ and $\dfrac{d^2y}{dx^2}$, and explain how each of these confirms that $y = \cos x$ has a stationary point at $x = \pi$.

6 Find the co-ordinates of the stationary points of the function $y = \sin x$ between $x = 0$ and $x = 2\pi$. Use the second derivative to determine the nature of these stationary points.

7 In **Chapter 2**, you used the quadratic model $y = 22x - x^2$ to model the number of people infected with a cold virus, where y is the number of people infected and x is the number of days since the outbreak started.
Use first and second derivatives to find how many days it took for the number of people infected by the cold virus to reach its peak.

8 In **Section 4.5**, you used the function
$h = 14e^{-0.01t}\left(1 + \cos\dfrac{\pi t}{4}\right) + 2$ to model the flight of a person on a skycoaster, where h metres is the height of the flyer above the ground t seconds after the start of the flight.

a Find an expression for the first derivative and show that
$\dfrac{d^2h}{dt^2} = 14e^{-0.01t}\left[-\dfrac{\pi}{4}\sin\dfrac{\pi t}{4} - 0.01\left(1 + \cos\dfrac{\pi t}{4}\right)\right]$.

b Show that the first derivative is zero when $t = 4$. Find the value of the second derivative at this point and say what this tells you about the motion of the flyer.

Points of inflection

In **Section 4.1** you learnt about points of inflection. At a point of inflection the sign of the first derivative, $\dfrac{dy}{dx}$, is either

- **positive** before the stationary point and decreasing, and **positive** after the stationary point and increasing, or
- **negative** before the stationary point and increasing, and **negative** after the stationary point and decreasing.

The simplest example of a point of inflection is the one that occurs in the function $y = x^3$ when $x = 0$.

Discussion point
What is the difference between a turning point and a stationary point?

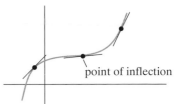

point of inflection

Point of inflection with the gradient positive on either side

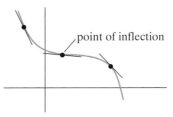

point of inflection

Point of inflection with the gradient negative on either side

---

Activity 4.8C

1 **a** Show that, for the function $y = x^3$, $\dfrac{dy}{dx}$ is zero when $x = 0$,

and that both before and after the stationary point $\dfrac{dy}{dx}$ is positive by substituting $x = -0.1$ and $x = 0.1$ into your expression for $\dfrac{dy}{dx}$.

 b What is the value of the second derivative at this stationary point?

2 In **Activity 4.1**, you showed that the function $y = x^3 + 6x^2 + 12x$ has a point of inflection.
Find the co-ordinates of this point of inflection and find the value of the second derivative at this point.

At a point of inflection, the second derivative of the function, $\dfrac{d^2y}{dx^2}$, is zero.

In the examples above, the points of inflection have occurred where the first derivative, $\dfrac{dy}{dx}$, is also zero, but this does not always have to be the case, as you can see in the next activity.

Discussion point
Here is a sketch of the graph of the function $y = x^4$. The second derivative of $y = x^4$ is zero when $x = 0$ but the function appears to have a minimum at the origin, not a point of inflection. Can you explain what is happening?

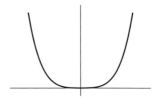

Activity 4.8D

Show that $x = \sin t$ has points of inflection at $t = 0, \pi, 2\pi$ and so on by examining $\dfrac{d^2x}{dt^2}$. Explain why $x = \sin t$ has a point of inflection whenever it crosses the t-axis.

Activity 4.8E

1 Sketch a copy of the graph below. On it mark clearly points of inflection and maximum and minimum turning points.

This graph shows the difference between the time that the sun is at noon (its highest point in the sky) and noon as indicated by a clock that shows local 'mean time'.

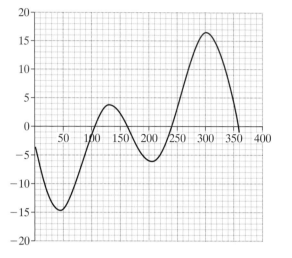

2 a Sketch a graph of $f(x) = 3x^5 - 5x^3$ for $-2 \leqslant x \leqslant 2$. (Use your graphic calculator to help you.) On your sketch indicate all maximum and minimum points and points of inflection.

b Find where $f'(x) = 0$. Use this result to mark clearly the co-ordinates of the maximum and minimum points.

c Find where $f''(x) = 0$. Use this result to confirm that the point you have indicated as a point of inflection is actually one.

3 a Sketch a graph of $y = e^{-x^2}$.

b Find $\dfrac{dy}{dx}$ and $\dfrac{d^2y}{dx^2}$ and use your results to find the co-ordinates and nature (whether maximum or minimum or points of inflection) of all stationary points. Mark these clearly on your sketch graph.

4 a Find the x co-ordinates of the stationary points $\left(\dfrac{dy}{dx} = 0\right)$ of the quartic function $y = \frac{1}{4}x^4 - 3x^3 + 12x^2 - 16x$.

b Use the second derivative of this function to find out whether each stationary point is a maximum, a minimum or a point of inflection.

c Use the second derivative to find any points of inflection that are not stationary points $\left(\text{i.e. } \dfrac{d^2y}{dx^2} = 0, \text{ but } \dfrac{dy}{dx} \neq 0\right)$.

d Use the information you have found in **a**, **b** and **c** to sketch a graph of $y = \frac{1}{4}x^4 - 3x^3 + 12x^2 - 16x$.
Check your answer by plotting the function on your graphic calculator.

5 Investigate the turning points and points of inflection of the decaying wave given by $y = 10e^{-\frac{x}{2}} \sin 5x$.

You may find it useful to plot a graph of this using a graphic calculator window of:

```
RANGE
↕ xMin=0
↕ xMax=6
↕ xSc1=1
↕ yMin=-10
↕ yMax=10
↕ ySc1=1
y(x)= | RANGE | ZOOM | TRACE | GRAPH ▶
```

Activity 4.8F

In this activity there are a selection of models to investigate using calculus. You will have met some of these before in *Algebra and Graphs* or earlier in this book.

1 You can model the height, h mm, of a seedling after n days using $h = -0.04(n - 35)^2 + 51.5$.

a Find $\dfrac{dh}{dn}$ and $\dfrac{d^2h}{dn^2}$.

b By putting $\dfrac{dh}{dn} = 0$ show that according to this model the height of the seedling is a maximum when $n = 35$.

c How does the value of $\dfrac{d^2h}{dn^2}$ when $n = 35$ confirm that this is a maximum value of h?

2 The height of a swing, h metres, above its initial position during the first t seconds of a ride can be modelled by $h(t) = 0.1t(1 + \sin t)$.

a Find $h'(t)$ and $h''(t)$.

b Sketch graphs of $h(t)$, $h'(t)$ and $h''(t)$ for $0 \leqslant t \leqslant 2\pi$ one under the other aligning carefully the t-axes and significant features of each graph.

c Use your graphs to explain how the height, rate of change of height (vertical velocity) and vertical acceleration are related.

d Find when
  i $h'(t) = 0$
  ii $h''(t) = 0$
and the height of the swing at each of these times.

4.9 Revision summary

Stationary points

At places on a graph where the gradient is zero, the graph is parallel to the *x*-axis for a short instant.

These points, where $\dfrac{dy}{dx} = f'(x) = 0$, are called stationary points.

There are three possible types of stationary points:

A maximum, where the gradient is positive before the stationary point and negative after it.

A minimum, where the gradient is negative before the stationary point and positive after it.

A point of inflection, where either:
- the gradient is positive before the stationary point and positive after it; or
- the gradient is negative before the stationary point and negative after it.

point of inflection

point of inflection

Maxima and minima are turning points.

Differentiating functions of functions

If *y* is a function of *u* and *u* is a function of *x* then: $\dfrac{dy}{dx} = \dfrac{dy}{du} \times \dfrac{du}{dx}$

This is sometimes called 'the chain rule' because it can be extended to a 'chain' of functions.
For example, if *y* is a function of *u*, *u* is a function of *v*, *v* is a function of *w* and *w* is a function of *x* then:

$$\frac{dy}{dx} = \frac{dy}{du} \times \frac{du}{dv} \times \frac{dv}{dw} \times \frac{dw}{dx}$$

The chain rule gives useful relationships between rates of change.

For example, if *V* is the volume of a sphere, then $V = \dfrac{4}{3}\pi r^3$.

If the volume and radius change with time then $\dfrac{dV}{dt} = \dfrac{dV}{dr} \times \dfrac{dr}{dt}$, which gives $\dfrac{dV}{dt} = 4\pi r^2 \times \dfrac{dr}{dt}$.

Differentiating trigonometric functions

For calculus, trigonometric functions must be written in terms of radians rather than degrees.

A **radian** is the angle subtended at the centre of a circle by an arc that is equal in length to the radius.

$$\pi \text{ radians} = 180°$$

To convert between the two systems use: $1 \text{ rad} = \dfrac{180°}{\pi}$ or $1° = \dfrac{\pi}{180} \text{ rad}$

Learn the derivatives of sine and cosine functions given below:

Sine function	Derivative		Cosine function	Derivative
$\sin x$	$\cos x$		$\cos x$	$-\sin x$
$A \sin \omega t$	$\omega A \cos \omega t$		$A \cos \omega t$	$-\omega A \sin \omega t$
$A \sin(\omega t + \alpha) + c$	$\omega A \cos(\omega t + \alpha)$		$A \cos(\omega t + \alpha) + c$	$-\omega A \sin(\omega t + \alpha)$

The last two rows are obtained using function of a function.

Differentiating exponential functions

The exponential function $y = e^x$ remains the same when differentiated (or integrated) i.e. $\dfrac{dy}{dx} = e^x$. This and other important results are given below:

Growth function	Derivative		Decay function	Derivative
e^x	e^x		e^{-x}	$-e^{-x}$
Ae^{kt}	kAe^{kt}		Ae^{-kt}	$-kAe^{-kt}$

All these results are obtained from the first using function of a function.

Differentiating products

If y is a product of u and v, where both u and v are functions of x, then: $\dfrac{dy}{dx} = \dfrac{du}{dx} \times v + u \times \dfrac{dv}{dx}$

Differentiating more than once

When a function, f(x) or y, is differentiated, the result is another function, f$'$(x) or $\dfrac{dy}{dx}$.

This gives the gradient function.

You can often differentiate this again to give the second derivative, f$''$(x) or $\dfrac{d^2y}{dx^2}$.

This gives the gradient of the gradient function.

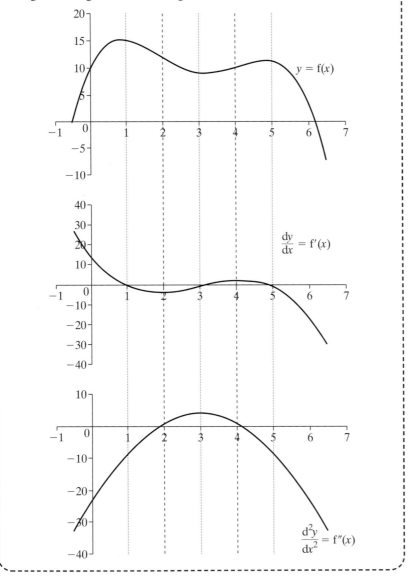

Applications

Examples:

The second derivative of a function giving the distance of a moving object from a fixed point is the acceleration of the object.

The second derivative of the function of retail prices over time is the rate at which inflation is increasing or decreasing.

Stationary points

At a stationary point, the first derivative of a function is zero. If the value of the second derivative at the stationary point is negative, the stationary point is a maximum.

If the value of the second derivative at the stationary point is positive, the stationary point is a minimum.

If the value of the second derivative at the stationary point is zero, the stationary point is a point of inflection.

It is possible for the second derivative to have a value of zero at a point where the first derivative is not zero – such a point is a point of inflection but not a stationary point.

4.10 Preparing for assessment

Your coursework portfolio

Portfolio work relating to this chapter should show your ability to do some advanced differentiation – finding the derivatives of trigonometrical or exponential functions and/or using the function of a function method or the product rule to differentiate functions that are combinations of two or more simpler functions.

You could also compare different ways of finding the gradient of a curve – by drawing tangents by eye, by using the formula for the gradients of chords close to the curve, gradient $= \dfrac{f(a + h) - f(a)}{h}$, or by differentiation. You could compare these different methods and discuss the circumstances in which one or other method may be appropriate.

You need some data that can be modelled with a polynomial, trigonometric or exponential function, or a composite function made up of simpler ones. In the chapter (and in the relevant sections of the *Algebra and Graphs* book) there are lots of possible ideas for situations that may generate such data – tide tables, sunrise and sunset times, wave motion of various kinds, growth and decay, as well as Ferris wheels and other theme park rides. Could you observe such a situation and collect some time–height or time–mass data?

Make sure your report includes discussion of how the use of gradient functions gives you information about the original situation and how realistic your models and their gradient functions are for the whole of your data set or parts of it. Consider the key features of your function(s) that are identified by putting $f'(x)$ or $\dfrac{dy}{dx}$ equal to zero: maxima, minima and points of inflection. You could use second derivatives to determine the nature of these stationary points.

Show that you have checked your work, perhaps by using different methods to do the same thing.

Practice exam questions

Funnel

Data

1 A funnel holding liquid has the shape of a cone as shown in the sketch.
   The liquid runs out of a small hole at the vertex at a steady rate.
   When the depth of liquid in the funnel is h cm, the volume of
   liquid remaining in the funnel is given by $V = \dfrac{\pi h^3}{9}$.

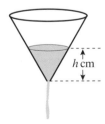

Question

a i Draw a sketch of V against h for $h \geqslant 0$.
   ii Describe how the gradient of the graph changes as h increases.

b Find $\dfrac{dV}{dh}$.

The liquid runs out of the hole at the vertex of the funnel at a steady rate of 2 cm^3 per second.

c Find a formula for $\dfrac{dh}{dt}$ in terms of h.

d **i** Sketch a graph of $\dfrac{dh}{dt}$ against h.

ii Describe what the graph shows in terms of the real situation.

e Find the depth of the liquid and the rate at which it is decreasing when there is 10 cm^3 of liquid left in the funnel.

Investment

Data

Some investments are more risky than others. The value of an investment can go down as well as up.

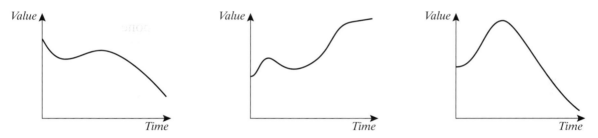

Question

2 The function $V(t) = e^{-t}(1 + t)^3$ models the value of an investment in thousands of pounds t months after the investment is made.

a According to the model, what is the value of the investment:
   i initially;
  ii after 1 month;
 iii after 6 months?

b **i** Show that $V'(t) = e^{-t}(1 + t)^2(2 - t)$
  ii Find a positive value of t for which $V'(t) = 0$.
 iii For what positive values of t is $V'(t) > 0$?
  iv For what positive values of t is $V'(t) < 0$?

c **i** Sketch the graph of $V(t)$ for $0 \leqslant t \leqslant 12$.
  ii What is the maximum value of the investment predicted by the model?
Give your answer to the nearest pound.
 iii Describe in general terms what happens to the investment during the course of the year shown on your graph.

5 More Integration

Contents

In earlier chapters of this book, you explored the key ideas of calculus – learning how to differentiate and integrate.

You have also seen in this book and *Algebra and Graphs* how exponential and trigonometric functions are very useful when modelling certain situations. For example,

- exponential functions are useful when modelling the growth of a population

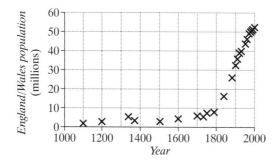

Year	Population
1100	2 000 000
1200	2 800 000
1340	5 500 000
1370	3 300 000
1500	3 000 000
1600	4 500 000
1700	5 800 000
1731	5 200 000
1751	7 300 000
1790	8 000 000
1841	16 000 000
1881	26 000 000
1901	32 500 000
1911	36 000 000
1921	39 000 000
1931	40 000 000
1951	43 800 000
1961	46 200 000
1971	49 000 000
1981	50 000 000
1991	51 000 000
1998	52 400 000

England/Wales population from 1100-1998

- trigonometric functions are useful for modelling how the height of the sea at the entrance to a harbour varies with time.

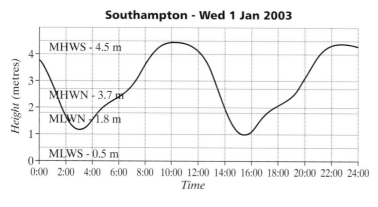

Water levels at Port Dover, Ontario 1–3 July, 2003

You should now know how to differentiate exponential and trigonometric functions. In this chapter you will consider how to integrate these. Before reading any further you might like to predict what $\int e^x \, dx$ and $\int \sin x \, dx$ might be from what you learned about differentiation in the previous chapter.

5.1 Integrating trigonometric functions

Integrating sin x and cos x

In **Section 4.3**, you saw that $\frac{d}{dx}(\cos x) = -\sin x$ when the angle x is in radians.

So the integral of $-\sin x$ must be $\cos x$. Therefore:

$$\int \sin x \, dx = -\cos x + c$$

where c is the constant of integration.

In the following activity you will use a spreadsheet to calculate areas under the sine graph to confirm this result.

Integrating sin x and cos x
|
Integrating general sine and cosine functions

Activity 5.1A

The spreadsheet below shows the formulae that you can use to calculate areas between the graph of $y = \sin x$ and the x-axis.

	A	B	C	D	E
1	x	$f(x) = \sin x$	**Strip area**	**Area between 0 and x**	
2	0	=SIN(A2)	0	0	
3	=A2+PI()/20	=SIN(A3)	=0.5*(B2+B3)*PI()/20	=SUM($C$2:C3)	
4	=A3+PI()/20	=SIN(A4)	=0.5*(B3+B4)*PI()/20	=SUM($C$2:C4)	
5	=A4+PI()/20	=SIN(A5)	=0.5*(B4+B5)*PI()/20	=SUM($C$2:C5)	
6	=A5+PI()/20	=SIN(A6)	=0.5*(B5+B6)*PI()/20	=SUM($C$2:C6)	
7	=A6+PI()/20	=SIN(A7)	=0.5*(B6+B7)*PI()/20	=SUM($C$2:C7)	
8	=A7+PI()/20	=SIN(A8)	=0.5*(B7+B8)*PI()/20	=SUM($C$2:C8)	
9	=A8+PI()/20	=SIN(A9)	=0.5*(B8+B9)*PI()/20	=SUM($C$2:C9)	
10	=A9+PI()/20	=SIN(A10)	=0.5*(B9+B10)*PI()/20	=SUM($C$2:C10)	
11	=A10+PI()/20	=SIN(A11)	=0.5*(B10+B11)*PI()/20	=SUM($C$2:C11)	

The spreadsheet below shows the values calculated by the spreadsheet above.

	A	B	C	D	E	F
1	x	$f(x) = \sin x$	**Strip area**	**Area between 0 and x**		
2	0	0	0	0		
3	0.157079633	0.156434465	0.012286334	0.012286334		
4	0.314159265	0.309016994	0.036556472	0.048842806		
5	0.471238898	0.4539905	0.059926468	0.108769275		
6	0.628318531	0.587785252	0.081820876	0.190590151		
7	0.785398163	0.707106781	0.101700582	0.292290733		
8	0.942477796	0.809016994	0.119076083	0.411366816		
9	1.099557429	0.891006524	0.133519535	0.544886351		
10	1.256637061	0.951056516	0.144675293	0.689561644		
11	1.413716694	0.987688341	0.152268665	0.841830309		

Discussion point

What method is used to find the areas of the strips?

1 The formula in cell A3 is '=A2 + PI()/20'.

    a By how much is the value of this cell greater than the value of cell A2?

    b The area is found by dividing it into strips. How wide is each strip?

2 Set up your own spreadsheet using these formulae and fill down the table to find the area between $x = 0$ and $x = 2\pi$.

3 **a** Use columns A and B to draw the graph of $y = \sin x$.

    b Use your graph to explain why the values in cells C23 to C42 are negative.

4 Use columns A and D to draw a graph of the area function against x to confirm that this is $y = -\cos x$.

5 **a** Use the integral of $\sin x$ given above to find an expression for $\int_0^x \sin x \, dx$.

    b Calculate values of this expression in column E of your spreadsheet and compare the results with those in column D.

    c Why are the values in columns D and E not *exactly* the same?

From **Section 4.3** we know that $\dfrac{d}{dx}(\sin x) = \cos x$.

In the next activity deduce the integral of $\cos x$ and then set up a spreadsheet to check using areas under the cosine curve.

Excel
Activity

Activity 5.1B

1 What is $\int \cos x \, dx$?

2 Set up a spreadsheet similar to that used in **Activity 5.1A** to calculate areas between the graph of $y = \cos x$ and the x-axis between 0 and x for $0 \leqslant x \leqslant 2\pi$.

Check that your spreadsheet supports the answer you gave for **question 1**.

Integrating general sine and cosine functions

From above you have the result that:
$$\int \sin x \, dx = -\cos x + c$$
where c is the constant of integration.

See **Section 4.3**.

The derivative of the general cosine form $y = A \cos(\omega t + \alpha)$ is:

$$\frac{dy}{dt} = -\omega A \sin(\omega t + \alpha)$$

Therefore:

$$\int A \sin(\omega t + \alpha)\, dt = -\frac{A}{\omega}\cos(\omega t + \alpha) + k$$

where k is the constant of integration in this case.

In this case the variable is t. A, ω and α are constants that will probably have numerical values in any problem you have to solve.

Discussion point
Make sure that you understand this result.

Activity 5.1C

1 This table gives the integrals deduced above.

Copy the table and use similar reasoning to complete it.

Revise derivatives from **Section 4.3** first if you need to.

Function	Integral
$\sin t$	$-\cos t + k$
$\cos t$	$\sin t + k$
$\sin \omega t$	
$\cos \omega t$	
$A \sin \omega t$	
$A \cos \omega t$	
$\sin(\omega t + \alpha)$	
$\cos(\omega t + \alpha)$	
$A \sin(\omega t + \alpha)$	$-\dfrac{A}{\omega}\cos(\omega t + \alpha) + k$
$A \cos(\omega t + \alpha)$	

2 Find the following integrals.

a $\displaystyle\int \sin 2t\, dt$ **b** $\displaystyle\int \cos 3t\, dt$

c $\displaystyle\int \sin \tfrac{1}{2}t\, dt$ **d** $\displaystyle\int 4 \cos 5t\, dt$

e $\displaystyle\int 15 \sin 0.3t\, dt$ **f** $\displaystyle\int 6 \cos \tfrac{1}{3}t\, dt$

3 Find these integrals.

a $\displaystyle\int \sin(2t + 3)\, dt$ **b** $\displaystyle\int \cos(4t - 1)\, dt$

c $\displaystyle\int \sin\left(5t - \frac{\pi}{6}\right) dt$ **d** $\displaystyle\int \cos\left(\frac{1}{2}t + \frac{\pi}{3}\right) dt$

e $\displaystyle\int 2 \sin(7t + 1)\, dt$ **f** $\displaystyle\int 8 \cos(t - 6)\, dt$

g $\displaystyle\int 3 \sin\left(2t + \frac{\pi}{4}\right) dt$ **h** $\displaystyle\int 5 \cos\left(4t - \frac{\pi}{4}\right) + 1\, dt$

i $\displaystyle\int [5 \cos(3t + \pi) + 4]\, dt$ **j** $\displaystyle\int \left[\frac{1}{2}\sin(10t + 3) + 5\right] dt$

Activity 5.1D

1 The graph below is of the function $y = \sin t$ for $0 \leqslant t \leqslant 2\pi$.

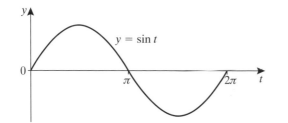

The area under the graph for $0 \leqslant t \leqslant \pi$ is given by $\int_0^\pi \sin t \, dt$.

You can evaluate this as follows:

$$\int_0^\pi \sin t \, dt = [-\cos t]_0^\pi = (-\cos \pi) - (-\cos 0) = 1 + 1 = 2$$

a Show that the total area under the function $y = \sin t$ for $0 \leqslant t \leqslant 2\pi$, found by evaluating $\int_0^{2\pi} \sin t \, dt$, is zero.

b Find the numerical value of the total area.

2 Find the values of the following integrals. For each, sketch a graph and shade the area that you are finding.

a $\int_0^{\frac{\pi}{2}} \cos t \, dt$

b $\int_0^{\pi} \cos t \, dt$

c $\int_0^{\frac{\pi}{2}} \sin_2 t \, dt$

d $\int_0^{\frac{\pi}{6}} 6 \cos 3t \, dt$

e $\int_0^{\frac{\pi}{4}} \sin 4t \, dt$

f $\int_{-\pi}^{\pi} \cos 2t \, dt$

g $\int_0^{4\pi} 5 \sin \frac{1}{2} t \, dt$

h $\int_0^{0.5} \sin(2t + 1) \, dt$

i $\int_{0.2}^{0.4} \cos(5t - 1) \, dt$

j $\int_{-\frac{\pi}{3}}^{\frac{\pi}{3}} \sin\left(t + \frac{\pi}{6}\right) dt$

3 a Sketch the graph of the function $y = 2 \sin 3t$.

b Find the area between the graph and the t-axis between the values $t = 0$ and $t = \dfrac{\pi}{3}$.

4 a Sketch the graph of the function $y = 5 \cos 4t$.

b Find $\int_0^{\frac{\pi}{2}} 5 \cos 4t \, dt$ and explain why this does not give the total area between the curve and the t-axis between $t = 0$ and $t = \dfrac{\pi}{2}$.

c Use integration to find the total area between the function $y = 5 \cos 4t$ and the t-axis between $t = 0$ and $t = \dfrac{\pi}{2}$.

Remember that when you use your calculator, it must be in *radian* mode.

Discussion point
Can you explain the answer to **1a**?

Discussion point
Can you explain your answers to **2b**, **2f** and **2g**?

Graphs may help you.

Checkpoint
Use your graphic calculator to check your answers.

5 a Sketch the graph of the function $y = 4 \sin\left(t + \dfrac{\pi}{6}\right)$.

   b Find the area between the graph and the t-axis between the values $t = 0$ and $t = \dfrac{5\pi}{6}$.

6 a Find $\displaystyle\int_{0}^{\frac{\pi}{2}} (\cos 2t + 1)\, dt$.

   b Sketch a graph and shade the area you have found.

7 A model for the vertical speed of a pod on a Ferris wheel rotating at a constant speed is $v = \dfrac{\pi}{3} \sin \dfrac{\pi t}{30}$ where v ms^{-1} is the vertical speed after t seconds.

   a Use integration to find the vertical distance travelled after 30 seconds.

   b A complete revolution of this wheel takes 1 minute. Integration appears to show that the vertical distance travelled in one revolution is zero. Explain this result.

Discussion point
Is calculus the best way of calculating the vertical distance travelled in **question 7a**? How else could you find the distance?

8 Part of a rollercoaster ride has a track profile that can be modelled by the trigonometric function

$y = 7 \sin \dfrac{\pi(x - 25)}{50} + 8$, where x metres is the horizontal distance and y metres is the vertical height.

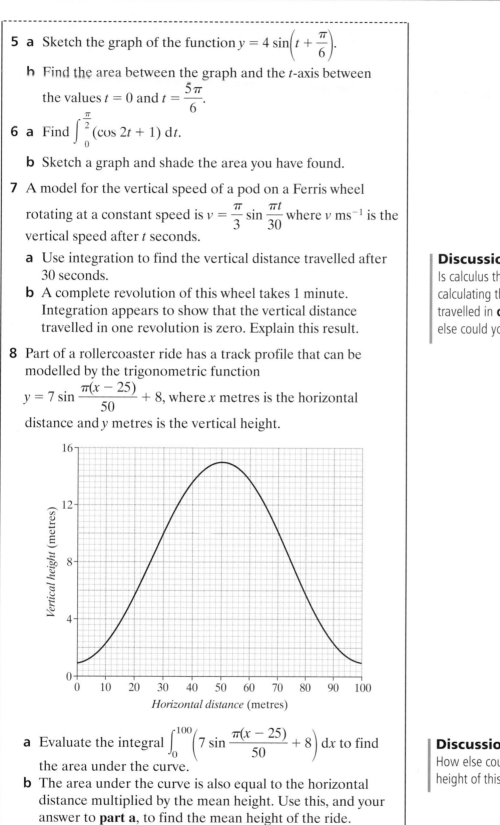

a Evaluate the integral $\displaystyle\int_{0}^{100} \left(7 \sin \dfrac{\pi(x - 25)}{50} + 8 \right) dx$ to find the area under the curve.

   b The area under the curve is also equal to the horizontal distance multiplied by the mean height. Use this, and your answer to **part a**, to find the mean height of the ride.

   c What would be different about the model and the mean height if the ride only went up to a maximum height of 10 metres? Could you find the new mean height without integrating again?

Discussion point
How else could you find the mean height of this part of the ride?

5.2 Integrating exponential functions

Integrating e^x and e^{-x}

We know that a very special feature of the exponential function is that it is its own derivative, i.e. $\frac{d}{dx}(e^x) = e^x$

So the integral of e^x must also be e^x,

i.e. $\qquad \int e^x \, dx = e^x + c$

$\qquad$ where c is the constant of integration.

☞

In the following activity you will use a spreadsheet to calculate areas under the graph of the exponential function to confirm this result.

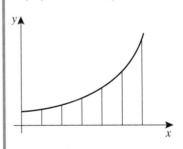

Integrating e^x and e^{-x}

Integrating general exponential functions

See **Section 4.4**.

Activity 5.2A

1 The spreadsheets below show how you can calculate the area enclosed by the graph of the exponential function and the x-axis. The second spreadsheet shows formulae that you can use.

	A	B	C	D	E	F
1	x	$y = \exp(x)$	Strip area	x	Area between 0 and x	
2	0	1	0	0	0	
3	0.01	1.010050167	0.020201003	0.02	0.020201003	
4	0.03	1.030454534	0.020609091	0.04	0.040810094	
5	0.05	1.051271096	0.021025422	0.06	0.061835516	
6	0.07	1.072508181	0.021450164	0.08	0.08328568	
7	0.09	1.094174284	0.021883486	0.10	0.105169165	
8	0.11	1.11627807	0.022325561	0.12	0.127494727	
9	0.13	1.138828383	0.022776568	0.14	0.150271294	
10	0.15	1.161834243	0.023236685	0.16	0.173507979	
11	0.17	1.185304851	0.023706097	0.18	0.197214076	

	A	B	C	D	E	
1	x	$y = \exp(x)$	Strip area	x	Area between 0 and x	
2	0	=EXP(A2)	0	0	0	
3	0.01	=EXP(A3)	=0.02*B3	=D2+0.02	=SUM($C$3:C3)	
4	=A3+0.02	=EXP(A4)	=0.02*B4	=D3+0.02	=SUM($C$3:C4)	
5	=A4+0.02	=EXP(A5)	=0.02*B5	=D4+0.02	=SUM($C$3:C5)	
6	=A5+0.02	=EXP(A6)	=0.02*B6	=D5+0.02	=SUM($C$3:C6)	
7	=A6+0.02	=EXP(A7)	=0.02*B7	=D6+0.02	=SUM($C$3:C7)	
8	=A7+0.02	=EXP(A8)	=0.02*B8	=D7+0.02	=SUM($C$3:C8)	
9	=A8+0.02	=EXP(A9)	=0.02*B9	=D8+0.02	=SUM($C$3:C9)	
10	=A9+0.02	=EXP(A10)	=0.02*B10	=D9+0.02	=SUM($C$3:C10)	
11	=A10+0.02	=EXP(A11)	=0.02*B11	=D10+0.02	=SUM($C$3:C11)	

Excel Activity

Discussion point

The area is found by dividing it into strips parallel to the y-axis.

How wide is each strip? What method is being used to find the strip areas?

   a Set up your own spreadsheet using these formulae and fill down all columns as far as $x = 2.99$.

   b Use the values in columns A, B and E to draw a graph of $y = e^x$ and a graph of the area function on the same axes.

   c What transformation of the graph of $y = e^x$ would give the graph of the area function?

   d Use your answer to **part c** to write down the area function in terms of x.

   e It is suggested above that $\int e^x \, dx = e^x + c$.

      Use this to find $\int_0^x e^x \, dx$.

2 a What is the derivative of e^{-x}?

   b Deduce the integral of e^{-x}.

   c Use your answer to **2b** to find an expression for $\int_0^x e^{-x} \, dx$.

   d Make a copy of the spreadsheet you used in **question 1**.

   e Alter the formulae in Column B to give values of e^{-x}.

   f Re-label and re-scale the graphs.

   g Explain how the graphs confirm your answer to **2c**.

Integrating general exponential functions

From above we have the results that:

See **Section 4.4**.

$$\int e^x \, dx = e^x + c \text{ and } \int e^{-x} \, dx = -e^{-x} + c$$

where c is the constant of integration.

The derivative of the general exponential form $y = Ae^{kt}$ is

$$\frac{dy}{dt} = kAe^{kt}.$$

Here the variable is t and A and k are constants that will take fixed positive or negative values in any particular problem.

When differentiated, Ae^{kt} is *multiplied* by k.
When integrated, Ae^{kt} will be *divided* by k.

i.e.
$$\int Ae^{kt} \, dt = \frac{A}{k} e^{kt} + c$$
where c is the constant of integration.

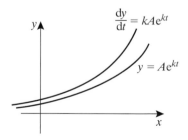

Activity 5.2B

1 Find expressions for these integrals.

   a $\int e^{5t} \, dt$ **b** $\int e^{-2t} \, dt$ **c** $\int e^{\frac{1}{2}t} \, dt$

   d $\int 6e^{3t} \, dt$ **e** $\int 4e^{-5t} \, dt$ **f** $\int 2e^{-\frac{2}{5}t} \, dt$

   g $\int (3e^{6t} + 5) \, dt$ **h** $\int (1 - 3e^{-0.5t}) \, dt$ **i** $\int 12(1 - e^{-0.2t}) \, dt$

2 Evaluate the following:

a $\int_0^1 e^{-x}\, dx$ b $\int_0^1 e^{2x}\, dx$ c $\int_{-1}^1 e^{5x}\, dx$

d $\int_2^6 e^{-\frac{1}{2}t}\, dt$ e $\int_0^{0.5} 8e^{4t}\, dt$ f $\int_0^{2.5} 3e^{0.2t}\, dt$

g $\int_0^1 (5e^{2t} + 3)\, dt$ h $\int_0^{0.25} 20(1 - e^{-4t})\, dt$ i $\int_{-1}^1 (e^{3t} + 4t)\, dt$

3 Find the value of each of the following integrals.
In each case draw a sketch of the function and shade the area
you have found.

a $\int_0^3 e^{-2x}\, dx$ b $\int_1^4 2e^{0.5x}\, dx$ c $\int_2^4 e^{-\frac{1}{2}t}\, dt$

d $\int_{-1}^1 (2e^{4x} + 1)\, dx$ e $\int_0^1 (e^{3t} - 1)\, dt$ f $\int_0^2 5(1 - e^{-2t})\, dt$

4 a i Show that $e^{3(x+1)}$ can be written as ae^{3x}, where a is a
constant.

ii Hence find $\int_0^1 e^{3(x+1)}\, dx$.

b Sketch the graph of $y = e^{3(x+1)}$ and shade the area you have
found in **part a ii**.

5 In **Chapter 3** of *Algebra and Graphs* and in Chapter 4 of this
book you may have done some work about the growth of the
cane toad population in Australia. A model of the rate of
growth of the area occupied
by the toads is $\dfrac{dA}{dt} = 2.839e^{0.0779t}$, where $1000A$ km² is the
area occupied by the toads t years after 1939.

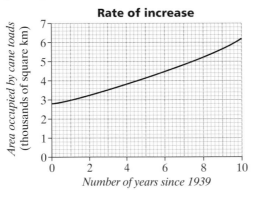

Rate of increase

Number of years since 1939

Area occupied by cane toads (thousands of square km)

a What does the area under the graph from $t = 0$ to $t = 10$
represent?

b Calculate the area under the graph by evaluating the
integral $\int_0^{10} 2.839e^{0.0779t}\, dt$.

c The area occupied by cane toads in 1939 was 32 800 km².
What was the area occupied in 1949, according to this model?

5.3 Applications of integration

Areas

You can use integration to find the area between a graph and the horizontal axis. This provides a useful method of finding areas, if the boundary of the area can be modelled by a function or functions that can be integrated.

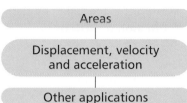

Areas

Displacement, velocity and acceleration

Other applications

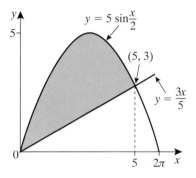

For example, suppose the shaded part of the sketch represents the plan of a reservoir with x and y both measured in kilometres.

The boundaries are represented by the curve $y = 5 \sin \dfrac{x}{2}$ and the straight line $y = \dfrac{3x}{5}$.

The points of intersection of the curve and line are the origin and the point (5, 3).

The area between the line and curve is the area under the curve between $x = 0$ and $x = 5$ minus the area under the straight line between $x = 0$ and $x = 5$.

You can calculate this as follows:

$$\text{Area} = \int_0^5 \left(5 \sin \frac{x}{2} - \frac{3x}{5} \right) dx$$

$$\left[-10 \cos \frac{x}{2} - \frac{3x^2}{10} \right]_0^5$$

$$[-10 \cos 2.5 - 7.5] - [-10 \cos 0 - 0]$$

$$8.01 - 7.5 + 10$$

$$10.51$$

The area of the reservoir is approximately 10.5 km².

Check the points of intersection by drawing the graphs on your graphic calculator and using the zoom and trace facilities. You should find that the second point is (5.00, 3.00) correct to 2 decimal places.

Alternatively you could find the areas separately and then subtract one from the other.

Discussion point
What other method is there of finding the area under the straight line?

Check this answer using the integration facility on your graphic calculator.

Activity 5.3A

1 The outline of the wing of an aircraft is modelled by the function $y = 10 \cos x$

for $-\dfrac{\pi}{2} \leqslant x \leqslant \dfrac{\pi}{2}$ where

both x and y are in metres.

Find the area of the wing.

Discussion point
What different ways are there of using integration to calculate this area?

2 The cross-section of a stream is modelled by the area between the curve $y = -0.5 \sin x$ and the x-axis between 0 and π.

  a Sketch the cross-section.

  b Use integration to find its area given that x and y are in metres.

Discussion point
If the water travels at a speed of 2 metres per second, how much water flows down the stream per minute?

3 The sketch shows the shape of a piece of land with the dimensions given in metres. The curved boundary is modelled by the graph of the function $y = 12e^{-0.2x} + 8$.

Find the area of the land.

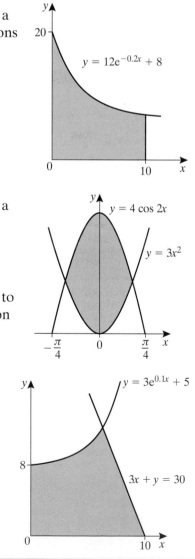

4 The sketch shows the shape of a leaf. Its outline is modelled by the curves $y = 4 \cos 2x$ and $y = 3x^2$ where both x and y are measured in centimetres.

  a Use your graphic calculator to find the points of intersection of these curves, giving your answers to 3 d.p.

  b Hence find the shaded area.

5 The shaded area in the sketch represents the shape of a lawn. The dimensions are given in metres.

Find the area of the lawn.

Displacement, velocity and acceleration

In **Section 3.3** you learnt that the area under an acceleration–time graph gives the change in velocity of a moving object and the area under a velocity–time graph gives the displacement. It follows that if acceleration is modelled by a function involving time, t, then integrating this function with respect to t gives an expression for velocity and integrating again gives an expression for displacement.

Sometimes the functions used to model acceleration may involve trigonometric or exponential terms. Suppose, for instance, a train is approaching a signal at a speed of 10 ms^{-1} when the signal changes from 'go' to 'stop'. The train's acceleration after the train driver applies his brakes is modelled by the function $a = -2e^{-0.2t}$ where t is the time in seconds after the brakes were applied and a is the acceleration in ms^{-2}.

Integrating this function gives the velocity:

$$v = \int a \, dt = \int (-2e^{-0.2t}) \, dt$$

$$v = \frac{-2}{-0.2} e^{-0.2t} + c$$

$$v = 10e^{-0.2t} + c$$

> Note we use 'a' for 'acceleration', even though the fact that it is negative means that the train is actually slowing down.

Substituting $v = 10$ when $t = 0$ gives $c = 0$ and so:

$$v = 10e^{-0.2t}$$

> The initial conditions allow you to find the value of c.

Integrating again gives the displacement:

$$d = \int v \, dt = \int (10e^{-0.2t}) \, dt$$

$$d = \frac{10}{-0.2} e^{-0.2t} + c$$

$$d = -50e^{-0.2t} + c$$

Substituting $d = 0$ when $t = 0$ gives $c = 50$ and so:

$$d = 50(1 - e^{-0.2t})$$

> **Discussion point**
> What happens to a, v and d as time goes by? What do the graphs of a, v and d plotted against time look like? Do you think this model is realistic?

Activity 5.3B

1 When a car accelerates away from a set of traffic lights its acceleration can be modelled by $a = 3e^{-0.25t}$ where a ms^{-2} is the acceleration after t seconds.

 a Use integration to find functions that model the velocity and displacement of the car t seconds after it sets off from the traffic lights.

 b Draw graphs to illustrate how the acceleration, velocity and displacement change with time.

 c Explain what your graphs predict will happen in the real situation.

 d Do you think this is realistic? Give reasons for your answer.

> Remember to include a constant of integration each time you integrate. To find the values of these constants assume that $v = 0$ and $d = 0$ when $t = 0$.

2 A parachutist is free-falling at a velocity of 25 ms^{-1} when he opens his parachute. The acceleration, a ms^{-2}, t seconds after the parachute opens, is modelled by $a = -20\mathrm{e}^{-t}$.

   a Find functions to model the velocity and displacement.

   b Draw graphs to illustrate how the acceleration, velocity and displacement change with time.

   c Explain what your graphs predict will happen in the real situation.

3 A toy train travels between two stations A and B positioned at the ends of a straight track. The acceleration, a in ms^{-2}, of the train t seconds after it leaves station A is modelled by

$$a = \frac{\pi}{8} \cos \frac{\pi}{4} t.$$

   a Use integration to find functions that model the velocity and displacement of the train t seconds after it sets off from station A.

   b Draw sketch graphs to illustrate how the acceleration, velocity and displacement change with time.

   c **i** Briefly describe the train's motion.
      ii What is the maximum speed of the train?
      iii How long is the track between the stations A and B?

4 The function $a = 5\pi \cos \frac{\pi}{3} t$ is used to model the upward acceleration a ms^{-2} of a bungee jumper t seconds after she rebounds from her lowest position.

   a Use integration to find functions to model her upward velocity and her distance above the lowest position.

   b Draw sketch graphs showing how these functions predict that the acceleration, velocity and distance will change with time.

   c **i** Explain, in terms of the real situation, what your graphs predict will happen to the bungee jumper after the first rebound.
      ii Do you think the model is realistic? Explain your answer.

Other applications

There are other situations where the rate of change of a variable can be modelled by a function and integration can give further information about the variable concerned.

For example, when current flows through a wire, its strength is measured as the *rate* at which electrical charge flows along the wire. Charge is measured in coulombs where 1 coulomb is the charge carried by 6.24×10^{18} electrons. Current is measured in amperes, usually abbreviated to 'amps'. One amp is the current when 1 coulomb of charge flows along the wire per second.

Alternating currents can be represented by sine functions. For example, the function $I = 20 \sin 100\pi t$, where t is the time in seconds, represents an alternating current that has a peak value of 20 amps as shown in the sketch below.

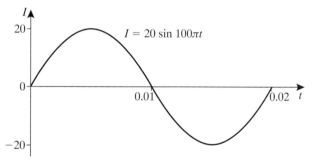

Since I amps is the rate of flow of charge, integrating I with respect to t gives information about the amount of charge that flows, Q coulombs.

$$Q = \int 20 \sin 100\pi \; dt$$

$$= -\frac{20}{100\pi} \cos 100\pi t + c$$

$$= -\frac{1}{5\pi} \cos 100\pi t + c$$

If you assume that no charge has flowed when $t = 0$

$$0 = -\frac{1}{5\pi} \cos 0 + c$$

$$\Rightarrow \quad c = \frac{1}{5\pi}$$

and the charge that has flowed after t seconds is given by the function:

$$Q = \frac{1}{5\pi}(1 - \cos 100\pi t)$$

This can be used to find the amount of charge that flows in the first hundredth of a second by substituting $t = 0.01$:

$$Q = \frac{1}{5\pi}(1 - \cos \pi) = \frac{2}{5\pi} = 0.127$$

The amount of charge is 0.13 coulombs (to 2 s.f.).

The convention chosen by early scientists, and still used today, is that current flows from the positive terminal to the negative terminal. In fact the actual flow of electrons is in the opposite direction.

Discussion points

What is happening during each part of the cycle shown in the graph?

How many cycles are there per second?

What transformations of the basic sine curve give this graph?

Alternatively the charge that flows in the first hundredth of a second can be found by integrating I from 0 to 0.01:

$$\int_0^{0.01} 20 \sin 100\pi t$$

$$= \left[-\frac{20}{100\pi} \cos 100\pi t \right]_0^{0.01}$$

$$= \left[-\frac{1}{5\pi} \cos \pi \right] - \left[-\frac{1}{5\pi} \cos 0 \right]$$

$$= \frac{1}{5\pi} + \frac{1}{5\pi} = \frac{2}{5\pi} = 0.127$$

Discussion point

What part of the graph represents this charge?

What would be the value of the integral over a full cycle (i.e. from 0 to 0.02)? Can you explain this in terms of the real situation?

133

Activity 5.3C

1 An alternating current, I amps, is given by $I = 12 \sin 40\pi t$ where t is the time in seconds.
   a Sketch a graph of I against t.
   b Shade the part of the graph that represents the charge that flows in the first hundredth of a second.
   c Use integration to find this charge.
   d i Find the charge that flows in the second hundredth of a second.
      ii Why is this not the same as the answer for **part c**?

2 When an electrical circuit is switched on a direct current flows given by $I = 13(1 - e^{-50t})$ where I is the current in amps t seconds after the switch is thrown.
   a Sketch a graph of I against t and explain briefly what the graph predicts will happen to the current.
   b Use integration to find an expression in terms of t for the charge, Q coulombs, that has travelled through the circuit after t seconds.
   c Sketch a graph of Q against t and explain briefly what the graph predicts.

3 The rate at which a worker packs components is modelled by the function $p(t) = 40 - 25e^{-0.5t}$, where t is the number of days since he started the job and $p(t)$ is the number of components packed on day t.
   a Sketch a graph of $p(t)$ and explain what it shows in terms of the real situation.
   b Find the area under the curve for $0 \leqslant t \leqslant 10$ and explain what this area represents.

4 A house is initially valued at £75 000. The rate, $r(t)$ pounds per month at which the price of the house rises is modelled by the function $r(t) = 1500e^{0.02t}$, where t is the time in months after its initial valuation.
   a Use integration to find an expression in terms of t for the price of the house.
   b Sketch a graph of the function you have found in **part a** and briefly explain what your graph predicts will happen in the real situation. Do you think this is realistic?

5 The rate at which the population of a seaside resort changes is modelled by the function $r(t) = \dfrac{\pi}{15} \cos \dfrac{\pi}{180} (t - 90)$, where t is the number of days since the beginning of the year and $r(t)$ gives the rate of change in thousands of people per day. The population on 1 January (i.e. $t = 0$) is estimated to be 18 000.
   a Use integration to find an expression in terms of t for the population of the resort t days after the beginning of the year.
   b Sketch a graph of the function you have found in **part a**.
   c Briefly explain what your graph predicts in terms of the real situation. How realistic do you think this is?

Remember to use your graphic calculator to help you sketch graphs.

Discussion point
What percentage increase per month does this represent?

5.4 Revision summary

Integrating trigonometric functions

The key results for trigonometric functions are:

$$\int \sin x \, dx = -\cos x + c$$

and

$$\int \cos x \, dx = \sin x + c$$

More generally:

$$\int A \sin(\omega t + \alpha) dt = -\frac{A}{\omega} \cos(\omega t + \alpha) + c$$

and

$$\int A \cos(\omega t + \alpha) dt = \frac{A}{\omega} \sin(\omega t + \alpha) + c$$

Integrating exponential functions

For exponential functions, the key result is:

$$\int e^x \, dx = e^x + c$$

which leads to the general results:

$$\int A e^{kt} \, dx = \frac{A}{k} e^{kt} + c$$

and

$$\int A e^{-kt} \, dx = -\frac{A}{k} e^{-kt} + c$$

5.5 Preparing for assessment

Your coursework portfolio

This chapter is about the integration of exponential and trigonometrical functions so your portfolio work should reflect this.

You need some data that can be modelled with a trigonometric or exponential function. There are many examples in earlier chapters of situations that generate such data, but in the case of this chapter you need to be able to interpret the area under the graph.

So, your data should be about rates – the area under a speed–time graph is the distance travelled, the area under a graph showing rates of increase of a quantity will give the total amount of the quantity, and so on.

Or possibly you could use integration to find the area of a shape such as the cross-section of a river-bed if you have data that is best modelled by an exponential or trigonometrical function. If you know a shape's cross-sectional area, you can perhaps find its volume. Could you apply this to the volume of earth to be removed to build a tunnel or a pool?

You should compare the use of calculus methods to solve your problem with other ways in which you could find the result. What are the advantages and disadvantages of the different methods?

Remember to show that you have checked your work.

Practice exam questions

Heights

Data

1 The data table shows information about the heights of 122 women aged 17–20.

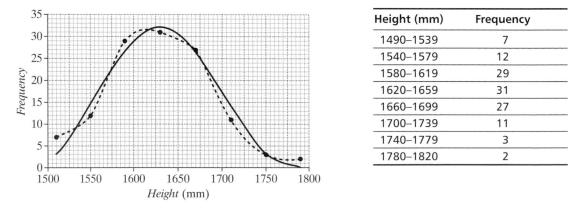

Height (mm)	Frequency
1490–1539	7
1540–1579	12
1580–1619	29
1620–1659	31
1660–1699	27
1700–1739	11
1740–1779	3
1780–1820	2

The graph shows this data, plotted against the mid-point of each interval, and a trigonometrical function that models it,

$$y = 16 \sin\left(\frac{\pi}{180}(x - 55)\right) + 16.$$

Question

1 a Show that the area under the sine graph for $x = 1510$ to 1790 is approximately 5000.

b The proportion of these young women that have heights between 1520 mm and 1700 mm can be estimated by dividing the area under the graph between these two limits by the total area, 5000. Find the area by integration and hence estimate the proportion of these women that have heights between 1520 mm and 1700 mm.

c Use the same method to estimate the probability that one of these women chosen at random will have a height less than 1.60 m.

Restaurant

Data

2 A restaurant uses a cool room to keep food fresh for as long as possible. If the refrigeration unit breaks down, the temperature of the cool room gradually returns to the temperature of the surrounding environment.

The rate of change of temperature is given by $\dfrac{dT}{dt} = 4e^{-0.25t}$,

where $T°C$ is the difference in temperature between the cool room and the surrounding environment and t is the number of hours since the refrigeration unit broke down.

Question

a i What is the significance of the negative sign in the formula for the rate of change of the difference in temperature?

ii Sketch a graph of $\dfrac{dT}{dt}$ against t.

b i Use integration to find the change in temperature in the first 5 hours after the warming-up starts.

ii The initial temperature of the cool room is 4°C. Will the temperature after 5 hours still be within the safety limit, a temperature of no greater than 8°C?

6 Differential Equations

▶ Contents

Another contribution that Newton made to science and mathematics was his law of cooling. Newton suggested that the rate of decrease of the temperature of a body is proportional to the difference between its temperature and that of its surroundings. This statement is very important because it tells you about a rate of change rather than how one variable changes with one other.

It can be expressed symbolically as $\dfrac{dT}{dt} = -k(T - T_s)$ where T is the temperature of the body (for example a hot cup of coffee or tea), T_s is the temperature of the surroundings and k is the constant of proportionality.

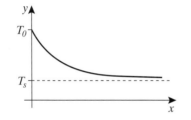

This is a differential equation – sometimes it is possible to write down a differential equation as a model of a situation, so you will need to be able to solve these. To do this, you will need to bring together all you have learned so far about differentiation and integration. You will learn some techniques that will allow you to solve straightforward differential equations in this chapter.

The acceleration, or rate of change of velocity (downwards), for a free-falling skydiver is $a = \dfrac{dv}{dt} = g$, where g is the acceleration due to gravity. Another differential equation!

6.1 Direction field diagrams

Population growth

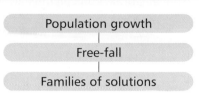

In this section you will see how you can use ideas of calculus to investigate population growth. The ideas you develop here – those of differential equations – are very powerful and you will see how you can use them in other situations where you know about how the rate of change of one variable varies with another.

In *Algebra and Graphs* you investigated the growth of different populations. For example, in Chapter 7 you used recurrence relations to model the growth of the population of England and Wales. Earlier you used exponential functions to model such growth. The data for the population of England and Wales over the years 1811 to 2001 is repeated here. The graph also shows the data together with models

i $P_n = P_{n-1} + 0.13P_{n-1}$
   ($P_0 = 10\,164$ (thousand), $n = 0$ in 1811, $n = 1$ in 1821 and so on)

ii $P = 0.0022e^{0.0086t}$, where t is the year.

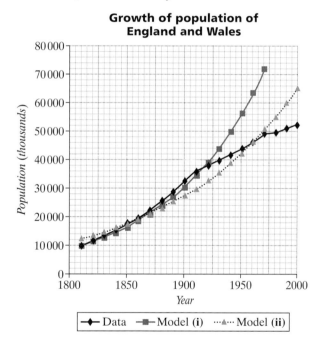

Growth of population of England and Wales

— Data   —■— Model (i)   ···▲··· Model (ii)

Population growth	
Year	England & Wales Population (thousands)
1811	10 164
1821	12 000
1831	13 897
1841	15 914
1851	17 928
1861	20 066
1871	22 712
1881	25 974
1891	29 002
1901	32 612
1911	36 136
1921	37 932
1931	39 988
1941	41 748
1951	43 815
1961	46 196
1971	49 152
1981	49 634
1991	51 099
2001	52 211

The most important factor that influences how a population grows is how many of the population actually exist – or more importantly how many of the population can reproduce. A reasonable assumption might be that the rate of increase of a population is proportional to the size of the population.

The implications of this are:
● when a population is small, its rate of increase is small;
● when a population is large its rate of increase is large.

For these reasons an exponential function in many instances is a suitable model for the size of a population over time.

Discussion point
What other factors influence the size of a population?

139

Consider carefully the phrase, 'the rate of increase of a population is proportional to the size of the population'. You can express this using algebraic and calculus notation as

$$\frac{dP}{dt} \propto P$$

or $\quad \dfrac{dP}{dt} = kP$

where P is the size of population at time t, and k is the constant of proportionality.

This is a differential equation.

In the next activity you will explore what this means.

Discussion point

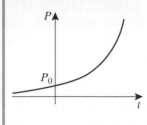

How is an exponential function suitable for population growth when the rate of increase of the population is proportional to its size?

Activity 6.1A

Resource Sheet 6.1A

The differential equation $\dfrac{dP}{dt} = P$ tells you that, for any point on a function that is a solution, the gradient is equal to P.

A set of axes is shown here with P on the vertical axis and t on the horizontal axis.

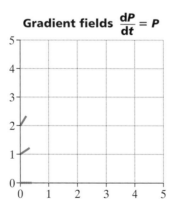

Gradient fields $\dfrac{dP}{dt} = P$

For $t = 0$ and $P = 0, 1, 2$ a small line segment has been drawn that satisfies the equation $\dfrac{dP}{dt} = P$.

So at $(0, 0)$ the line segment has gradient 0, at $(0, 1)$ the line segment has gradient 1, at $(0, 2)$ the line segment has gradient 2.

On a copy of the diagram:

a for $t = 0$, sketch line segments at $(0, 3)$, $(0, 4)$ and $(0, 5)$

b for $t = 1$, sketch line segments at $(1, 0)$, $(1, 1)$, $(1, 2)$, $(1, 3)$, $(1, 4)$, $(1, 5)$

c sketch line segments at $t = 2, t = 3, t = 4, t = 5$ for integer values of P.

Discussion point

The solution of $\dfrac{dP}{dt} = kP$ is an exponential function $P = P_0 e^{kt}$. Show that this is true by finding $\dfrac{dP}{dt}$ and checking that this is equal to kP.

The diagram you now have is shown opposite. It is known as a direction field diagram, or compass needle diagram. You can draw such a diagram when you know a differential equation that describes a situation.

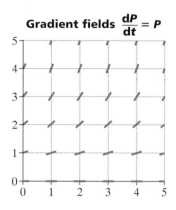

Gradient fields $\dfrac{dP}{dt} = P$

Your teacher may have a computer spreadsheet or other software that will draw direction field diagrams for you.

If you know just one set of values of P and t, this diagram allows you to sketch a graph of the solution. For example, if $P = 1$ when $t = 0$, the small line segments on the direction field show you how to get to the next point. If you draw such line segments frequently – say every 0.25 along the t-axis, you can more easily see how to move from one point to another.

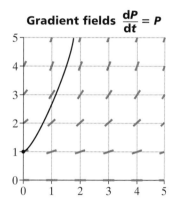

Gradient fields $\dfrac{dP}{dt} = P$

If your teacher has a computer spreadsheet or other software that draws direction field diagrams it is likely that it will plot the solution if you input the co-ordinates of one set of values of P and t.

If you sketch in the curve of the solution you can see it has the shape of an exponential function.

$P = e^t$ is a solution of $\dfrac{dP}{dt} = P$.

You can show this by finding $\dfrac{dP}{dt}$.

Since $P = e^t$, $\dfrac{dP}{dt} = e^t$ (**Section 5.4**), so $\dfrac{dP}{dt} = P$.

$P = P_0 e^t$ is also a solution of $\dfrac{dP}{dt} = P$.

You can show this by finding $\dfrac{dP}{dt}$.

Since $P = P_0 e^t$, $\dfrac{dP}{dt} = P_0 e^t$, so $\dfrac{dP}{dt} = P$.

So there is a **family of solutions** of this differential equation. To find an exact solution you need to know more information – for example, a point that the solution curve passes through.

141

Activity 6.1B

1 On your direction field diagram for $\dfrac{\mathrm{d}P}{\mathrm{d}t} = P$, mark solutions that pass through the points that have these initial conditions.

   a $P = 1$ **b** $P = 2$ **c** $P = 3$

2 Find the equations of the functions that you have drawn as solutions.

Note that, when time is involved, initial conditions are when $t = 0$.

Free-fall

Near the surface of the Earth the acceleration of an object is constant at approximately 10 ms^{-2} – the acceleration due to gravity.

This means that the rate of change of velocity, $v \text{ ms}^{-1}$, of the object is constant, $\dfrac{\mathrm{d}v}{\mathrm{d}t} = 10$.

Note that $\dfrac{\mathrm{d}v}{\mathrm{d}t} = 10$ tells you that the acceleration (rate of change of velocity) is downwards. If vertically upwards was taken as the positive direction then $\dfrac{\mathrm{d}v}{\mathrm{d}t} = -10$.

Activity 6.1C

1 On a copy of the set of axes below, draw a direction field diagram for the differential equation for a free-falling object, i.e. $\dfrac{\mathrm{d}v}{\mathrm{d}t} = 10$.

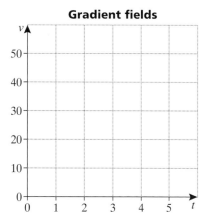

Gradient fields

2 **a** On your direction field diagram, sketch the solution that passes through $(0, 0)$.

   b Explain what the fact that the solution passes through $(0, 0)$ tells you about the real situation of the falling ball.

   c Give the equation of your solution (i.e. find v in terms of t).

   d Check that your answer to **part c** is correct by differentiating v with respect to t and showing that your answer satisfies the differential equation $\dfrac{\mathrm{d}v}{\mathrm{d}t} = 10$.

3 a Show by differentiation that $v = 20 + 10t$ is a solution of the differential equation $\dfrac{dv}{dt} = 10$.

b Explain all you know about an object that has a velocity given by $v = 20 + 10t$ and how this is different to the object you investigated in **question 2**.

4 a Show by differentiation that $v = 10t + k$ is a general solution of the differential equation $\dfrac{dv}{dt} = 10$.

b Explain what you know about an object that has a velocity given by $v = 10t + k$.

Families of solutions

You have seen that for the differential equations you have investigated there are many solutions. It is only when you know something about the situation (such as what is happening when $t = 0$) that you can arrive at a **particular solution**.

For example, in the previous activity $v = 10t + k$ is the general solution. By taking different values of k you obtain a **family of solutions**.

In this next activity you will explore a number of different differential equations by finding the general solution, sketching direction field diagrams for a family of solutions and considering a particular solution.

Resource
Sheet
6.1D

Activity 6.1D

For each differential equation:

a sketch a direction field diagram using a copy of the grid shown;

b find a general function $g = f(x)$ for the family of solutions;

c check your solution by finding $\dfrac{dy}{dx}$ and making sure that it can be substituted back into the original differential equation;

d find a particular solution that passes through $(0, 1)$.

1 $\dfrac{dy}{dx} = x$ **2** $\dfrac{dy}{dx} = 10x$ **3** $\dfrac{dy}{dx} = x^2$ **4** $\dfrac{dy}{dx} = x^3$

5 $\dfrac{dy}{dx} = 0$ **6** $\dfrac{dy}{dx} = 1$ **7** $\dfrac{dy}{dx} = y$ **8** $\dfrac{dy}{dx} = 2y$

9 $\dfrac{dy}{dx} = y^2$ **10** $\dfrac{dy}{dx} = \dfrac{1}{y}$

You might like to share the work out within a group so that each individual tackles only one or two of the differential equations and then reports back on what he or she finds.

Activity 6.1E

Prepare a summary of what you found as the result of the previous activity. This should clearly identify what you know about solutions to differential equations under two headings:

$$\frac{dy}{dx} = f(x) \text{ and } \frac{dy}{dx} = f(y) \text{ where } f(y) = ay^n.$$

You may like to present all your results in a table before you summarise these.

This summary should be for all of the functions that were explored in the previous activity. If you shared the work across a group make sure that you have details of all the work and that your summary covers this.

6.2 Solving differential equations

$$\frac{dy}{dx} = f(x)$$

At the end of the previous section you investigated solutions of differential equations of the form

$$\frac{dy}{dx} = f(x) \quad \text{e.g.} \quad \frac{dy}{dx} = 10x$$

You will have recognised that you solve these using integration in the ways you have done throughout this book.

So, for example, if $\frac{dy}{dx} = 10x$ then $y = 5x^2 + c$.

This gives rise to a family of solutions:

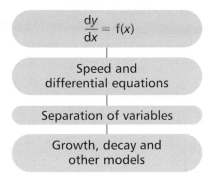

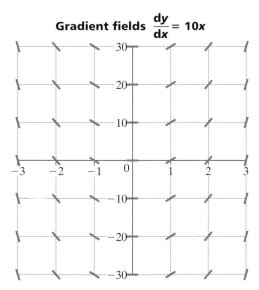

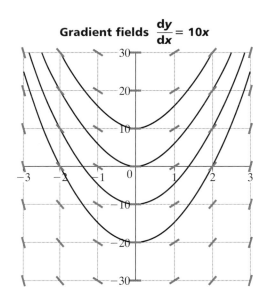

To find a particular solution you need to know information about one particular point. For example, if you know that when $x = 0, y = 0$:

$0 = 5 \times 0^2 + c$ so $c = 0$ and the particular solution is $y = 5x^2$.

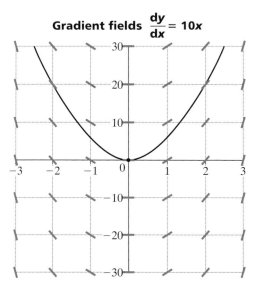

Activity 6.2A

Solve each differential equation below so that the solution passes through the given point. *Sketch* a graph of your solution marking on it all key features. (Use your graphic calculator to help you.)

1 $\dfrac{dy}{dx} = x$ $(0, 0)$ **2** $\dfrac{dy}{dx} = 2x$ $(0, 0)$

3 $\dfrac{dy}{dx} = x^2$ $(0, 1)$ **4** $\dfrac{dy}{dx} = e^x$ $(0, 1)$

5 $\dfrac{dy}{dx} = \sin x$ $(0, 1)$ **6** $\dfrac{dy}{dx} = \cos 2x$ $(0, 1)$

Speed and differential equations

At times you will perhaps start your investigation of a situation with a differential equation (when you know something about the rate of change of one quantity with another).

Time (seconds)	Distance (metres)
0.0	0.00
0.1	0.04
0.2	0.23
0.3	0.69
0.4	1.45
0.5	2.57
0.6	4.00
0.7	5.60
0.8	7.62
0.9	10.12
1.0	12.77

For example, if you were to investigate the performance of cars you may have speed data which tells you how the speed of the car varies with time rather than how its distance varies with time.

Speed–time data for a car accelerating from rest is given here. The speed of the car, v ms^{-1}, t seconds after it starts to move can be modelled by the function $v = 24t$.

If x metres is the distance that the car has moved after t seconds then another way of expressing this is $\dfrac{dx}{dt} = 24t$, a differential equation.

Activity 6.2B

A car accelerates from rest so that its speed can be modelled by $\dfrac{dx}{dt} = 24t$, where x metres is the distance that the car has moved after t seconds.

1 Find an expression for x in terms of t. You will need to use the fact that $x = 0$ when $t = 0$ to find a particular solution.

2 Sketch a graph of x plotted against t for $0 \leqslant t \leqslant 2$. Check that this is what you would expect.

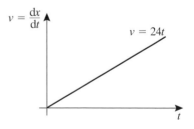

Separation of variables

So far in this section you have investigated solving differential equations of the form $\frac{dy}{dx} = f(x)$, for example $\frac{dx}{dt} = 24t$, which you can solve using integration techniques that you have learnt throughout this book.

So if $\frac{dx}{dt} = 24t$, $x = 12t^2 + c$. To find c you need to know a value of x at a specific time.

How can you solve differential equations of the form $\frac{dy}{dx} = f(y)$ such as $\frac{dP}{dt} = P$? P is not a function of t so you cannot just integrate with respect to t.

You have already met this particular differential equation earlier in this chapter and may know that a possible solution is $P = e^t$. What is the method for arriving at this solution?

Note we have not presented the mathematics behind this method. You can look this up in a pure maths text book.

If $\frac{dP}{dt} = P$ then **separating the variables** and rearranging gives

$\frac{dP}{P} = dt$ so that integrating each side of the equation gives

$\int \frac{dP}{P} = \int dt$

$\Rightarrow \ln P = t + c$

So, $P = e^{t+c}$ or $P = Ae^t$ (since $e^{t+c} \equiv e^c e^t$ and e^c is a constant which can be written as A).

This method is known as **separating the variables** and can be used to solve differential equations of the form $\frac{dy}{dx} = f(y)$. In this next activity you will explore and practise this for a number of functions before going on to explore its use in some common mathematical models in the next section.

Checkpoint

You can check that $P = Ae^t$ is a solution of $\frac{dP}{dt} = P$ by differentiating P.

$\frac{dP}{dt} = Ae^t$ which confirms

$\frac{dP}{dt} = P$.

Activity 6.2C

1 $\frac{dm}{dt} = -m$

a Show that this can be rearranged by separating the variables to give $\int \frac{dm}{m} = -\int dt$.

b By integrating show that $m = e^{-t+c}$.

c Explain why you can write the general solution as $m = Ae^{-t}$.

d Check, by differentiating that, $m = Ae^{-t}$ is the general solution of $\frac{dm}{dt} = -m$.

If you have access to a spreadsheet or other graph plotting software that will draw direction field diagrams, check that these differential equations have the solutions that you find by inspecting their direction field diagrams and superimposing the function you find as a solution.

2 $\dfrac{dP}{dt} = 0.01P$

   a Show by using the method of separating the variables and integrating that the general solution of this differential equation is $P = Ae^{0.01t}$.

   b Find A given that, when $t = 0$, $P = 1000$. Hence find P when $t = 500$.

3 $\dfrac{dy}{dx} = y^2$

   a **i** By separating the variables and integrating show that this differential equation has solutions given by $-\dfrac{1}{y} = x + c$.

     ii Given that $y = 1$ when $x = 0$, show that the particular solution of the differential equation is $y = \dfrac{1}{1 - x}$.

   b By differentiating $y = \dfrac{1}{1 - x}$ show that this solution satisfies the differential equation $\dfrac{dy}{dx} = y^2$.

Growth, decay and other models

Growth and decay are two very important situations that you can model using differential equations. An example of one such situation is worked through below. When you feel comfortable with this, work through the questions of the next activity where differential equations are used to model such situations.

The radioactive isotope carbon-14 is present in small quantities in all living organisms. This decays but is constantly replaced whilst the organism is alive. However, when the organism dies it decays and is not replaced, and that the rate of decay of the mass of carbon-14 present is proportional to the mass present, m. As a differential equation, $\dfrac{dm}{dt} = -km$.

When $t = 0$, $m = m_0$ and after 5730 years $m = \dfrac{m_0}{2}$.

5730 years is the half-life of the radioactive isotope carbon-14, the time taken for half of it to have decayed.

$$\dfrac{dm}{dt} = -km$$

Separating the variables and integrating:

$$\int \dfrac{dm}{m} = \int -k \, dt$$

So, $\ln m = -kt + c$

$$m = e^{-kt+c}$$

or $m = Ae^{-kt}$

When $t = 0$, $m = m_0$, so

$$m_0 = Ae^{-k \times 0} = A$$

$$\therefore m = m_0 e^{-kt}$$

When $t = 5730$, $m = \dfrac{m_0}{2}$, so

$$\frac{m_0}{2} = m_0 e^{-k \times 5730}$$

$$\frac{1}{2} = e^{-5730k}$$

$$\ln \frac{1}{2} = -0.6931 = -5730k$$

$$k = 1.21 \times 10^{-4}$$

$$\therefore m = m_0 e^{-1.21 \times 10^{-4}t}$$

Graph of radioactive decay

The decay of radioactive carbon-14 allows scientists to estimate the age of materials that were living at one time (e.g. wood).

For example, if scientists find that a piece of material contains 62% of the amount of carbon-14 in living organisms then

$$0.62m_0 = m_0 e^{-1.21 \times 10^{-4}t}$$

$$\ln 0.62 = -1.21 \times 10^{-4}t$$

$$t = 3950$$

So the piece of material is 3950 years old.

Activity 6.2D

1 Warfarin is a drug given to thin the blood of patients who are at risk of blood clotting. The rate of decrease of warfarin in a patient's body is proportional to the amount present, ω.

That is $\dfrac{d\omega}{dt} = -k\omega$.

a Show by splitting the variables and integrating that $\omega = \omega_0 e^{-kt}$ where ω_0 is the concentration of warfarin at $t = 0$ (i.e. initially).

b The half-life of warfarin is 37 hours (so when $t = 37$, $\omega = \dfrac{\omega_0}{2}$). Use this information to show that $k = -0.0187$.

c After how many hours will the amount of warfarin in a patient's body have reduced to $\frac{1}{8}$ of its original value?

d Sketch a graph showing how the amount of warfarin in a patient's body will decay with time.

e On your diagram sketch a graph showing how the concentration of a different drug in a patient's body will vary given that this drug will have a lower initial concentration and longer half-life.

2 The growth of money deposited in a bank can be modelled using a differential equation. If the interest rate is 3% then $\frac{dP}{dt} = 0.03P$, where £P is the amount of money in the account after t years.

a Show by separating the variables and integrating that the amount of money you would have in the bank is given by $P = P_0 e^{0.03t}$, where £P_0 is the amount you initially have invested.

b Show that you would need to keep your initial investment in the bank for between 23 and 24 years for it to have doubled in time.

c Show that if the interest rate doubles, the time taken for your initial investment to have doubled in value is half the original time.

d Sketch a graph that shows how P varies with t for interest rates of 3% and 6%, marking each solution clearly.

3 The rate at which the thickness of ice forming on a pond increases slows down with time, t hours. Assume that the rate of increase of the thickness, h mm, of ice is inversely proportional to the existing thickness, i.e. $\frac{dh}{dt} = \frac{k}{h}$.

a By separating the variables and integrating show that
$$\frac{h^2}{2} = kt + c.$$

b Given that $h = 0$ when $t = 0$ and $h = 1$ when $t = 1$, show that $h = \sqrt{t}$.

c Sketch a graph showing how h varies with t.

d Explain why in the long run this is an unlikely model for the growth of thickness of ice covering a pond.

4 The rate of decrease of height of water in a rectangular tank is proportional to the height of water in the tank, so, $\frac{dh}{dt} = -kh$. Assume that $k = 0.01$, so $\frac{dh}{dt} = -0.01h$.

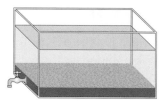

a Solve the differential equation to show that $h = e^{-0.01t}$, given that $h = 1$ when $t = 0$, where t hours is the time.

b Sketch a graph of how the height of water varies with time.

c Write a sentence or two to explain how the rate of change of height of water in the tank varies with time according to this model.

d Find the time taken for the depth of water in this tank to halve.

Discussion point

Is this what you would expect?

5 The rate at which a cold item heats up to room temperature when stored in a cool bag is directly proportional to the difference, $T°C$, between its temperature and that of the room. $\frac{dT}{dt} = -kT$, where t is the time in hours.

a For a certain cool bag, $k = 0.5$. Show that $T = Ae^{-0.5t}$.

b Given that the room is at a temperature of 20°C and that the items in the cool bag are initially at a temperature of 2°C, show that $T = 18e^{-0.5t}$ and hence find how long it will take items in the cool bag to reach a temperature of 15°C.

6.3 Revision summary

Direction field diagrams

This chapter introduces differential equations and their solution.

A differential equation gives information about the gradient of a function, such as $\dfrac{dv}{dt} = 10$, i.e. the gradient of the function $v(t)$ is always 10, or $\dfrac{dP}{dt} = kP$, i.e. the rate of change of P with respect to t is proportional to P.

The differential equation can be used to draw a direction field or compass needle diagram. Short lines with gradients calculated according to the equation are drawn at many points on a grid. They suggest the direction of the graphs in the family of graphs that form the general solution to the differential equation.

For example, if $\dfrac{dP}{dt} = P$, the gradient is equal to P, whatever the value of t.

In the diagram, the greater the value of P, the steeper the compass needle.

The slopes do not change as you go across the diagram, (the value of t makes no difference to the gradient), but the slopes increase as you go up the diagram (the gradient has the same value as P).

The curves follow the direction of the compass needles.

Other information about the function (such as a pair of (t, P) values) determines which curve in the family is the particular one required.

Such information is called **initial conditions** or **boundary conditions.**

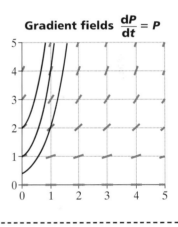

Gradient fields $\dfrac{dP}{dt} = P$

Solving differential equations

Differential equations can be solved by integration.

For example, if $\dfrac{dv}{dt} = 10$, integrating with respect to t gives $v = 10t + c$. Different values of c give different solutions in the family. An initial condition, such as $v = 1$ when $t = 0$, determines the value of c and hence the particular solution $v = 10t + 1$.

For some equations, it is necessary to separate the variables before integrating.

For example, $\dfrac{dP}{dt} = kP$.

Separating the variables, $\displaystyle\int \frac{dP}{P} = \int 2 \, dt$.

Integrating (on the left with respect to P and on the right with respect to t), $\ln P = 2t + c$.

Raising each side to the power e, $P = e^{2t+c}$ or $P = e^{2t}e^{c} = Ae^{2t}$.

A particular value of A, determined from the initial or boundary conditions, gives the particular solution.

6.4 Preparing for assessment

Your coursework portfolio

In this chapter you have been looking at differential equations, which give information about the gradient of a function which you can then use to deduce the function itself.

Have you got, or could you collect in an experiment or by observation, data about, for example, the rate at which something changes? You need to get to the point where you have a formula connecting the rate at which one variable changes with respect to another, such as acceleration (the rate at which velocity changes with respect to time) or interest rates (the rate at which the amount of money in an account changes with respect to time).

Then you need to use your formula to construct a compass needle diagram and draw some members of the family of possible solution curves using the direction of the compass needles to guide you. Which of the family of curves is the correct one that fits your problem? Can you find a formula for your curve?

Can you now find the general solution by integrating your gradient formula, either directly or by separating the variables? If so, you will then need to determine the value of the constant of integration using initial or boundary conditions to determine the particular equation that satisfies your differential equation and enables you to move on further with your problem.

As always, interpret your solution in the light of the real situation and comment on how good your models are for the data you are working with.

Practice exam question

Building society account

Data

A sum of money, £P, is invested in a building society account. Its rate of increase is given by the differential equation $\frac{dP}{dt} = 0.0296P$, where t is the number of years since the money was invested.

Question

a **i** On the grid, draw 'compass needles' to show $\frac{dP}{dt}$ at the points marked.

> Resource Sheet 6.4

ii Draw two possible solution curves on the grid.

b **i** Use integration to show that the general solution of the differential equation $\frac{dP}{dt} = 0.0296P$ is $P = Ae^{0.0296t}$, where A is a constant.

ii The original amount of money invested was £150. Find the particular solution of the differential equation.

iii Use your solution to find the amount of money in the account after 10 years.

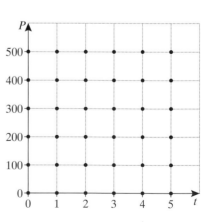

Using Technology

Throughout this course you will find it useful to use technology to help you not only to find the solutions to problems but also to investigate situations and learn new mathematics.

In addition to using your **graphic calculator**, you will find **graph plotting software** and a **spreadsheet** on a computer helpful. These are particularly useful when you want to print out your work.

Your teacher may have some ready-made spreadsheets available to assist your learning of topics throughout the book.

You need to have a graphic calculator when you are working through this book and when you are preparing work for your coursework portfolio and when you are sitting the written examination paper.

Graphic calculators

You will find a graphic calculator helpful when carrying out all calculations but particularly useful when investigating the graphs of functions and their features such as turning points.

You will find the **Trace** and **Zoom** facilities of your graphic calculator useful when working with such graphs – you can use them, for example, to investigate gradients at a point.

Consider the following graphic calculator screens which show the graph of $y = x^2$ and zooming in at the point $x = 3$. This demonstrates that when you look at just a small part of a curve you can consider it to be straight.

Discussion points

How many times do you need to use the **Zoom** facility to make a curved function such as $y = x^2$ appear to be straight?

Why does the **Trace** function give such awkward values for x and y?

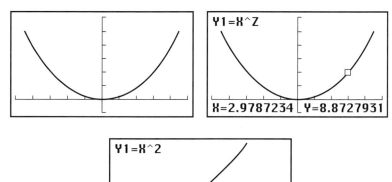

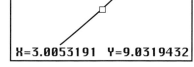

Using the **Trace** facility you can calculate an estimate of the gradient at this point ($x = 3.005\ 319\ 1$) by finding the co-ordinates of two points that lie on the curve and using these values in your calculations.

In this case you know that when $x = 3.005\,319\,1$, $y = 9.031\,943\,2$, and when $x = 3.031\,914\,9$, $y = 9.192\,507\,9$ (see the screen shots below), so you can calculate the gradient of the straight line joining these two points using your graphic calculator

$$\left(\text{gradient} = \frac{9.192\,507\,9 - 9.031\,943\,2}{3.031\,914\,9 - 3.005\,319\,1} = 6.037\,220\,163 \right).$$

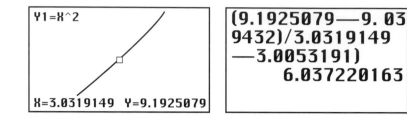

Discussion point
How can you calculate a better estimate of the gradient at this point?

Many graphic calculators have features that allow you to evaluate the gradient (value of the derivative) at a point and the area (value of the integral) under a graph. You can often find these values numerically on the graphic calculator's home screen and some calculators allow you to display what you are doing on the graph screen.

The screens below show how you can use a graphic calculator to calculate the gradient (derivative) at $x = 3$ for the function $y = x^2$, and how this graphic calculator can display this on a graph of the function.

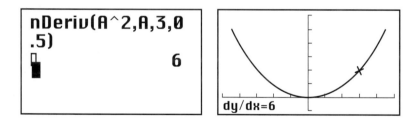

The screens below show two ways in which you can use a graphic calculator to evaluate the area enclosed by the curve $y = x^2$ from $x = 0$ to $x = 3$. One of these is evaluated on the home screen and the other shows a graph of the function with the area shaded and the area calculated.

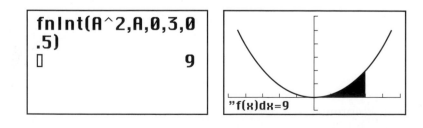

Spreadsheets

You will need to use a spreadsheet at various points of this course.

For example, in **Chapter 2** it is suggested that you use a spreadsheet to find the gradient between two points on a function to find the speed of an accelerating car. The spreadsheet allows you to evaluate this gradient as the two points approach each other.

Your teacher may have access to some ready-prepared spreadsheets which will allow you to investigate the process of differentiation. For example, the spreadsheet shown here allows you to plot a function and see a tangent dynamically drawn as the value of x increases and the gradient function plotted. In this screen shot you can see both the original function $f(x) = x^3$ and the gradient function $f'(x) = 3x^2$ with a tangent to $f(x)$ at $x = -3.2$.

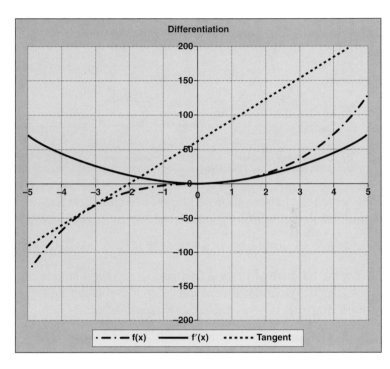

This process can be extended to the gradient function of the gradient function (the second differential). This second screen shot shows $f(x) = x^3$, $f'(x) = 3x^2$ and $f''(x) = 6x$ together with a tangent drawn to the original function, $f(x)$, at $x = 5$.

Other graph plotting software, such as Autograph, can also allow you to investigate gradients in this way (see below).

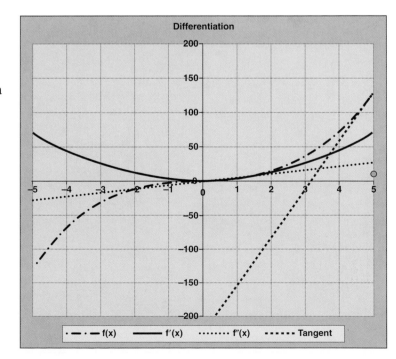

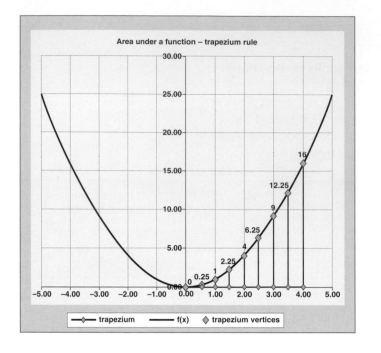

Of course, another important use of spreadsheets in this course will be to calculate the area enclosed by the graph of a function and the x-axis when you investigate the important process of integration.

You may use a spreadsheet yourself to carry out the calculations required to sum the areas of small strips using methods such as the trapezium or mid-ordinate rules. Alternatively your teacher may again have pre-prepared spreadsheets that allow you to do this.

The screen shot above shows a graph of the function $f(x) = x^2$ with 8 trapezia drawn so as to calculate the area under the curve $\left(\int_0^4 x^2 \, dx\right)$. With this number of strips the area is calculated to be 21.5.

When the number of strips is increased to 16 this value is calculated to be 21.375. As you will learn in this course you can find the exact value using integration – this exact value is $21\frac{1}{3}$.

Another important use of pre-prepared spreadsheets is to draw direction field diagrams quickly such as the one shown here for $\frac{dy}{dx} = x$.

Discussion point

How can you get more and more accurate estimates of the area under a curve?

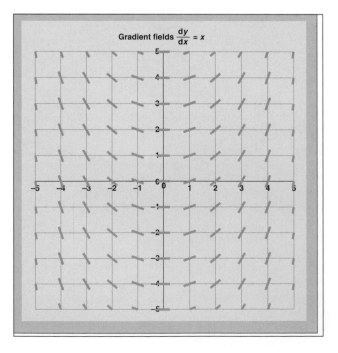

This second screen shot shows the general direction field diagram for the differential equation $\dfrac{dy}{dx} = x$ together with a particular solution passing through the origin (i.e. the solution that satisfies the condition $y = 0$ when $x = 0$).

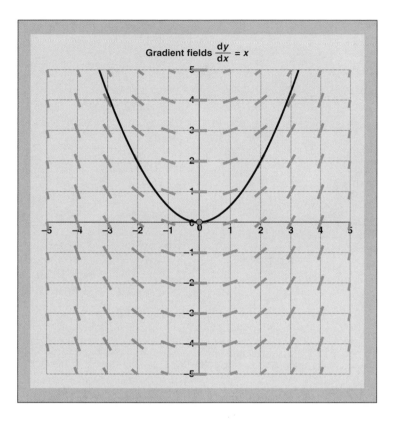

Graph plotting software

You can use graph plotting software such as Autograph on a computer to explore the graphs of functions. This software also allow you to explore differentiation and integration – some of the features of this software have been recreated by the pre-prepared spreadsheets described above.

In the screen shot shown here you can see the function $y = x^2$ together with its gradient function plotted and a tangent dawn to the original function at $x = 1.4$.

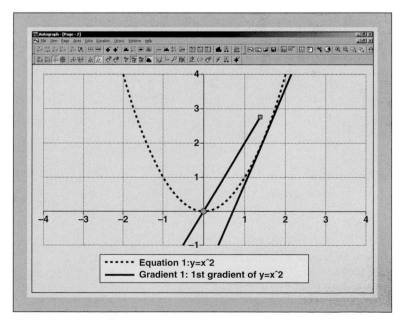

Answers

1 Introduction to Calculus

1.1 Interpreting gradients

1.1A

a *Height, h*

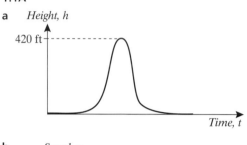

b *Speed, v*

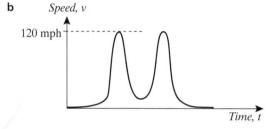

1.1B

1 a *T*

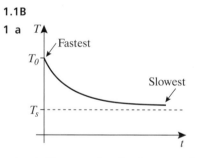

b i The rate of cooling is constantly decreasing with time.
ii The rate of cooling decreases as the temperature of the tea approaches the temperature of the room.

2 a There is no mould initially, when the bread was fresh.

b

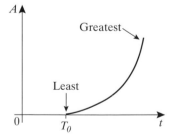

c i The rate of growth of mould is continually increasing with time.
ii The rate of growth of mould is increasing with the area of mould (i.e. greater area, greater rate of growth).

1.1C

1 2

2

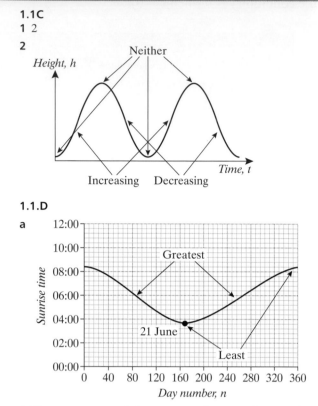

1.1.D

a

b The greatest rate of change means that, over the year, the sunrise times from one day to the next at these points change the most.
c Conversely, the least rate of change means that over the year, the sunrise times from one day to the next change the least at the points indicated above.

1.1E

1 B – The ride slows as it reaches its maximum height on each swing and reaches its greatest speed as it passes through the bottom of each swing.
2 C – The ride has the greatest acceleration as it reaches the top of each swing as it has to change directions, and acceleration is least when it reaches maximum speed.

1.2 Measuring gradients

1.2A

1 0.625   **2** $m = 0.625k$ **3** m

1.2B

1 *Total cost, C (£)*

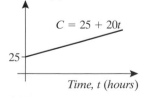

20, additional cost/hour

2 *Amount owing, A* (£)

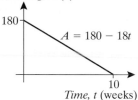

18, amount paid back/week

3 *Speed, v* (ms^{-1})

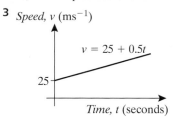

0.5, increase in speed (measured in ms^{-1}) per second

4 *Height, h* (cm)

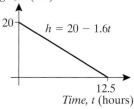

-1.6, change in height (cm) per hour

5 *Temperature, T* (°C)

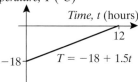

1.5, increase in temperature (°C) per hour

1.2C
1 & 2 See **1.1A Q2**

1.2D
1 **a** Always positive
  b The gradient (rate of growth) increases as x increases.
2 **b** (Answers will vary depending on your tangent lines.)
   $x = 40$, gradient = 0.14 approx.
   $x = 80$, gradient = 0.56 approx.
   $x = 120$, gradient = 2.22 approx.
   Gradients are increasing by a factor of 4 every 40 minutes.
  c The gradient should be similar to that found in **2b**, i.e. approx. 0.14.

1.2E
2 **a** 225 s and 525 s, gradient = -0.2; 375 s, gradient = 0.2
  b 0 metres/second

c *Rate of change of height* (ms^{-1})

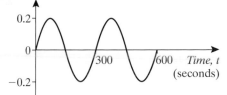

d The gradient graph tells you the speed of the passenger.
e Similar (sinusoidal) shapes, but out of phase.

3 a

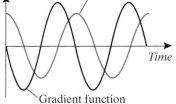

b

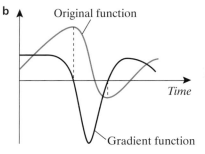

c

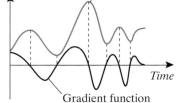

1.2F

1 1B, 2A, 3C
   (The slimmer the base of the cylinder, the less time it takes the cylinders to reach the same height.)
2 **d** It takes increasingly longer to raise the water level a fixed amount because the cross-section is increasing from the base.
3 **a** Bottle
  b Vase
  c Conical flask
  d Mug
   Bottle of ink:

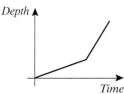

1.3 Areas under graphs

1.3A

1 a & b *Speed, v (mph)*

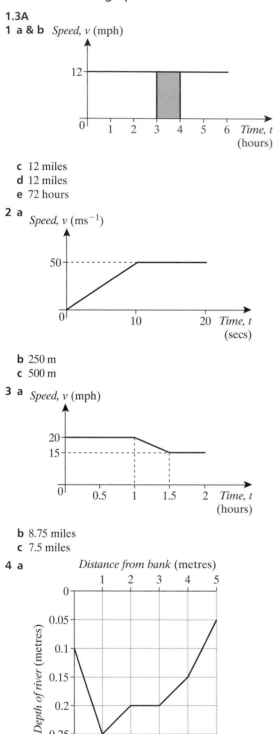

c 12 miles
d 12 miles
e 72 hours

2 a *Speed, v (ms⁻¹)*

b 250 m
c 500 m

3 a *Speed, v (mph)*

b 8.75 miles
c 7.5 miles

4 a *Distance from bank (metres)*

b 1.75 m²
5 20 ms⁻¹

1.3B

1 7000 cm²
2 630 m³h⁻¹

1.3C

1 London: 4480 hrs; Glasgow: 4500 hrs
2 London: 12.3 hrs; Glasgow: 12.3 hrs
3 Very similar amounts of daylight in total, but Glasgow has the greatest range in hours of daylight through the year.

2 Gradient Functions

2.1 Calculating gradients accurately

2.1A

2 Approx. 10, 15, 20
3 The car's speed is always increasing over the time interval $0 \leqslant t \leqslant 1$.

2.1B

3 a i 1.92 m   **ii** 3 m
b 10.8 ms⁻¹
c 10.2 ms⁻¹
d 9.9 ms⁻¹

2.1C

1 a with Q_1 at $t = 0.7$, approx. speed = 15.6 ms⁻¹
    with Q_1 at $t = 0.65$, approx. speed = 15 ms⁻¹
    with Q_1 at $t = 0.625$, approx. speed = 14.7 ms⁻¹
b with Q_1 at $t = 0.9$, approx. speed = 20.4 ms⁻¹
    with Q_1 at $t = 0.85$, approx. speed = 19.8 ms⁻¹
    with Q_1 at $t = 0.825$, approx. speed = 19.5 ms⁻¹

2.1D

1

Time t (seconds)	Distance x (metres)	Model d (metres)	Speed v (metres per second)
0.0	0	0.0	0.012
0.1	0.04	0.1	2.412
0.2	0.23	0.5	4.812
0.3	0.69	1.1	7.212
0.4	1.45	1.9	9.612
0.5	2.57	3.0	12.012
0.6	4	4.3	14.412
0.7	5.6	5.9	16.812
0.8	7.62	7.7	19.212
0.9	10.12	9.7	21.612
1.0	12.77	12.0	24.012

2

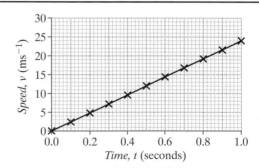

3 $v = 24t$
4 The speed is constantly increasing with time.

2.2 Gradient functions – differentiation

2.2A

Original function, f(x)	Gradient function, g(x)
$f(x) = x^2$	$g(x) = 2x$
$f(x) = x^3$	$g(x) = 3x^2$
$f(x) = x^4$	$g(x) = 4x^3$
$f(x) = x^5$	$g(x) = 5x^4$
$f(x) = x^{-1} = \dfrac{1}{x}$	$g(x) = -x^{-2} = \dfrac{-1}{x^2}$
$f(x) = x^{\frac{1}{2}} = \sqrt{x}$	$g(x) = \frac{1}{2}x^{-\frac{1}{2}} = \dfrac{1}{2\sqrt{x}}$

2.3 Applying differentiation

2.3A

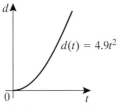

The distance and the rate of increase in distance both increase with time.

2.3B

1 The speed of the skydiver is directly proportional to the length of time spent in free-fall.

2

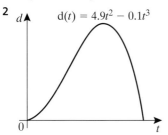

3 Speed of the skydiver slows after a similar acceleration – and actually returns to zero! The gradient decreases as the speed slows down and then goes negative, whereas in the original model, the gradient just goes on increasing.

4 $d'(t) = 9.8t - 0.3t^2$

5

Time (s)	Speeds for Model 1, $d(t) = 4.9t^2$	Speeds for Model 2 $d(t) = 4.9t^2 - 0.1t^3$
0	0	0
1	9.8	9.5
2	19.6	18.4
3	29.4	26.7
4	39.2	34.4
5	49	41.5
6	58.8	48
7	68.6	53.9
8	78.4	59.2
9	88.2	63.9
10	98	68

6 The first model has the speed increasing at a constant rate with time, whereas the rate of speed increase in the second model actually slows with time. The first model has no limit to the speed that can be reached (provided you can be in free-fall for long enough) but although the second model can be taken to model the effect of wind resistance over the 10 s, over the longer term, this model has the speed reaching zero eventually, and going negative (flying upwards!).

2.3C

1 a $\dfrac{dh}{dt} = 2.8 - 0.08x$

  b 2 mm/day

2 a

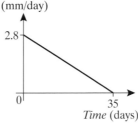

  b The quadratic model eventually stops increasing at day 35 and then decreases, so that the height of the seedling will eventually return to zero and go negative.

2.3D

2 a $\dfrac{dy}{dx} = 22 - 2x$

  b The rate at which people have the infection has been decreasing since the outbreak started.

  c 22 infections/day at day 0

  d Day 22

  e Day 11

3 −22 infections/day at day 22, meaning there are 22 fewer people with infections over the course of the 22nd day.

2.3E

2

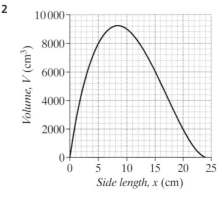

3 a 8.33

  b 9260 cm^3 to 3 s.f.

4 0

6 $x = 8\frac{1}{3}$, 25 (both are points where the gradients of the volume curve are zero)

7 9260 cm^3 to 3 s.f.

2.3F

1 a

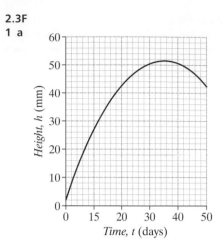

b $\dfrac{dh}{dt} = -0.08t + 2.8$

c **i** 2.4 mm/day

ii 0.8 mm/day

d $t = 35, h = 51.5$ refers to the maximum point on the graph.

2 a **i** $\dfrac{dt_r}{dn} = 0.0006n - 0.03$

ii $\dfrac{dt_s}{dn} = -0.0007n + 0.035$

b **i** 19 June ($n = 50$)

ii 04:39

c **i** Also 19 June ($n = 50$)

ii 21:11 (to nearest minute)

2.5 Practice exam questions

1 a **i** Approx. 30 ft/s

ii 3600/5280 × answer from **part i.**

b **i** $t = 0$ and $t = 8.6$

ii The car is at rest at these times.

iii At approx. 6 s.

c **i** $d'(t) = -10.5 + 16.4t - 1.41t^2$

iii $d(0) = 4$ means the car is 4 feet from the start, before it has started to move and $d'(0) = -10.5$ means the car starts at time $t = 0$ by reversing.

iv 11.0 s and 0.680 s to 3 s.f.

2 a **i** 5.9

ii 3.51% to 3 s.f.

b **i** 1 at $t = 150$ s

ii

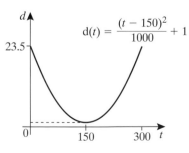

$$d(t) = \dfrac{(t - 150)^2}{1000} + 1$$

iii The volume increases for $t > 150$

c **ii** -0.14

3 Areas Under Curves

3.1 Calculating areas accurately

3.1A

1 a $0.82\,\text{m}^2$ **b** $295.2\,\text{m}^3\text{h}^{-1}$

2 F $1.67\,\text{m}^2$

3 $4.6\,\text{m}^2$ (2 s.f.)

3.1B

2 a 55 miles   **b** 51 miles (2 s.f.)

3.2 Numerical methods for finding areas under graphs

3.2A

1 $1.45\,\text{m}^2$

2 a $\frac{1}{2} \times 1 \times (f_0 + 2f_1 + 2f_2 + 2f_3 + 2f_4 + f_5)$

b $\frac{1}{2} \times 1 \times (f_0 + 2f_1 + 2f_2 + 2f_3 + 2f_4 + 2f_5 + 2f_6 + f_7)$

3.2B

7.96 m

3.2C

1 a 292.5 m

2 a **i** 70 squared units   **ii** 71.5 squared units

3 b 7.68 m

3.2D

1 a

t	v
0	0
1	10.6
2	18.5
3	24.2
4	28
5	30.3
6	31.5
7	31.9
8	32

b **i** 191 m   **ii** 194 m

c **i** 191.75 m   **ii** 192.5m

2 b Mid-ordinate rule: $2312.5\,\text{cm}^2$
Trapezium rule: $2250\,\text{cm}^2$

c Mid-ordinate rule: $1062.5\,\text{cm}^2$
Trapezium rule: $1000\,\text{cm}^2$

3.3 Area functions

3.3A

a **i** $10\,\text{ms}^{-1}$ **ii** $20\,\text{ms}^{-1}$ **iii** $50\,\text{ms}^{-1}$ **iv** $10t\,\text{ms}^{-1}$

b

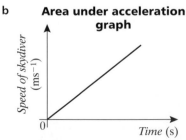

c Distance the skydiver has fallen

3.3B

1 a 37.5 m

b 24 m

2 a The gradient of the straight-line speed graph is 3.

b $\dfrac{3t^2}{2}$

2 c 24 m evaluate **2b** with $t = 5$ and $t = 3$ and subtract.

3 a $\dfrac{mx^2}{2}$

4 Area of a rectangle

3.3C

1

x	y	Area under graph between this x-value and the previous one	Area under curve from 0 up to x
0	0	0	0
1	1	0.5	0.5
2	4	2.5	3
3	9	6.5	9.5
4	16	12.5	22
5	25	20.5	42.5
6	36	30.5	73
7	49	42.5	115.5
8	64	56.5	172

2 a

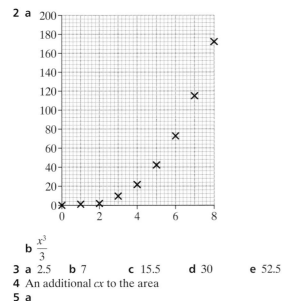

b $\dfrac{x^3}{3}$

3 a 2.5   **b** 7   **c** 15.5   **d** 30   **e** 52.5

4 An additional cx to the area

5 a

x	y	Area under graph between this x-value and the previous one	Area under curve from 0 up to x
0	0	0	0
1	3	1.5	1.5
2	12	7.5	9
3	27	19.5	28.5
4	48	37.5	66
5	75	61.5	127.5

6 A factor of m times the area

7 & 8

Function, $f(x)$	Area function, $A(x)$	Derivative of $A(x)$
$y = c$	cx	0
$y = mx$	$\dfrac{mx^2}{2}$	m
$y = x^2$	$\dfrac{x^3}{3}$	$2x$
$y = mx^2$	$\dfrac{mx^3}{3}$	$2mx$
$y = mx^2 + c$	$\dfrac{mx^3}{3} + cx$	$2mx$

3.3D

2 a $y = \dfrac{x^3}{3} + 3x$

b $y = \dfrac{5x^2}{2} - 4x$

c $y = \dfrac{x^3}{6} - 10x$

3.3E

1 a $4x^3$

b Divide by 4

c $\dfrac{x^4}{4}$

2 a $\dfrac{x^4}{2}$

b x^4

c $\dfrac{x^4}{8}$

d $\dfrac{ax^4}{4}$

3 a $\dfrac{81}{4}$

b 27

c 136

4 a $A(x) = \dfrac{x^4}{4} + 2x$

b There is the additional area under the line $y = 2x$ over the same range of x-values.

5 a $A(x) = \dfrac{x^3}{3} + x^2 + x$

b $A(x) = \dfrac{x^4}{4} - \dfrac{x^2}{2}$

c $A(x) = \dfrac{ax^4}{4} + \dfrac{bx^3}{3} + \dfrac{cx^2}{2} + dx$

d $A(x) = \dfrac{x^5}{5}$

3.4 Integrating polynomial functions

3.4A
2 14

3 a $A(x) = \dfrac{x^2}{2} - 4x$

b The line lies below the x-axis for $x < 4$.

c i
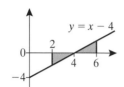

Area = 0 squared units (by symmetry of problem, or calculating areas of triangles)

3.4B
1 a 57.5　　**b** 0　　**c** 12　　**d** −2

2 a $\displaystyle\int_4^7 \left(4 - \dfrac{x}{2}\right) dx = 3.75$

b $\displaystyle\int_2^5 \left(\dfrac{x}{2} + 8\right) dx = 29.25$

4 a ii 0.8 joules　　**iii** 0.6 joules
　b 47.25 joules

3.4C
1 a $\dfrac{91}{3}$　　**b** $\dfrac{98}{3}$

2 $\dfrac{1}{6}$

3 $5000^{\frac{1}{4}} = 8.409$ to 3 d.p.

3.4D
1 a x^3　　**b** $-\dfrac{x^3}{3}$　　**c** $\dfrac{x^3}{9}$

　d $\dfrac{x^4}{2}$　　**e** x^4　　**f** $-\dfrac{x^4}{8}$

2
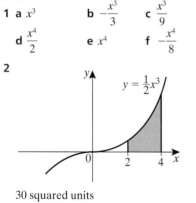

30 squared units

3 a $\dfrac{215}{9}$　　**b** 28　　**c** $-\dfrac{490}{3}$

3.4E
1 a 14　　**b** 17.5　　**c** 4.5

2 b
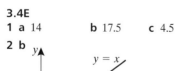

c 0.9

3.4F
1 a 2.75
　b 48.6

2 a
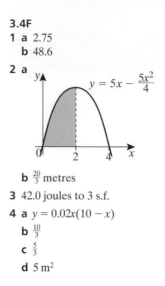

b $\dfrac{20}{3}$ metres

3 42.0 joules to 3 s.f.

4 a $y = 0.02x(10 - x)$
　b $\dfrac{10}{3}$
　c $\dfrac{5}{3}$
　d $5\,\text{m}^2$

3.5 Applying integration

3.5A
3 300 m
4 Over-estimate – look at areas under the graphs for the data and model.

3.5B
1 & 2 & 3

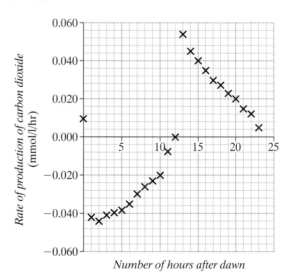

In the first 12 hours after dawn, i.e. during sunlight hours, photosynthesis by the plants uses carbon dioxide at a greater rate than the animals' respiration produces it, hence the negative production rates. After sunset, both plants and animals respire carbon dioxide, hence the positive production rate.

4 0.2995 mmols/litre (depends on number of trapeziums used to approximate area)

5 Carbon dioxide is being used up quicker by the plants than being produced by the animals.

6 −0.337 mmols/litre

7 Less

3.5C

1 c 192 m

d

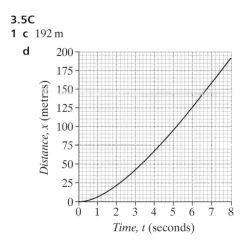

Time, t (seconds)

2 a $2291\frac{2}{3}$, 1250

  b $1041\frac{2}{3}$

3.6 Integration as the reverse of differentiation

3.6A

1 $y = 2x + 2$
2 $y = 6 - x^2$
3 $y = -3$

3.6B

1 a i $10x + 2$ **ii** $10x + 2$ **iii** $10x + 2$
  b The addition of a constant makes no difference to the gradient function.

3.6C

  a $\dfrac{x^3}{3} + 3x + c$

  b $\dfrac{5x^2}{2} + 3x + c$

  c $x^4 + c$

3.6D

1 $y = 2x^2 - x + 2$
2 $y = 5x - 5$
3 $C = 0.08t + 12$
4 $C = \frac{5}{9}(F - 32)$

3.6E

1 a $\dfrac{x^3}{3} + \dfrac{3x^2}{2} + c$

  b $\dfrac{x^6}{6} - 2x + c$

  c $2x + \dfrac{3x^2}{2} - \dfrac{x^3}{3} + c$

2 a 544   **b** 2.5   **c** 0

3.6F

1 a $s = ut + \frac{1}{2}at^2$
  b 48 m
  c 10.5 m
2 The integral represents the area under the speed–time graph which gives the distance travelled.

3.8 Practice exam questions

1 a i 15 December
    ii 500 tonnes/hour (estimate)
  b i 18–19 December
    ii 15–16 December
  c i 33 090 tonnes
    ii 47 900 tonnes
  d 12–19 December estimate, because there are more frequent readings over the time-period. The readings clearly can change quite dramatically, but there is an assumption that the emission rose steadily over 6 days from 1–6 December for the first estimate.
2 a i $3.9 \, \text{m}^3\text{s}^{-1}$
    ii 8.5 hours after storm began
    iii 6 hours after storm began
    iv 10 hours after storm began
  b 975%
  c 97 000 m³ to 3 s.f.
  d i 12 700 m³ to 3 s.f.
    ii 34 600 m³ to 3 s.f.
    iii 267% to 3 s.f.

4 Differentiation Techniques

4.1 Using gradients to identify key features of functions

4.1A

1 a $x < 0$ **b** 0   **c** $x > 0$
2 Can be read from the gradient function ($y = 2x$)

4.1B

1 a $\dfrac{dy}{dx} = 2x - 2$ **b** $x = 1$ **c** minimum
2 (0, 10)
3 (1.5, −0.25)
4 $x = 25$, maximum area = 625 m²

4.1C

1 a $\dfrac{dy}{dx} = 6x^2 + 6x - 12$
  d Maximum at $x = -2$, minimum at $x = 1$
2 a & b Maximum at $x = 0$ and minimum at $x = \frac{2}{3}$
3 Minimum at $x = -1$, maximum at $x = 1$
4 b After the minimum at about week 7, the model for the value of the pound rises without limit against the euro.
  c Max (1.67, 1.66), min (7, 1.58)

4.1D

2 b

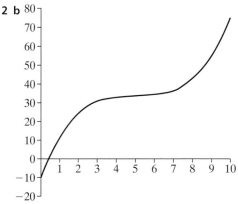

4.2 Differentiating functions of functions

4.2A

1 $\dfrac{dy}{dx} = 12(6x + 1)$

2 $\dfrac{dy}{dx} = 14(7x - 3)$

3 $\dfrac{dy}{dx} = 4x(x^2 + 5)$

4 $\dfrac{dy}{dx} = -6x^2(1 - x^3)$

5 $\dfrac{dy}{dx} = 18(6x + 1)^2$

6 $\dfrac{dy}{dx} = 21(7x - 3)^2$

7 $\dfrac{dy}{dx} = 6x(x^2 + 5)^2$

8 $\dfrac{dy}{dx} = -9x^2(1 - x^3)^2$

4.2C

1 a $\dfrac{dy}{dx} = 20(5x - 2)^3$

b $\dfrac{dy}{dx} = 10x(x^2 + 3)^4$

c $\dfrac{dy}{dx} = 18x^2(5 + 2x^3)^2$

d $\dfrac{dh}{dt} = \dfrac{-9}{(9t - 4)^2}$

e $\dfrac{dv}{dt} = \dfrac{2t^3}{\sqrt{t^4 - 1}}$

f $\dfrac{dy}{dx} = \dfrac{6}{(5 - 3x)^3}$

2 a i $p(0) = 18$; current population of the town

ii

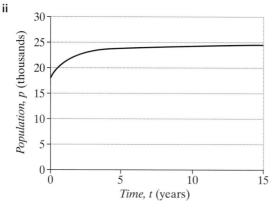

iii The town population gets ever closer to 25 thousand.

b i $p'(t) = \dfrac{7}{(t + 1)^2}$

ii 7 thousand/year; represents rate of population increase at time $t = 0$

iii

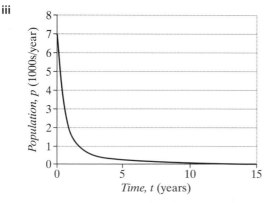

iv The rate of change in population remains positive, but approaches 0 as $t \to \infty$.

3 a $\dfrac{dy}{dx} = 9 - \left(1 - \dfrac{t}{5}\right)^2$

b

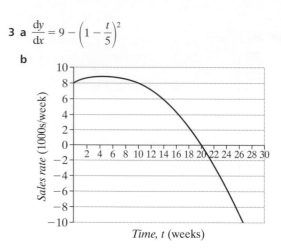

c The sales rate reaches a peak of 9000/week about 5 weeks after release, and the sales reach a maximum at week 20 (sales rate = 0). Beyond this point the model makes no sense in the real situation (CDs being returned!!)

4 a $\dfrac{dV}{dt} = 3(0.5t + 1)^{\frac{1}{2}}$

b i $V = 0$; $\dfrac{dv}{dt} = 3$; initially no paint has been used and the painter sets off at a rate of 3 litres/hour

ii $V = 28$; $\dfrac{dV}{dt} = 6$; 28 litres of paint has been used after 6 hours, and the painter is now using the paint at a rate of 6 litres/hour.

c i

Graph of model for paint used and its gradient function

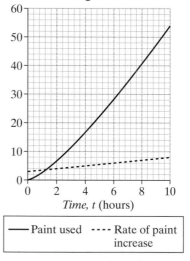

ii Both graphs of the rate of paint being used and the total volume of paint used are increasing with time. This makes sense as the total volume of paint used will only increase (paint cannot be removed after being used!) and it is not unusual to work faster as the job goes on. However, both graphs increase without limit but in the real situation, the job must finish (i.e. limit to paint use) and a physical limit to how fast you can paint.

4.2D

1 a i 0.0159 to 3 s.f.

  ii 0.001 77 to 3 s.f.

  iii 0.000 637 to 3 s.f.

 b i 0.04

  ii 0.013

  iii 0.008

 c i $\dfrac{dS}{dt} = \dfrac{0.004}{r}$

  ii

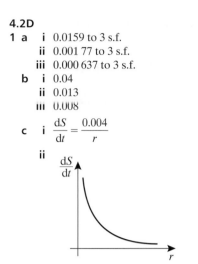

It shows that (when the volume is being increased at a constant rate) the rate at which the surface area increases most is when the balloon radius is smallest.

2 a i $\dfrac{dS}{dt} = \dfrac{8\pi r}{5}$ or 1.6 πr **ii** $\dfrac{dV}{dt} = \dfrac{4\pi r^2}{5}$ or 0.8 πr²

 b When $r = 10$, the rate at which the surface area changes,

$\dfrac{dS}{dt} = 16\pi$ cm²/s and the rate at which the volume changes,

$\dfrac{dV}{dt} = 80\pi$ cm³/s.

 c i

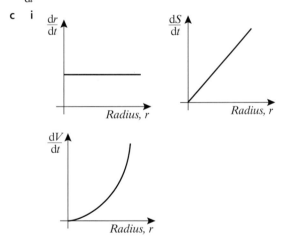

  ii It shows that as the radius increases at a constant rate, the volume of gas supplied must increase quadratically with r. (The surface area grows linearly with r.)

  iii This is possible to start with but for larger balloons it is impractical to sustain an ever increasing supply rate of helium gas.

3 a i $\dfrac{dr}{dt} = -\dfrac{1}{400\pi r}$ **ii** $\dfrac{dS}{dt} = -0.02$

 b $\dfrac{dV}{dt} = -0.02,\ \dfrac{dr}{dt} = \dfrac{-0.01}{8\pi} = -0.000398,\ \dfrac{dS}{dt} = -0.02$

This shows that the volume, radius and surface area are all decreasing when $r = 2$.

(The volume at 0.02 m³/min, the radius at approx. 0.4 mm/min and the area at 0.02 m²/min.)

c i

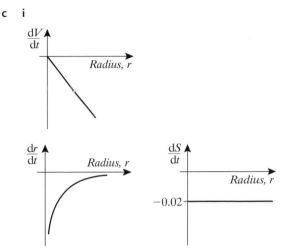

  ii The surface area is decreasing at the same rate whatever the radius size, that the radius changes fastest when it is smallest and the rate of volume leaking is directly proportional to the radius size.

4.2E

1 a i $\dfrac{dA}{dt} = 6\pi r$

  ii

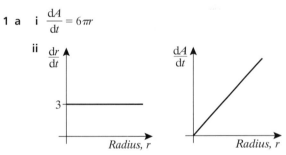

The rate at which the radius of the stain increases remains constant (unaffected by value of current radius) but the area is increasing at a rate directly proportional to the current radius.

 b i $\dfrac{dA}{dt} = 20\pi$

  ii

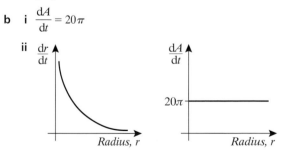

The area is increasing at a constant rate, independent of radius size, but the radius size increases fastest when it is smallest and its rate of growth decreases as r increases.

 c The second model – as the stain gets larger, you would expect it to take longer for the radius to increase by similar amounts (unless for some reason the rate of leakage is increasing with time to keep the rate of radius increase steady).

2 a Pressure, P

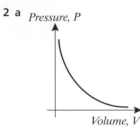

Volume, V

As the volume increases, the pressure decreases and vice versa, so that their product (PV) remains a constant 8000.

2 b ii -80

c i $\dfrac{dP}{dt} = -\dfrac{80\,000}{V^2}$

ii -800. Pressure is decreasing at 800 cm of mercury per second.

3 a i $V = l^3$ **ii** $S = 6l^2$

b i $\dfrac{dV}{dl} = 3l^2$ **ii** $\dfrac{dS}{dl} = 12l$

c i $\dfrac{dV}{dt} = -0.3l^2$ **ii** $\dfrac{dS}{dt} = -1.2l$

d $\dfrac{dV}{dt} = -120, \dfrac{dS}{dt} = -24$

When the ice cube has sides of 20 mm, the volume of the ice cube is decreasing at a rate of 120 mm³/second, and the surface area is decreasing at the rate of 24 mm²/second.

e i

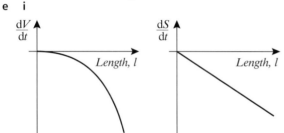

ii With the length of the sides decreasing at a constant rate, the surface area is decreasing at a rate proportional to the length, whereas the rate at which the volume decreases is quickest initially, and decreases with the size of the ice cube.

4 a i $\dfrac{dV}{dt} = 5$ **ii** $\dfrac{dh}{dt} = \dfrac{5}{\pi h(20 - h)}$

b i 0.0838 cm/s to 3 s.f. **ii** 0.0212 cm/s to 3 s.f.

c i

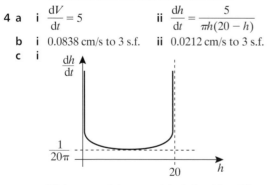

Note: – graph is symmetrical about $h = 10$
– graph approaches the vert. axis and $h = 20$ but never touches them
– graph has min. at $(10, \frac{1}{20\pi})$

ii Valid for h up to 10 (rate at which the depth is increasing slows as h increases from 0 to 10). Note also the real situation has the hemispherical bowl of radius (and hence height) of 10 cm.

4.3 Differentiating trigonometric functions

4.3A

1 a $\dfrac{2\pi}{3}$ **b** $\dfrac{3\pi}{4}$ **c** $\dfrac{5\pi}{6}$ **d** 4π

2 a 150° **b** 225° **c** 540° **d** 900°

3 a i 14°
ii 74°
iii 146°
b i 1.40 rads
ii 4.12 rads
iii 6.98 rads

4

x (rads)	sin x	cos x
0	0.000	1.000
1	0.841	0.540
2	0.909	-0.416
3	0.141	-0.990
4	-0.757	-0.654
5	-0.959	0.284
6	-0.280	0.960

5 b

t (seconds)	h (metres)
0	0.00
10	5.00
20	8.66
30	10.00
40	8.66
50	5.00
60	0.00
70	-5.00
80	-8.66
90	-10.00
100	-8.66
110	-5.00
120	0.00

c

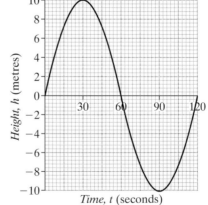

Time, t (seconds)

d The pod goes through 1 revolution in the 2 minutes.

4.3B

2 a 0
 b 0

3 Answers approximately:

x	Gradient
0	1.00
1	0.54
2	−0.42
3	−0.99
4	−0.65
5	0.28
6	0.96
π	−1.00
2π	1.00

4 b $\cos x$

4.3C – Spreadsheet activity
2 b ii $-\sin x$

4.3D
1 a $2\cos(2t)$ **b** $-3\sin(3t)$
c $\frac{1}{2}\cos(\frac{1}{2}t)$ **d** $-20\sin(5t)$
e $1.5\cos(0.3t)$ **f** $-2\sin(\frac{1}{3}t)$
2 b i $2\cos(2t+3)$ **ii** $-4\sin(4t-1)$
iii $5\cos\left(5t-\frac{\pi}{6}\right)$ **iv** $-\frac{1}{2}\sin\left(\frac{1}{2}t+\frac{\pi}{3}\right)$
v $14\cos(7t+1)$ **vi** $-8\sin(t-6)$
vii $6\cos\left(2t+\frac{\pi}{4}\right)$ **viii** $-20\sin\left(4t-\frac{\pi}{4}\right)$
ix $-15\sin(3t+\pi)$ **x** $5\cos(10t+3)$

4.3E
1 b $\frac{dh}{dt}=4.5\pi\cos\left(\frac{\pi t}{15}\right)$

c
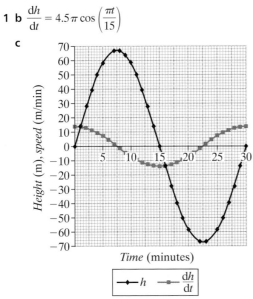

Time (minutes)

Legend: ◆ h ■ $\frac{dh}{dt}$

d $7\frac{1}{2}$ minutes and $22\frac{1}{2}$ minutes into the ride – i.e. when the ride is at its highest and lowest points.
e 14 m/min (0 and 30 minutes) and −14 m/min (15 minutes) – i.e. when the ride is passing the centre of the eye.

2 a $\frac{dp}{dt}=210\cos 7t$

b
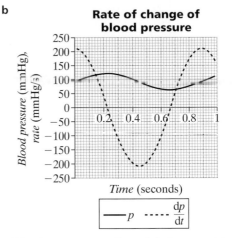

Rate of change of blood pressure

Time (seconds)

Legend: — p ---- $\frac{dp}{dt}$

c Blood pressure goes through just over one cycle between 60 and 120 mmHg/s

3 a $w'(t)=-\frac{\pi}{2}\sin\left(\frac{\pi}{6}t\right)$

b i $t=0, w=8, \frac{dw}{dt}=0$

ii $t=2, w=6.5, \frac{dw}{dt}=-1.36$

iii $t=4, w=3.5, \frac{dw}{dt}=-1.36$

iv $t=6, w=2, \frac{dw}{dt}=0$

v $t=8, w=3.5, \frac{dw}{dt}=1.36$

vi $t=10, w=6.5, \frac{dw}{dt}=1.36$

vii $t=12, w=8, \frac{dw}{dt}=0$

c & d

falling most rapidly   rising most rapidly

minimum   *Hours after midnight*

Legend: — w ---- $\frac{dp}{dt}$

4 a i $V_1=70.5$ V, $\frac{dV_1}{dt}=30.5$ V/ms

ii $V_1=114$ V, $\frac{dV_1}{dt}=11.6$ V/ms

iii $V_1=114$ V, $\frac{dV_1}{dt}=-11.6$ V/ms

b i $V_2=-119$ V, $\frac{dV_2}{dt}=3.94$ V/ms

ii $V_2 = -89.2$ V, $\dfrac{dV_2}{dt} = 25.2$ V/ms

iii $V_2 = -24.9$ V, $\dfrac{dV_2}{dt} = 36.9$ V/ms

4.4 Differentiating exponential functions

4.4A

1 d e^x

3 b $-e^{-x}$

c i

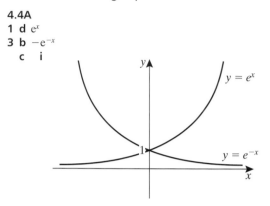

Note: graphs are reflections of one another in vertical axis both cut the vertical axis at 1

ii The graphs are reflections of one another in the y-axis, so the tangents are too. The magnitude of the gradients are still the original function but the negative sign is because the tangent to $y = e^{-x}$ now runs down from left to right.

4 b $2e^{2x}$

c i

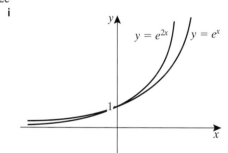

Note: $y = e^{2x}$ is below $y = e^x$ to the left of y-axis & above $y = e^x$ to the right of y-axis both cut y-axis at 1

ii The graph of $y = e^{2x}$ is that of $y = e^x$ compressed in the x-direction by a factor of 2.

4.4B

2 a $-5e^{-5t}$

b $6e^{3t}$

c $-5e^{-\frac{t}{6}}$

d $e^{0.25t}$

e $20e^{-4t}$

f $120e^{-5t}$

4.4C

1 a $\dfrac{dy}{dt} = 1.505e^{0.0646t}$

b i 38.0 megatonnes/year

ii 962 megatonnes/year

iii 24 300 megatonnes/year

2 b $\dfrac{dN}{dt} = 0.0347e^{0.0347t}$, this gives the rate of increase in the population of *E. coli*.

c i

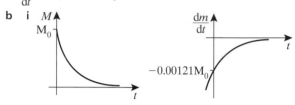

ii Stretch in the N-direction of factor 0.0347

3 a $\dfrac{dm}{dt} = -0.000\,121m_0e^{-0.000\,121t}$

b i

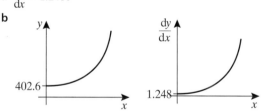

ii Both tend towards zero. The amount of C-14 can only decrease and the rate at which the C-14 decays drops as there is less and less C-14 about to decay.

4 a $\dfrac{dy}{dt} = -28.6e^{-0.0286t}$

b i 972 g, -27.8 g/1000 years

ii 867 g, -24.8 g/1000 years

iii 3.79×10^{-10} g, -1.09×10^{-11} g/1000 years

5 a $\dfrac{dy}{dx} = 1.1832 \times 10^{-13}e^{0.0136x}$

b i 0.006 30 billion, 8.56×10^{-5} billion/year

ii 5.65 billion, 0.0769 billion/year

iii 5080 billion, 69.0 billion/year

6 a $\dfrac{dy}{dx} = 1.248e^{0.48x}$

b

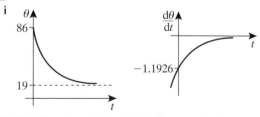

c Both the rate of waste increase and the amount of waste itself increase exponentially.

d One would expect the rate of increase (and possibly the actual amount) of waste to slow in future years wouldn't, simply for physical reasons – there won't be enough space for all the waste if it continued growing exponentially! Local Authorities aim to recycle more waste.

7 b $\dfrac{d\theta}{dt} = -1.1926e^{-0.0178t}$. Rate of cooling in °C/minute.

c i

ii Both the rate of temperature change and temperature itself decrease exponentially – the temperature tending towards the surrounding temperature of 19°C, with the rate of change tending to zero.

8 a **i** 0, 10

ii 40.0, 3.06 × 10⁻⁶

iii 40.0, 9.36 × 10⁻¹³

Skydiver starts from rest and accelerates at 10 ms⁻². After one minute they are travelling at 40 ms⁻¹ and only very slowly increasing in speed. After 2 minutes there is little change in velocity (from after 1 min) and acceleration is now negligible for the remainder of dive.

b **i**

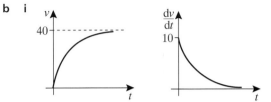

ii The model suggests that the skydiver falls with an initial acceleration of 10 ms⁻² (i.e. gravity) but is slowed exponentially to a terminal velocity of 40 m/s.

iii Very similar in practice. The slowing down of the acceleration above can be attributed to wind resistance.

4.5 Differentiating products

4.5A

1 $\dfrac{dy}{dx} = 5(x + 1) + 5x = 10x + 5$

2 $\dfrac{dy}{dx} = 4x^3(1 - 3x) - 3x^4 = 4x^3 - 15x^4$

3 $\dfrac{dy}{dx} = (x^2 - 4) + x(2x) = 3x^2 - 4$

4 $\dfrac{dy}{dx} = 6x^2(7 - x^5) + 2x^3(5x^4) = 42x^2 - 16x^7$

5 $\dfrac{dy}{dx} = 2(x + 4) + (2x + 5) = 4x + 13$

6 $\dfrac{dy}{dx} = -4x(x^3 + 5) + (1 - 2x^2)3x^2 = -10x^4 + 3x^2 - 20x$

4.5B

1 a $\dfrac{dy}{dx} = x^3 e^x (4 + x)$

b $\dfrac{dy}{dx} = 2x(\cos 4x - 2x \sin 4x)$

c $\dfrac{dy}{dx} = x^4(x^2 - 1)^2(11x^2 - 5)$

d $\dfrac{dy}{dx} = (x + 2)^4 e^x (7 + x)$

e $\dfrac{dy}{dx} = \dfrac{6x - 4}{\sqrt{x - 1}}$

f $\dfrac{dy}{dx} = 14(x - 4)^3(2x - 1)^2(x - 2)$

g $\dfrac{dy}{dx} = xe^{-x}(2 - x)$

h $\dfrac{dy}{dx} = e^{3x}(3 \sin x + \cos x) - 1$

i $\dfrac{dy}{dx} = 3x^2 + e^x(4 \sin 4x - \cos 4x)$

2 a $\dfrac{dy}{dx} = \dfrac{5}{(2x - 1)^2}$

b $\dfrac{dy}{dx} = e^{-5x}(9 - 20x)$

c **i** $\dfrac{dy}{dx} = \dfrac{x \cos x - 2 \sin x}{x^3}$

ii $\dfrac{dh}{dt} = \dfrac{e^t(2t - 9)}{(2t - 3)^4}$

iii $\dfrac{dv}{dt} = \dfrac{2t^3(t^2 - 6)}{(t^2 - 3)^2}$

4.5C

1 $\dfrac{dh}{dt} = e^{-0.01t}\left(-\dfrac{7\pi}{2} \sin\left(\dfrac{\pi t}{4}\right) - 0.14\left(1 + \cos\left(\dfrac{\pi t}{4}\right)\right)\right)$

2 a **i** −10.9

ii 10.2 to 3 s.f.

b The flyer is falling at time $t = 2$ and rising at $t = 6$ with the vertical speeds found in **part a**.

3 b The flyer is neither rising nor falling at time $t = 4$ (i.e. the flyer is at the point of changing direction).

4 a

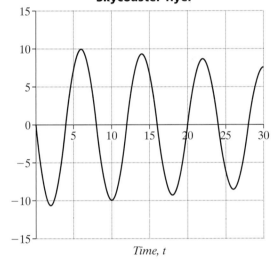

Rate of change of height of a Skycoaster flyer

Time, t

b The changes in direction of the flyer coincide with where the rate of change of height graph cuts the horizontal axis. The sections of the graph which lie above the horizontal axis relate to the upward motion of the flyer, and the sections of the graph which lie below the horizontal axis relate to the falling motion of the flyer.

4.5D

1 a **i**

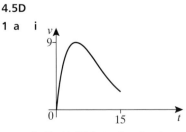

ii Fast initial acceleration to a maximum speed followed immediately by a more gradual deceleration.

b ii

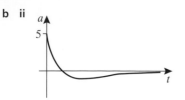

iii Initial acceleration of 5 ms^{-2} reduces to 0 after 5 seconds when the car reaches its maximum speed. After 5 seconds the car decelerates.

2 a i

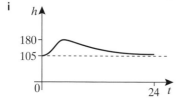

ii 08:00, 180 cm to 3 s.f.

b i $\dfrac{dh}{dt} = t^3e^{-0.5t}(4 - \tfrac{1}{2}t)$

This function gives the rate of change of the river depth for different times, t.

iii

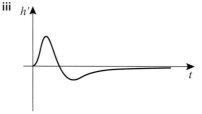

iv Time, t, between 0 and 8; the height of the river is increasing during this period.

v Maximum when $t = 4$ (the time at which the river height is increasing the fastest) and a minimum when $t = 12$ (the time at which the river height is decreasing the fastest).

3 a $h'(t) = 0.1(1 + \sin t + t \cos t)$

b i

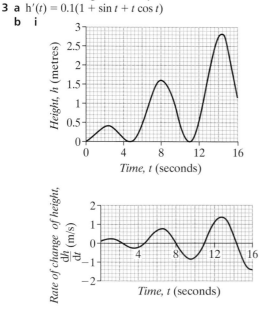

4 a i

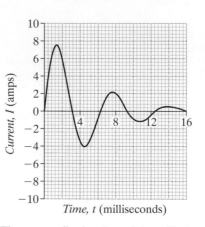

ii The current flowing through is oscillating and changing direction with the same period (time between successive zeros are the same), but the size of the current is decaying exponentially.

b i $\dfrac{dI}{dt} = 2e^{-0.2t}(5 \cos t - \sin t)$

ii

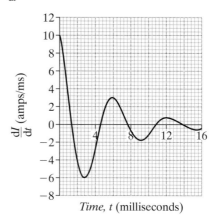

iii $t = 1.37$ to 3 s.f.
At this time, the current has reached a maximum and is about to start decreasing.

iv $t = 4.51$ to 3 s.f.
The current has dropped to a minimum and is about to start increasing.

5 a i 12; There are initially 12 000 fish in the lake.

ii

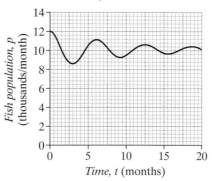

iii Approx. 8500 fish, after 3 months

iv The fish population will fluctuate but get closer and closer to a population of about 10 000.

b i $\dfrac{dp}{dt} = -2e^{-0.1t}(0.1 \cos t + \sin t)$

ii

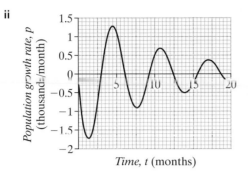

Time, t (months)

iii At $t = 3.04$ months, the fish population reaches a minimum and is about to go into a period of growth. At $t = 6.18$ months, the population reaches a maximum for this part of the cycle and is about to go into a period of population decline.

iv 1.27; the rate at which the fish population (according to the model) is growing fastest in thousands/month.

v -1.74; the rate at which the fish population (according to the model) is declining fastest in thousands/month.

vi $\dfrac{\mathrm{d}p}{\mathrm{d}t} \to 0$; the population growth rate tends to zero, so the population itself will settle to a steady population (of 10 000).

4.6 Second derivatives

4.6A

2 a For every fixed time-interval the velocity increases by the same amount.

b The acceleration (gradient of the velocity graph) is constant (and non-zero).

3 b $v = 10t + 10$ **c** $a = 10$

4.6C

1 a $\dfrac{\mathrm{d}^2y}{\mathrm{d}x^2} = 6$

b $\dfrac{\mathrm{d}^2y}{\mathrm{d}x^2} = 2$

c $\dfrac{\mathrm{d}^2y}{\mathrm{d}x^2} = 2$

2 a $\dfrac{\mathrm{d}^2y}{\mathrm{d}x^2} = -\sin t$

b $\dfrac{\mathrm{d}^2y}{\mathrm{d}x^2} = -9\cos 3t$

c $\dfrac{\mathrm{d}^2y}{\mathrm{d}x^2} = -2\sin t - 4\sin 2t$

d $\dfrac{\mathrm{d}^2y}{\mathrm{d}x^2} = 2\cos t^2 - 4t^2\sin t^2$

3 a $\dfrac{\mathrm{d}^2y}{\mathrm{d}t^2} = e^t$

b $\dfrac{\mathrm{d}^2y}{\mathrm{d}t^2} = 4e^{2t} + 2$

c $\dfrac{\mathrm{d}^2y}{\mathrm{d}t^2} = -2e^t\sin t$

4 a -4

b 9

4.7 Applications of second derivatives

4.7A

1 $t = 30, 90, 150, 210 \ldots$, i.e. when the pod is at the top or bottom of the wheel.

2 $t - 0, 60, 120, 180 \ldots$, i.e. when the pod is passing the level of the centre of the wheel.

4.7B

3 $t = 0, 60, 120, 180, 240, 300$

4.7C

1 a $\dfrac{\mathrm{d}y}{\mathrm{d}x} = 5$; the rate of inflation is constant.

b 0; the rate of change in the rate of inflation is zero – i.e. rate of inflation steady year on year.

2 $\dfrac{\mathrm{d}y}{\mathrm{d}x} = 4.2e^{0.04x}$; $\dfrac{\mathrm{d}^2y}{\mathrm{d}x^2} = 0.168e^{0.04x}$

4.8 Stationary points and points of inflection

4.8A

1 a $\dfrac{\mathrm{d}y}{\mathrm{d}x} = 2x - 4$

b $x = 2$

c Minimum

2 a $\dfrac{\mathrm{d}y}{\mathrm{d}x} = -2 - 2x$

b $x = -1$

c Maximum

3 a $\dfrac{\mathrm{d}y}{\mathrm{d}x} = 3x^2 - 4x - 5$

b $x = -0.786, 2.12$ to 3 s.f.

c Maximum, minimum respectively

4 a $\dfrac{\mathrm{d}y}{\mathrm{d}x} = \cos x$

b $x = \pm\dfrac{\pi}{2}, \pm\dfrac{3\pi}{2}, \pm\dfrac{5\pi}{2} \ldots$

c Alternating maximum, minimum

5 a $\dfrac{\mathrm{d}y}{\mathrm{d}x} = -\sin x$

b $x = 0, \pm\pi, \pm2\pi, \pm3\pi \ldots$

c Alternating maximum, minimum

4.8B

1 Positive; minimum

2 a $(1, 6)$

b Maximum

3 a $\dfrac{\mathrm{d}y}{\mathrm{d}x} = 3x^2 - 6$; $\dfrac{\mathrm{d}^2y}{\mathrm{d}x^2} = 6x$

b $x = -\sqrt{2}; x = \sqrt{2}$

c $y = 5 + 4\sqrt{2}; y = 5 - 4\sqrt{2}$

e Maximum, minimum respectively.

4 a $(-4.65, 79.0); (0.646, 4.96)$ to 3 s.f.

b Maximum, minimum respectively.

5 b

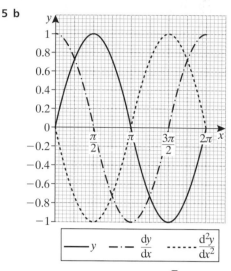

Graph of y shows a maximum at $\dfrac{\pi}{2}$, which is confirmed by the graph of $\dfrac{dy}{dx}$ which is zero at that point.

6 Maximum at $\left(\dfrac{\pi}{2}, 1\right)$, minimum at $\left(\dfrac{3\pi}{2}, -1\right)$

7 11 days

8 b 8.30 to 3 s.f., minimum

4.8C

1 b 0

2 $(-2, -8)$; 0

4.8D

Second derivative is zero when $x = \sin t$ crosses the t-axis.

4.8E

1

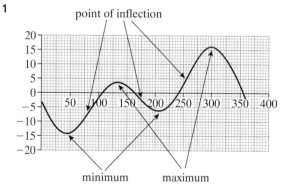

2 b Maximum at $(-1, 2)$; minimum at $(1, -2)$.
  c Point of inflection at the origin.

3 b Maximum at $(0, 1)$; points of inflection at $\left(\dfrac{-1}{\sqrt{2}}, e^{-\frac{1}{2}}\right)$
  and $\left(\dfrac{1}{\sqrt{2}}, e^{-\frac{1}{2}}\right)$.

4 a $x = 1$ and $x = 4$
  b Minimum, point of inflection respectively.
  c $x = 2$

5 x co-ordinates of turning points satisfy $\tan 5x = 10$ and alternate between maximum and minimum.
  x co-ordinates of inflection points satisfy $\tan 5x = -0.202$.

4.8F

1 a $\dfrac{dh}{dn} = -0.08(n - 35)$; $\dfrac{d^2h}{dn^2} = -0.08$

  c Second derivative is negative.

2 a $h'(t) = 0.1(t \cos t + 1 + \sin t)$;
  $h''(t) = 0.1(-t \sin t + 2 \cos t)$

  b

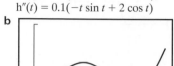

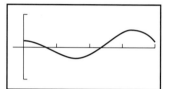

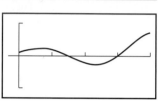

  d i $(2.37, 0.402)$; $(4.71, 0)$
    ii $(1.08, 0.203)$; $(3.64, 0.189)$

4.10 Practice exam questions

1 a i

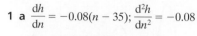

    ii The gradient is always greater than or equal to zero, and increases as h increases.

  b $\dfrac{dV}{dh} = \dfrac{\pi h^2}{3}$

  c $\dfrac{dh}{dt} = \dfrac{6}{\pi h^2}$

  d i

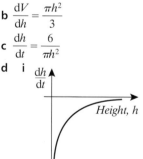

    ii It shows that the rate at which the height of the liquid in the funnel decreases quickest is when it is already at a smaller height. The greater the height, the smaller the rate of height decrease.

  e $h = \sqrt[3]{\dfrac{90}{\pi}} = 3.06\,\text{cm}$, to 3 s.f. $\dfrac{dh}{dt} = -0.204\,\text{cm/s}$, to 3 s.f.

2 a i £1000
    ii £2943 to nearest pound
    iii £850 to nearest pound

b ii $t = 2$ **iii** $0 < t < 2$ **iv** $t > 2$
c i

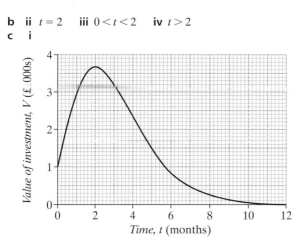

Time, t (months)

ii £3654
iii Any correct interpretation of the graph, e.g. from the initial investment of 1000, the investment rises quickly to its maximum of £3654 in 2 months before a slightly slower decline in its value over the next 10 months of the year ending well below its initial value and worth almost nothing.

5 More Integration

5.1 Integrating trigonometric functions

5.1A

1 a $\dfrac{\pi}{20}$ **b** $\dfrac{\pi}{20}$

3 b The graph of $\sin x$ falls below the x-axis.

5 a $\displaystyle\int_0^x \sin x\, dx = 1 - \cos x$

c The trapezium method is an approximation.

5.1B

1 $\displaystyle\int \cos x\, dx = \sin x + c$

5.1C

1

Function	Integral
$\sin t$	$-\cos t + k$
$\cos t$	$\sin t + k$
$\sin \omega t$	$-\dfrac{1}{\omega}\cos \omega t + k$
$\cos \omega t$	$\dfrac{1}{\omega}\sin \omega t + k$
$A\sin \omega t$	$-\dfrac{A}{\omega}\cos \omega t + k$
$\sin(\omega t + \alpha)$	$-\dfrac{1}{\omega}\cos(\omega t + \alpha) + k$
$\cos(\omega t + \alpha)$	$\dfrac{1}{\omega}\sin(\omega t + \alpha) + k$
$A\sin(\omega t + \alpha)$	$-\dfrac{A}{\omega}\cos(\omega t + \alpha) + k$
$A\cos(\omega t + \alpha)$	$\dfrac{A}{\omega}\sin(\omega t + \alpha) + k$

2 a $-\frac{1}{2}\cos 2t + k$

b $\frac{1}{3}\sin 3t + k$
c $-2\cos\frac{1}{2}t + k$
d $\frac{4}{5}\sin 5t + k$
e $-50\cos 0.3t + k$
f $18\sin\frac{1}{3}t + k$

3 a $-\frac{1}{2}\cos(2t + 3) + k$
b $\frac{1}{4}\sin(4t - 1) + k$
c $-\dfrac{1}{5}\cos\left(5t - \dfrac{\pi}{6}\right) + k$
d $2\sin\left(\dfrac{1}{2}t + \dfrac{\pi}{3}\right) + k$
e $-\frac{2}{7}\cos(7t + 1) + k$
f $8\sin(t - 6) + k$
g $-\dfrac{3}{2}\cos\left(2t + \dfrac{\pi}{4}\right) + k$
h $\dfrac{5}{4}\sin\left(4t - \dfrac{\pi}{4}\right) + k$
i $\frac{5}{3}\sin(3t + \pi) + k$
j $-\frac{1}{20}\cos(10t + 3) + k$

5.1D
1 b 4

2 a 1
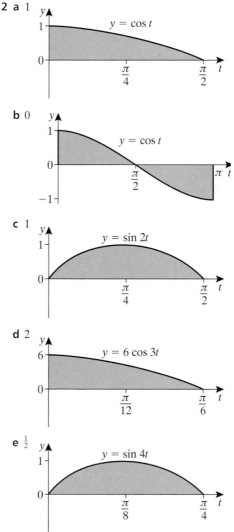

b 0

c 1

d 2

e $\frac{1}{2}$

f 0

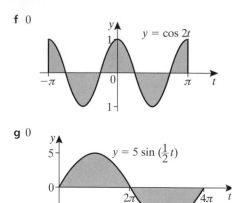

g 0

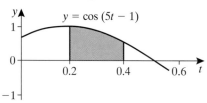

h $-\frac{1}{2}(\cos 2 - \cos 1) = 0.478$ to 3 d.p.

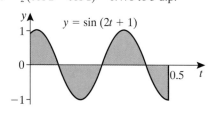

i $\frac{1}{5}\sin = 0.168$ to 3 d.p.

j 0.866 to 3 d.p.

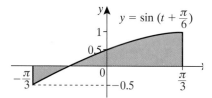

3 a

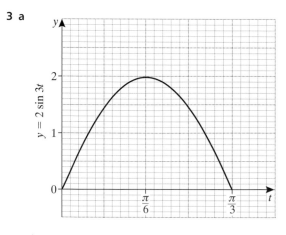

b $\frac{4}{3}$

4 a

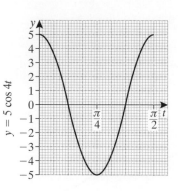

b 0; integration counts area above the horizontal axis as positive and the area below as negative.

c 5

5 a

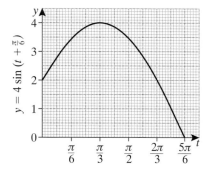

b 7.464 to 3 d.p.

6 a 1.57

b

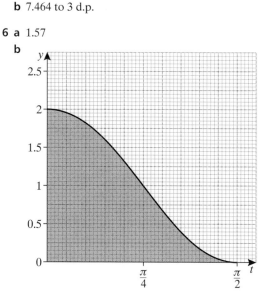

7 a 20 m

b Looking at the graph of v plotted against t, the areas above (0–30 s) and below (30–60 s) the t-axis are the same, so cancel each other out when integrating.

8 a 800

b 8 m

c $y = 4.5 \sin \dfrac{\pi(x - 25)}{50} + 5.5$; 5.5 m; Yes, because in the profile length here, 100 m, also happens to represent the period of the sine term in the model which over its period averages 0.

5.2 Integrating exponential functions

5.2A

1 c Translation − 1 parallel to y axis.

  e $e^x - 1$

2 a $-e^{-x}$

  b $-e^{-x} + c$

  c $1 - e^{-x}$

5.2B

1 a $\frac{1}{5}e^{5t} + c$

  b $-\frac{1}{2}e^{-2t} + c$

  c $2e^{\frac{1}{2}t} + c$

  d $2e^{3t} + c$

  e $-\frac{4}{5}e^{-5t} + c$

  f $-5e^{-\frac{2}{3}t} + c$

  g $\frac{1}{2}e^{6t} + 5t + c$

  h $t + 6e^{-0.5t} + c$

  i $12(t + 5e^{-0.2t}) + c$

2 a $1 - e^{-1} = 0.632$ to 3 s.f.

  b $\frac{1}{2}(e^2 - 1) = 3.19$ to 3 s.f.

  c $\frac{1}{5}(e^5 - e^{-5}) = 29.7$ to 3 s.f.

  d $-2(e^{-3} - e^{-1}) = 0.636$ to 3 s.f.

  e $2(e^2 - 1) = 12.8$ to 3 s.f.

  f $15(e^{0.5} - 1) = 9.73$ to 3 s.f.

  g $\frac{1}{2}(5e^2 + 1) = 19.0$ to 3 s.f.

  h $5e^{-1} = 1.84$ to 3 s.f.

  i $\frac{1}{3}(e^3 - e^{-3}) = 6.68$ to 3 s.f.

3 a $-\frac{1}{2}(e^{-6} - 1) = 0.499$ to 3 s.f.

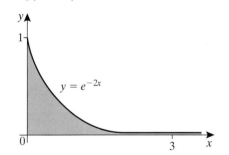

  b $4(e^2 - e^{\frac{1}{2}}) = 23.0$ to 3 s.f.

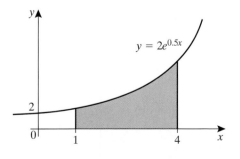

c $-2(e^{-2} - e^{-1}) = 0.465$ to 3 s.f.

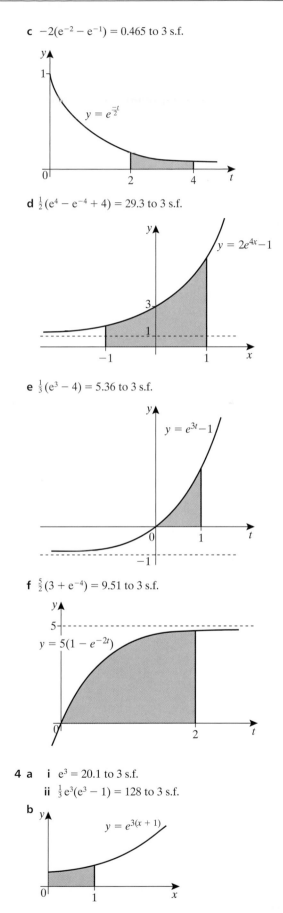

d $\frac{1}{2}(e^4 - e^{-4} + 4) = 29.3$ to 3 s.f.

e $\frac{1}{3}(e^3 - 4) = 5.36$ to 3 s.f.

f $\frac{5}{2}(3 + e^{-4}) = 9.51$ to 3 s.f.

4 a **i** $e^3 = 20.1$ to 3 s.f.

    ii $\frac{1}{3}e^3(e^3 - 1) = 128$ to 3 s.f.

  b

5 a Total *increase* in area (in 1000s of square kilometres) occupied since 1939.
b 43.0 to 3 s.f.
c 75 800 km² to 3 s.f.

5.3 Applications of integration

5.3A

1 20 m²
2 a

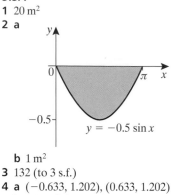

$y = -0.5 \sin x$

b 1 m²
3 132 (to 3 s.f.)
4 a (−0.633, 1.202), (0.633, 1.202)
b 3.3 cm² (to 2 s.f.)
5 78.3 m² to 3 s.f.

5.3B

1 a $v = 12(1 - e^{-0.25t}), d = 12t + 48(e^{-0.25t} - 1)$
b

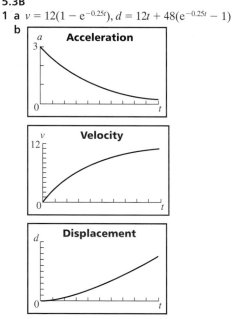

c Acceleration reduces towards 0, velocity approaches, displacement eventually increases at a linear rate.
2 a $v = 20e^{-t} + 5, d = 5t - 20e^{-t} + 20$
b

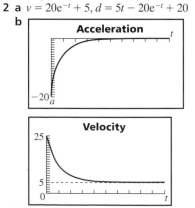

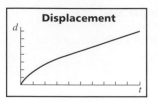

c Deceleration approaches 0, terminal velocity of 5 m s⁻¹, displacement increasing

3 a $v = \frac{1}{2} \sin \frac{\pi t}{4}, d = \frac{2}{\pi}\left(1 - \cos \frac{\pi t}{4}\right)$
b

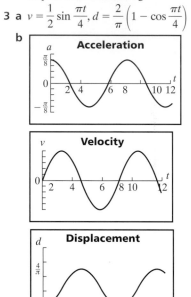

c **i** Train towards backwards and forwards between A and B.
ii $\frac{1}{2}$ ms⁻¹
iii $\frac{4}{\pi}$ m

4 a $v = 15 \sin \frac{\pi t}{3}, d = \frac{45}{\pi}\left(1 - \cos \frac{\pi t}{3}\right)$
b

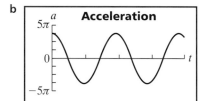

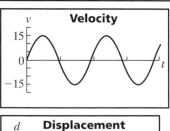

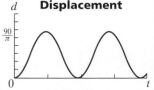

c i Return to their original height

ii No, energy will be lost and the height the jumper reaches on each successive rebound should decrease.

5.3C

1 a & b

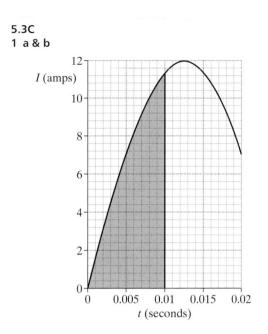

c $\dfrac{3}{10\pi}\left[1 - \cos\left(\dfrac{2\pi}{5}\right)\right] = 0.0660$ to 3 s.f.

d i $\dfrac{3}{10\pi}\left[\cos\left(\dfrac{2\pi}{5}\right) - \cos\left(\dfrac{4\pi}{5}\right)\right] = 0.107$ to 3 s.f.

ii Current has yet to reach its maximum at $t = 0.0125$, so area would be greater in the second hundredth of a second.

2 a

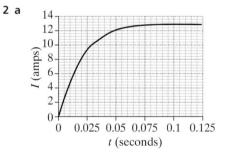

The current will tend to 13 as t increases.

b $Q = 13\left[t + \tfrac{1}{50}\left(e^{-50t} - 1\right)\right]$

c

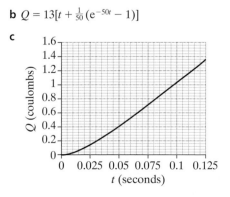

3 a

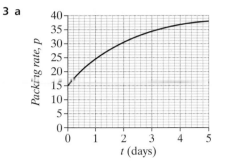

The graph shows that the worker's rate starts off low as he is new to the job, but then improves to a maximum level of 'performance' of 40 per day.

b 350 packs to nearest pack (assuming p is given in packs/day)

4 a $p(t) = 75\,000e^{0.02t}$

b

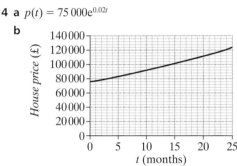

Growth would be exponential but the factor $e^{0.02}$ is equivalent to roughly 2%, which is probably a little on the high side for a monthly increase in price.

5 a $P(t) = 12\left[\sin\left(\dfrac{\pi}{180}(t-90)\right) + 1\right] + 18$

b

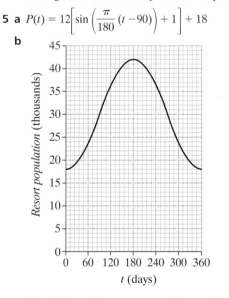

c Plausible, as it shows a seasonal, repeating change in resort population. However, the model has a period of 360 days, so will be unsuitable over a number of years.

5.5 Practice exam questions

1 a Integrating gives 4978 which is approx. 5000

b 4542; 91%

c 51%

2 a i For large values of t, the exponential term tends to zero because of the negative sign, otherwise it would increase exponentially and without limit.

ii

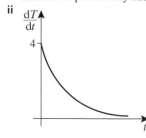

b i 11.4°C   **ii** No

6 Differential Equations

6.1 Direction field diagrams

6.1B

1 a, b & c

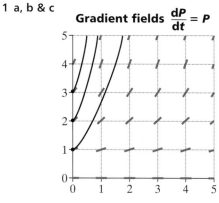

2 $P = e^x; P = 2e^x; P = 3e^x$

6.1C
1 & 2 a

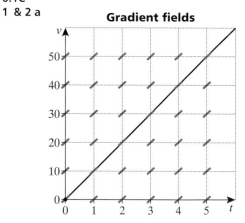

2 b Initially at rest.   **c** $v = 10t$
3 b Has an initial velocity of 10, rather than starting from rest. Acceleration is still 10.
4 b Has an initial velocity of k. Acceleration is still 10.

6.1D
1 $y = \frac{1}{2}x^2 + 1$
2 $y = 5x^2 + 1$
3 $y = \frac{1}{3}x^3 + 1$
4 $y = \frac{1}{4}x^4 + 1$

5 $y = 1$
6 $y = x + 1$
7 $y = e^x$
8 $y = e^{2x}$
9 $y = \dfrac{1}{1 - x}$
10 $y = (2x + 1)^{\frac{1}{2}}$

6.2 Solving differential equations

6.2A
1 $y = \frac{1}{2}x^2$
2 $y = x^2$
3 $y = \frac{1}{3}x^3 + 1$
4 $y = e^x$
5 $y = 2 - \cos x$
6 $y = \frac{1}{2}\sin 2x + 1$

6.2B
1 $x = 12t^2$
2

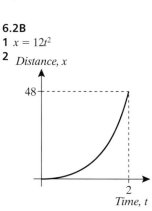

6.2C
1 c $e^{-t+c} = e^{-t}e^c = Ae^{-t}$, where $A = e^c$ is a constant that depends on initial conditions.
2 b $A = 1000; P = 148\,000$ to 3 s.f. when $t = 500$

6.2D
1 c 111 hours
d & e

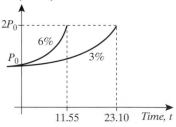

2 d

3 c

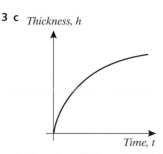

Thickness, h

Time, t

d There is no limit to the thickness, h, as t increases.

4 b

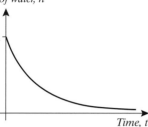

Height of water, h

1

Time, t

d 69.3 hours to 3 s.f.

5 b 2.56 hours or 2 hours 34 min

6.4 Practice exam question

a

Gradient fields $\dfrac{\mathrm{d}P}{\mathrm{d}t} = 0.0296P$

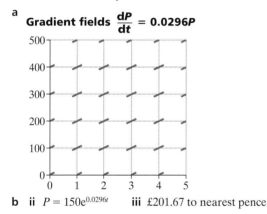

b ii $P = 150\mathrm{e}^{0.0296t}$ **iii** £201.67 to nearest pence

Comprehension Answers

Escape Velocity

2 $\dfrac{\mathrm{d}y}{\mathrm{d}x} = \dfrac{-2k}{x^3}$; No local maximum or minimum because $\dfrac{\mathrm{d}y}{\mathrm{d}x} = 0$ has no solutions

3 Acceleration is being measured upwards, so a downward acceleration is negative.

4 $\dfrac{\mathrm{d}r}{\mathrm{d}t} = v$

7 More because the poles are closer together – a smaller value for r increases value of F.

8 a 2370 ms^{-1} (to 3 s.f.)

  b i 1.62 ms^{-2} (to 3 s.f.)

Normal Distribution

1 The exponential function is always greater than zero for all values of the exponent.

5 The areas of strips beyond 5.6 are negligible (0 to 4 dps from the table) and because the graph is symmetrical about 0, you can double up.

6 Using value of $x = 1$ from the table, $2 \times 0.8536 = 1.7072$. As a proportion of the whole area under the graph, this is: $\dfrac{1.7072}{\sqrt{2\pi}} = 0.681$ to 3 s.f., which is approx. two-thirds.

7 For example:
- Translation right by μ units, followed by
- Stretch parallel to the x-axis with factor σ^2, followed by
- Stretch parallel to the y-axis with factor $\dfrac{1}{\sigma\sqrt{2\pi}}$.

Index

ESCAPE VELOCITY

If you throw a ball vertically upwards the height it reaches depends on the speed with which you release it – the greater the speed, the higher it goes. On its upward journey the force of gravity acts to decelerate the ball so that it eventually comes momentarily to rest before accelerating back downwards to Earth. Would it be possible to project a ball with great enough speed that it could escape the effect of the Earth's gravity? Of course, that is the question that space flight engineers need to ask when they wish to send a probe deep into space. For example, the rockets used to propel explorers to Mars need to overcome the Earth's gravity. To do this they need to be travelling at about 25 000 miles per second.

Figure 1: Launching a spaceship to Mars

We need to turn to the thinking of Newton to answer this question. It was Newton who realised that what we commonly refer to as 'gravity' is a special case of the force that acts between *any* two objects. His Universal Law of Gravitation may be written as

$$F = \frac{GMm}{d^2},$$

where F is the force experienced by each of two objects of masses M and m, because of the other when they are a distance d apart. G is the constant of universal gravitation, its value depending on the system of units you are using. When M and m are measured in kilograms, d in metres, F in newtons, then $G = 6.67 \times 10^{-11}\ \mathrm{Nm^2kg^{-2}}$.

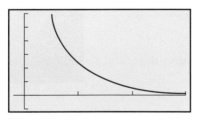

Figure 3: Sketch graph of $y = \dfrac{k}{x^2}$ for $x > 0$

As the sketch of the graph of $y = \dfrac{k}{x^2}$ (an inverse square law) in

Figure 3 illustrates, the force of attraction will quickly decrease as the distance between the two objects increases.

Figure 2: Sir Isaac Newton (1643–1727)

If you model the Earth as a sphere with radius $R = 6.378 \times 10^6$ metres with its entire mass ($M = 5.98 \times 10^{24}$ kg) concentrated at its centre, then the force acting on an object of mass m kilograms at the Earth's surface will be $F = 9.81m$ newtons.

In this case the value of $\dfrac{GM}{d^2} = 9.81\ \mathrm{Nkg^{-1}}$ (or $\mathrm{ms^{-2}}$) is what is

commonly known as g, the acceleration due to gravity. The value of g is usually taken to be constant at all points on the Earth's surface. This is not strictly the case as the Earth is not absolutely spherical – in fact it is an oblate spheroid with the poles not being as far from the centre as places on the equator.

To return to the original question of whether an object can be projected with sufficient speed to escape the Earth's gravity you need to consider another of Newton's important contributions to science – his Second Law of Motion. This is often expressed as $F = ma$, meaning that a force F acting on an object of mass m will give rise to an acceleration a. For an object that has been projected vertically upwards the only force that acts on it is that due to gravity as shown in **Figure 5**.

Figure 4: The Earth viewed from space appears to be spherical

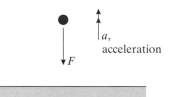

Figure 5: The force acting on a ball thrown vertically upwards

In this case Newton's Second Law results in

$$-\frac{GM\cancel{m}}{r^2} = \cancel{m}a.$$

So
$$a = \frac{dv}{dt} = -\frac{GM}{r^2}.$$

Since
$$\frac{dv}{dt} = \frac{dv}{dr} \times \frac{dr}{dt} = v\frac{dv}{dr}$$

So
$$\frac{dv}{dt} = -\frac{GM}{r^2} \text{ can be written as } v\frac{dv}{dr} = -\frac{GM}{r^2}.$$

You can then solve this differential equation by splitting the variables and integrating:

$$\int v\,dv = -\int \frac{GM}{r^2}\,dr$$

$$\therefore \qquad \frac{v^2}{2} = \frac{GM}{r} + c$$

If the object is just to escape the Earth's gravitational pull (so that $v = 0$ as $r \to \infty$) $c = 0$, and when $r = R$ (the radius of the Earth) the speed of the object will be v_{escape}.

Therefore, for the Earth $v_{escape} = \sqrt{\frac{2GM}{R}} = 11\ 180\ \text{ms}^{-1}$.

You can see from the expression for v_{escape}, i.e.

$v_{escape} = \sqrt{\frac{2GM}{R}}$, that escape velocity depends on the mass and

radius of the planet (assumed to be spherical).

The table in **Figure 6** gives data for the planets of the Solar System from which you can see that the escape velocity from Mars is considerably less than that from the Earth. This is just as well as any spaceship reaching Mars will have to take enough fuel with it for its launch from Mars for its return journey.

Figure 7: Planets of the Solar Sytem

Planet	Radius (m)	Mass (kg)	Escape velocity (ms^{-1})
Mercury	2.439×10^6	3.3×10^{23}	4250
Venus	6.052×10^6	4.87×10^{24}	10 400
Earth	6.378×10^6	5.98×10^{24}	11 200
Mars	3.397×10^6	6.4×10^{23}	5010
Jupiter	7.190×10^7	1.9×10^{27}	59 400
Saturn	6.000×10^7	5.67×10^{26}	35 500
Uranus	2.615×10^7	8.70×10^{25}	21 000
Neptune	2.475×10^7	1.03×10^{26}	23 600
Pluto	2.000×10^6	1.3×10^{22}	931

Figure 6: Planetary data giving radius, mass and escape velocity

Comprehension Questions

1   Use data from the table in **Figure 6** to show calculations to confirm that $g = 9.81 \text{ ms}^{-2}$.

2   Newton's Universal Law of Gravitation, $F = \dfrac{GMm}{d^2}$, is a function of the type $y = \dfrac{k}{x^2}$.

Find $\dfrac{dy}{dx}$ and use your result to explain how you know that $y = \dfrac{k}{x^2}$ has no local maximum or minumum.

3   Applying Newton's Second Law to an object that has been projected vertically upwards (see **Figure 5** in the article) gives rise to the expression $a = -\dfrac{GM}{r^2}$.

Explain the negative sign in this expression.

4   Use the chain rule to explain how $\dfrac{dv}{dt} = v\dfrac{dv}{dr}$.

5   Use the expression $\dfrac{v^2}{2} = \dfrac{GM}{r} + c$ together with the condition that $v = 0$ as $r \to \infty$ to show that $c = 0$.

6   Show calculations to confirm that for Mars $v_{escape} = 5010 \text{ ms}^{-1}$.

7   Is the force due to gravity likely to be more or less at the poles than at places on the equator? Explain your answer.

8   Consider the Moon to be spherical with radius 1.74×10^6 metres and mass 7.35×10^{22} kg.

   a   Calculate the escape velocity required for a spacecraft to escape the Moon's gravity.

   b   The gravity of the Moon is often quoted as being one-sixth that of the Earth.
   (i)   Calculate the acceleration due to gravity on the Moon.
   (ii) Confirm that this is approximately one-sixth the value of the acceleratiion due to gravity on the Earth.

NORMAL DISTRIBUTION

The bar chart in **Figure 2** shows the height of 211 children aged 16. Their heights have been measured to the nearest centimetre and grouped in 5-centimetre intervals. As you can see the distribution of heights approximately has a bell shape (see **Figure 3**). Many naturally occurring phenomena have such a distribution and are said to be 'normally distributed'.

Data about the dimensions of the human body are, of course, very important to designers of all manner of things that we wear and use – for example, such data is essential to designers of furniture when they have to decide how high a desk should be.

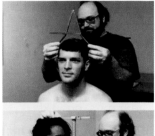

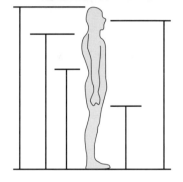

Figure 1: Collecting anthropometric data

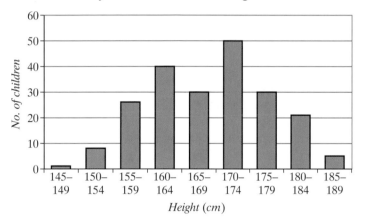

Figure 2: Distribution of heights of a sample of 16-year-old children

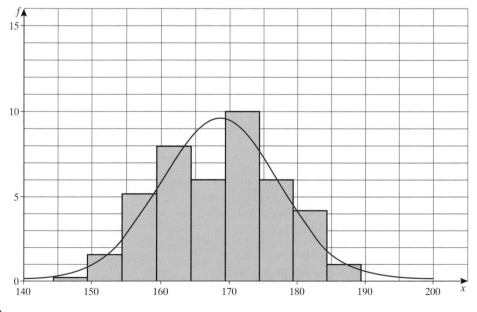

Figure 3: A normal distribution fitted to the children's height data plotted as a histogram. Note that in a histogram the frequency is given by the area of a bar so that between 169.5 and 174.5 cm, for example, there are 50 children – given by the area (10×5)

Statisticians use the **normal distribution** to study such data. This distribution is based on the function $y = e^{-\frac{x^2}{2}}$ which is shown in **Figure 4**. You can use the ideas of calculus to determine some of the significant features of the function $y = e^{-\frac{x^2}{2}}$.

To differentiate this you need to use the 'chain rule' or 'function of a function'.

Let $u = \dfrac{x^2}{2}$ so $y = e^{-u}$.

Therefore, $\dfrac{dy}{dx} = \dfrac{dy}{du} \times \dfrac{du}{dx} = -xe^{-\frac{x^2}{2}}$

Any turning points of the function $y = e^{-\frac{x^2}{2}}$ are found where $\dfrac{dy}{dx} = 0$. So this confirms that the function has a local maximum or minimum when $x = 0$.

To find the second differential of $y = e^{-\frac{x^2}{2}}$ you need to use the product rule together with the chain rule (or function of a function). This gives $\dfrac{d^2y}{dx^2} = e^{-\frac{x^2}{2}} (1 - x^2)$.

This allows you to confirm that when $x = 0$ the function has a *maximum* point and points of inflection at $x = \pm 1$ (see **Figure 5**).

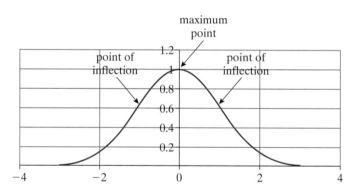

Figure 4: Function $y = e^{-\frac{x^2}{2}}$

Figure 5: Significant features of the normal distribution

A further property you might like to investigate is the area enclosed by the graph of the function and the x-axis. Statisticians do this because, as you might deduce from **Figure 3**, this area is related to the total number of children in the sample.

This would require finding or $\displaystyle\int_{-\infty}^{\infty} e^{-\frac{x^2}{2}} \, dx$ or $2 \times \displaystyle\int_{0}^{\infty} e^{-\frac{x^2}{2}} \, dx$.

As you can see this is a difficult integral to evaluate using algebraic methods. However, it is possible to do this numerically using methods such as the trapezium or mid-ordinate rules.

The spreadsheet in **Figure 6** shows the area enclosed by the function $y = e^{-\frac{x^2}{2}}$ and the x-axis evaluated using the trapezium rule from $x = 0$ for increasing values of x (in steps of 0.2) to $x = 5.6$.

	A	B	C	D
1	x	y	Area of strip	Area sum A(x)
2	0	1.0000		
3	0.2	0.9802	0.1980	0.1980
4	0.4	0.9231	0.1903	0.3884
5	0.6	0.8353	0.1758	0.5642
6	0.8	0.7261	0.1561	0.7203
7	1	0.6065	0.1333	0.8536
8	1.2	0.4868	0.1093	0.9629
9	1.4	0.3753	0.0862	1.0491
10	1.6	0.2780	0.0653	1.1145
11	1.8	0.1979	0.0476	1.1621
12	2	0.1353	0.0333	1.1954
13	2.2	0.0889	0.0224	1.2178
14	2.4	0.0561	0.0145	1.2323
15	2.6	0.0340	0.0090	1.2413
16	2.8	0.0198	0.0054	1.2467
17	3	0.0111	0.0031	1.2498
18	3.2	0.0060	0.0017	1.2515
19	3.4	0.0031	0.0009	1.2524
20	3.6	0.0015	0.0005	1.2529
21	3.8	0.0007	0.0002	1.2531
22	4	0.0003	0.0001	1.2532
23	4.2	0.0001	0.0000	1.2533
24	4.4	0.0001	0.0000	1.2533
25	4.6	0.0000	0.0000	1.2533
26	4.8	0.0000	0.0000	1.2533
27	5	0.0000	0.0000	1.2533
28	5.2	0.0000	0.0000	1.2533
29	5.4	0.0000	0.0000	1.2533
30	5.6	0.0000	0.0000	1.2533

Figure 6: Calculating numerically, using the trapezium rule, the area enclosed by the function from to $y = e^{-\frac{x^2}{2}}$ from $x = 0$ to $x = X$

As you can see this appears to be approaching the value 1.2533. It appears that the $\int_{\infty}^{\infty} e^{-\frac{x^2}{2}} \, dx$ then has the value 2.5066. It turns out that the exact value of the integral approaches $\sqrt{2\pi}$. This value has been found by mathematicians determining the integral by an exact method.

The information that you now know about the function $y = e^{-\frac{x^2}{2}}$ allows statisticians to use ideas associated with transformations of functions to find a function that fits data when drawn as a histogram. For data with a mean, μ, and standard deviation, σ, the function is $y = \dfrac{1}{\sigma\sqrt{2\pi}} e^{\frac{-(x^2 - \mu)^2}{2\sigma^2}}$. This transformed function has:

- a maximum point at $x = \mu$

- points of inflection at $x = \mu + \sigma$ and $x = \mu - \sigma$

- an area enclosed by the function and the x-axis of 1.

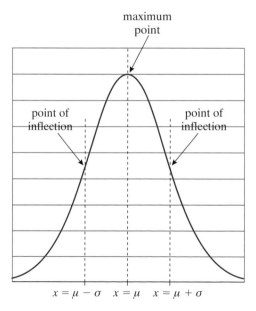

Figure 7: Significant features of the function that models the normal distribution

Comprehension Questions

1 For $y = e^{-\frac{x^2}{2}}$ explain why $y > 0$.

2 Show carefully, using the chain rule, that $\frac{dy}{dx} = -xe^{-\frac{x^2}{2}}$ for the function $y = e^{-\frac{x^2}{2}}$.

3 Starting with $\frac{dy}{dx} = -xe^{-\frac{x^2}{2}}$, show carefully, using the product and chain rules, that $\frac{d^2y}{dx^2} = e^{-\frac{x^2}{2}}(1 - x^2)$.

4 Use your answers to **questions 2** and **3** to confirm that $y = e^{-\frac{x^2}{2}}$ has

    a a local maximum at $x = 0$;

    b points of inflection at $x = 1$ and $x = -1$.

5 Explain how finding twice the area sum from $x = 0$ to $x = 5.6$ in the table in **Figure 6** gives approximately $\int_{\infty}^{\infty} e^{-\frac{x^2}{2}} dx$.

6 Statistics books often claim that the area under the graph of the normal distribution between $x = \mu - \sigma$ and $x = \mu + \sigma$ is approximately two-thirds of the total area under the graph. Use a value from the table in Figure 6 to show that this is approximately true.

7 Throughout the article the function $y = e^{-\frac{x^2}{2}}$ was explored as being the basic function on which functions
$y = \frac{1}{\sigma\sqrt{2\pi}} e^{\frac{-(x^2 - \mu)^2}{2\sigma^2}}$, that fit normally distributed data, are based.

Explain the geometric transformations that map $y = e^{-\frac{x^2}{2}}$ to $y = e^{-\frac{(x - \mu)^2}{2\sigma^2}}$.